TRANSLATION AS CITATION

GLOBAL ASIAS

Eric Hayot, Series Editor

TRANSLATION
AS CITATION

Zhuangzi Inside Out

HAUN SAUSSY

OXFORD
UNIVERSITY PRESS

Great Clarendon Street, Oxford, OX2 6DP,
United Kingdom

Oxford University Press is a department of the University of Oxford.
It furthers the University's objective of excellence in research, scholarship,
and education by publishing worldwide. Oxford is a registered trade mark of
Oxford University Press in the UK and in certain other countries

© Haun Saussy 2017

The moral rights of the author have been asserted

First Edition published in 2017
Impression: 1

Published in the United States of America by Oxford University Press
198 Madison Avenue, New York, NY 10016, United States of America

British Library Cataloguing in Publication Data
Data available

Library of Congress Control Number: 2017942139

ISBN 978-0-19-881253-1

Printed and bound by
CPI Group (UK) Ltd, Croydon, CR0 4YY

Links to third party websites are provided by Oxford in good faith and
for information only. Oxford disclaims any responsibility for the materials
contained in any third party website referenced in this work.

ACKNOWLEDGMENTS

I am grateful to the John Simon Guggenheim Foundation for a fellowship in 2014–15 and to the Division of the Humanities, University of Chicago, for an extension of leave time and many other kindnesses.

Kang-i Sun Chang, Yu Ying-shih, and the late Karl Kao Hsin-yung encouraged me to go on with Chinese studies: I always hope they were right, not just kind. Conversations with Qian Nanxiu, Zhang Longxi, Paul Farmer, Roger Hart, the late Michael Henry Heim, Martin Svensson Ekström, Christoph Harbsmeier, E. Bruce Brooks, Tina Smith MD, Steve Yao, the late Mark Southern, Li Sher-Shiueh, Victor Mair, Sandra Bermann, Timothy Brook, Robert Batchelor, Lucas Klein, Helen Huiwen Zhang, Salikoko Mufwene, Rob Campany, Hou Jue, Tom Kelly, Romain Graziani, and Eugenia Kelbert have been especially helpful. Helen Tartar's friendship and criticism have always meant a great deal to me. Despite this abundance of good advice, I have clung to some of my preconceptions, and can only hope that the resulting errors are not too grievous. In more or less chronological order, Mary Jacobus, Jane Gallop, Daniel Sherman, David Rolston, Timothy Billings, Isabelle Poulin, Ben Elman, Felicia McCarren, Eric Hayot, Victoria Kahn, Sandra Bermann, Thomas Hare, Qian Suoqiao, Panagiotis Roilos, Marc Maufort, Michael Syrotinski, Galin Tihanov, Nan Z. Da, Dorothy Chansky, Gu Ming Dong, Stefan Uhlig, Timme Kragh, and Anne Cheng have given me chances to present one or another part of these investigations to audiences. Jeffrey Tharsen shared with me an early version of his "Intertext" application for large-scale text comparisons. While writing, I've often thought about Jonathan Stalling's *Yingelishi* and *Pinying*, though they're not directly discussed here. The Neubauer Collegium at the University of Chicago supported a multi-year workshop, "History, Philology and the Nation in

China," to which this book is profoundly indebted: among my fellow participants, Judith Farquhar, Ge Zhaoguang, and Liu Dong have taught me a great deal.

Olga Viktorovna (the prophet of *Zaftrabudizm*), René Zosima, Constantin Hippolyte, and Kirill Anatole have been in my thoughts, and often within earshot, throughout the writing of this book.

The passage from the poetry of Gottfried Benn is reproduced with the kind permission of Klett-Cotta/J.G. Cotta'sche Buchhandlung Nachfolger GmbH, Stuttgart. I am grateful to the journal *Europe* for their gracious permission to cite an interview between Evelyne Grossman and Jacques Derrida, and to Carcanet Press for allowing me to quote from the *Collected Poems* of Hugh MacDiarmid. "Death and Translation" was previously published in *Representations* 94 (2006): 112–30. Earlier versions of other sections of the book have appeared as "Les macaroniques du XXe siècle. Auto-traduction, jargon, écriture bâtarde: la boîte noire des langues," 80–90 in Isabelle Poulin, ed., *Critique et plurilinguisme* (Paris: Société française de littérature générale et comparée, 2013); "Matteo Ricci the Daoist," 176–93 in Qian Suoqiao, ed., *Cross-Cultural Studies, China and the World: A Festschrift for Zhang Longxi* (Leiden: Brill, 2014); and "Macaronics as What Eludes Translation," *Paragraph* 38.2 (2015): 214–30. The translated poem "To Matteo Ricci of the Far West" was previously published in *A Book to Burn and a Book to Keep (Hidden)*, by Li Zhi, edited by Rivi Handler-Spitz, Pauline Lee, and Haun Saussy (copyright © 2016 Columbia University Press; reprinted with permission of Columbia University Press). I am grateful to *Representations*, Éditions Lucie, Koninklijke Brill N.V, Edinburgh University Press, and Columbia University Press for permitting the reuse of this material.

Eric Hayot, as series editor, and two anonymous reviewers for the Press gave much-needed encouragement in the late stages. I am also grateful for Drew Stanley's meticulous copy-editing.

CONTENTS

Adventuring beyond the scope of my previous training and going into the history of Buddhism in China, I have depended more than usually on the work of previous scholars, whose translations I cite with gratitude (and footnotes). I do, however, often modify their wording in pursuit of specific lexical echoes and continuities, and the reasons for my changes, where I have not added an explanation, can be found by consulting the Chinese texts usually given below the translations. I modify existing romanizations to the *pinyin* system without giving special notice. In citing traditionally bound Asian books, I give the fascicle (*juan* 卷) number followed by a virgule and the page number: thus 12/14b is page 14 verso of *juan* 12. Texts from the *Taishō Tripitaka* Chinese Buddhist canon are signaled by their T number, followed by volume, page, and column number: thus (T 87) 1: 910c–912a stands for text 87 in that collection, volume 1, from page 910 column c to column a of page 912. I drop the surname Shi 釋 conventionally attached to the names of monks: thus in the bibliography and elsewhere you will find not Shi Huijiao but simply Huijiao. Other monastic or ethnic surnames such as Zhu 竺 and Zhi 支 are retained.

Staatsbibliothek, Kaschemme,
Resultatverlies,
Satzbordell, Maremme,
Fieberparadies...
—Gottfried Benn, "Staatsbibliothek" (1925)

INTRODUCTION
Translation Inside Out

Translation is one of the favorite metaphors of our time. People ask how a slogan is to translate into reality, or how to translate Islamic morals into liberal-democratic form; my university boasts an Institute of Translational Medicine, the task of which is to speed up the practical application of biological discoveries; for a time anthropologists thought that the most economical way of characterizing their business was "translating among cultures"; historians of science, too, framed the incommensurability problem as a case of translation.[1] Such operations have little to do with translating among languages. The use of the word "translate" there is more of an unsecured promise that these mediations will occur in the same way and with the same regularity that interlinguistic translation does. Closer to my concern (and to literal translation of words and sentences), it is often suggested that translation is the real subject of comparative literature.[2] Certainly translation takes up a great deal of space in the world of words today—but not all the space, for like everything, it has an edge and an Other. It is this other thing, non-translation, that I would like to investigate.

By non-translation I do not mean the realm of untranslated works, because they could always find a translator; nor do I intend a claim that is sometimes heard, that we can't or shouldn't translate, or that certain people should refrain from translating. Walter Benjamin sought "translatability" in the original work itself, in its essence, in its "intention toward the language into which the work is to be translated."[3] Some hold certain texts to be so holy that translation would defile them. Some translations are apparently doomed to failure. Prasenjit Gupta contends that asymmetries in wealth, power, authority, and receivability are fatal to the project of translation between Third World authors and First World audiences:

> Even with the best intentions in the world, with the aim of giving Bengali writing a voice in the West, the Western translator, merely by being Western and a member of the global ruling class, usurps that voice.... The humanistic motives of the Western translator are parallel to those of the British colonizer who thought he was bringing progress to India.[4]

We often hear that certain words in a language are untranslatable (by which is usually meant, "not translatable by a single word of English": the meanings appear to be describable enough). All these cases amount to a single kind of claim. These traditional negatives of translation—what cannot be translated or must not be translated—are not the Other I mean to explore. The Other I have in mind is vanishingly close to translation, so much so that it is often mistaken for translation, as it happens usually at close quarters to it and achieves, more or less, the same ends. To see this Other, we have to examine translation, but to look askance, to look away from the specific operation that translation, in the classic formulations of that term, performs. "Interlingual translation or *translation proper* is an interpretation of verbal signs by means of some other language."[5] Assuming that we know what "verbal signs," "interpretation," and a "language" are (which is already assuming quite a lot, as I shall endeavor to show), "translation proper" leaves considerable resources to the Other of translation—this non-translation has its own distinct effects, makes its receivers do different things and engage with bits of the world in a different way.

We usually understand by "translation" the creation, in language B, of an expression that will be the equivalent of a pre-existing expression in language A. The utterance may be a word, a sentence, a poem, a novel; and what counts as "equivalent" varies with the context and genre of the expression. Thus, as everyone admits, translating poetry is difficult because so many operative features would need to be replicated in the new language.

I am interested in aspects of translation that run counter to that common understanding. Let me reiterate the definition above with differing emphasis: "the *creation* of an expression *in language B* that will be the *equivalent* of a *pre-existing* expression in language A." For centuries now, theorists of translation have objected that there can be no true "equivalence" between languages, and so one school of translation studies explores how translations inevitably modify the original. I appreciate this objection but am not focusing on it. Rather, here I consider a series of translations that do not so much *make* an expression in the target language as *find* it (thus reversing the sequence in which the original necessarily precedes the translation), as well as renderings that do not express the original content in words that already existed in the target language, but *import* words or constructions (via loan words, calques, transliterations) directly from the source to the target language.

Both these features—citation and transliteration—are found to a greater or lesser degree in any translation and modify, indeed pervert, the definition of what it means to translate. Since "translation" has in recent years come to be such a prestigious metaphor for cultural exchange, communication, or enlargement, to work out the consequences of these non-classical translation modes ought to be worth someone's while.

Ever since the word "intertextuality" began to circulate among literary theorists in the 1970s, it has often been said that language is always citational—but this thesis tends to be articulated broadly rather than pursued in detail.[6] Following the growth of the field of translation studies in the 1970s and 1980s, we are accustomed to see a translated work as validated not only by its relation to the original it represents, but also (even mainly) by reference to norms of the language and culture into which it is introduced (the "target" context).[7] Machine translation has permitted a modification of our understanding of what a "language" is, what grammar, vocabulary, and meaning are. With the ability to search and point up correlations among sequences in collections of digitized material, we can begin to imagine "the problem of induction" in language-learning differently. That is, rather than imagining that learning a language is a matter of abstracting rules from examples (the problem of induction being, roughly: how many examples can ever be enough?), a probabilistic view of language lays out a terrain of more and less likely outcomes that speakers make their way through by emulation and analogy (when it's not by cutting and pasting).[8] I venture that combining these three points of view—translation as reception, translation as citation, the corpus approach to meaning—in reference to specific examples will lead to a better understanding of translation, at once formally more precise and culturally more suggestive than the standard view.

When describing a text as put together from bits of other texts, we naturally reach for such similes as the patchwork and the mosaic; but to represent the double perspective here put forth, we would have to add that every piece of the mosaic retains a vestigial string connecting it to its previous home in the slab of (linguistic) stone. Imagine, then, that by tugging on the strings we could cause the mosaic pieces to pivot between their two contexts. However technically improbable, that would be the model of the kind of reading I plan to offer.

An illustration of the principle of citation: *Moby-Dick* has been translated into French at least four times in the last seventy years. The earliest version (1939), by the novelist Jean Giono and two collaborators, is known for being the freest, and also often the most incomplete. Numerous critics have blamed Giono for taking liberties with the text, a complaint that has served to justify

the production of further translations, notably those of Armel Guerne (1954)
and Philippe Jaworski (2006). Readers impatient with Melville's style may
find Giono's version with its many cuts an improvement. But a look at the
novel's famous opening words, where Giono is already diverging from the
English sentence structure, shows that what is at stake is not literalness,
but acclimation. "Je m'appelle Ishmaël. Mettons." ("My name's Ishmaël. Let's
say." Or: "For example"; "Why not.") With this small linguistic gesture, Giono
claims a place for this novel alongside existing narratives in the French
tradition of the "récit," where the authorial voice and the question of fictionality
are foregrounded. The "Mettons" puts Melville in the company of Gide, Paulhan,
Céline, Giono himself, and beginners like Maurice Blanchot or Louis-René
des Forêts: unlikely, transfiguring company. Keeping consistency with this
generic decision may have mandated Giono's other changes to the text
he was translating. Had the translator modeled himself on the style of, say,
Jules Verne, the result would have accommodated some obvious features of
Melville (the adventure tale, the fascination with technology, the appetite
for digressions) but blurred many others. However close in other aspects to
Melville's English, a translation in the Verne manner would have been differently different. Moreover, in the literary world of 1939, a Jules Verne version
of *Moby-Dick* would have had little appeal. My proposal (aided by the passage
of time since both 1851 and 1939, which reveals the period quality of style) is
that translators and publics do not really have the option of faithfulness, only
choices among more or less suitable "manners." That is why translation is
(nearly) citation.

To demonstrate the other dynamic I am tracing, transliteration, let me
call up a few sentences from Ngũgĩ wa Thiong'o's *A Grain of Wheat* (1967):

> The school sports and races were followed by traditional dances. Uncircumcised
> boys and girls delighted the crowd with vigorous Muthuo; they had painted
> their faces with chalk and red-ochre and tied jingles to their knees; younger
> men and women did Mucung'wa: older women, in Mithuru, Miengu and
> layers of beads, danced Ndumo.[9]

For this passage describing costumes and dances, Ngugi could certainly have
used words in the *Oxford English Dictionary*; elsewhere in the novel he does
so, though most of his characters are inhabitants of a Kenyan village and use
English only occasionally. But here he makes his narrator address (although
in English) an audience for whom the Gikuyu terms are familiar and need
no gloss. The *entre-nous* effect fits the occasion described, the festival marking
Kenya's independence: it tacitly separates the ignorant reader like myself from
the narration's implied public at the moment that the nation is separating
from its colonizers.

Mithuru, Miengu, and Ndumo were not, as of 1967, common words in English, but the device of directly importing a foreign word for which there is no obvious equivalent is responsible for much of the English we speak today: *amen, amok, avocado, berserk, orangutan, sprezzatura, watusi, yacht,* and so many other familiar words for things that were once exotic. Sometimes the use of a foreign term is meant to keep the thing referred to at an artificial distance: *Führer,* for example. ("Leaders," on the other hand, are homegrown and unremarkable.) To a lesser degree, calques organize English words into sequences that would not make sense without a reference to a foreign context: "mandate of heaven," "enemy of the people," "Sublime Porte." Importation always accompanies translation, but on a local scale it stops translation (the "interpretation of verbal signs by means of some other language") from happening. Translation includes transliteration as if the latter were an imperfectly muffled dissent, or an avowal of the incompleteness of translating. It is the RNA to the DNA of a translated text, so to speak.[10]

Languages are constantly under construction. Languages are composite. They diverge and converge. The elements that make up a language are constantly modified through translations or transliterations. No language actually has a border or a center, although we speak as if they do when categorizing translations as "nativizing," "foreignizing," and the like. The English of 1300 or 1600, the English of Lagos, Kolkata, Glasgow, or Melbourne, the English of some neighborhoods of my own city require paraphrase, indeed translation, if they will be turned into my language. It is nonsense to lump them all into the category "English." "English," like all languages, is a variable object stretched across expanses of time and space that include a great deal of difference. Attention to such forms of distance should provoke us to restore the macaronic to its rightful place both in literary language and in the processes of language change. And, as was observed above, the macaronic's gains are often at the expense of translation.

The transliteration-and-citation dynamic cuts across much of what we know as translation and may, if we attend to it, deeply modify the preconceptions of translation theory. Since a theoretical argument in literary studies is most often the lengthened shadow of an example, it is important to have good examples, be prepared to argue for their usefulness, and work out what exactly they exemplify. My main examples, taken from the history of translation in China, are three episodes in which something new came into Chinese culture from outside through translations-as-citations. Remarkably, in each case the translations pilfered from a single book, the Daoist philosophical text *Zhuangzi* 莊子. The *Zhuangzi,* said to be the work of one Zhuang Zhou 莊周 (also known as Zhuangzi, "Master Zhuang"; traditional dates 369–286 BCE) but certainly incorporating the work of many later hands, exhibits an unusual freedom in rewriting the legends it takes as objects of parody and derision, and in imagining counterfactual scenarios to confound common sense. This exorbitance perhaps designated the *Zhuangzi* to be the gateway text through which unknown and exotic ideas—for example Buddhist doctrine, Jesuit teachings, and Baudelairean poetic modernism—could first become citable and speakable in Chinese. To vary somewhat Benjamin's proposal, translation belongs "essentially" to the *Zhuangzi*—but not in the sense that it would one day be translated, rather that its purposes would include aid in translating other texts. When we look more closely at the *Zhuangzi* itself (or: "itself"), we will see operations of citation and rewriting as responsible for large parts of that text, as if it had accumulated through successive parodies of a purported original "Zhuangzi." Perhaps translation-as-citation in this case goes, if not all the way down, at least a long way below the surface of history as we know it.

I hope that *Translation as Citation: Zhuangzi Inside Out* will make room for a different relation between works or translations and the languages we commonly imagine them to inhabit; that it will suggest that translation-histories outside the well-known European and Near Eastern cultural areas have something to tell us about the work translation does in culture; and that it will argue for a new status for the *Zhuangzi*, often considered *sui generis* or assimilated to a Daoist doctrinal tradition, but here described as the gateway of an open-ended exotic textual series responsible for much of the innovation in Chinese literature over the last two thousand and more years.

HS

Chicago,
August 2016

1

Norns and Norms

RENUNCIATION

A poem by Stefan George, made famous by Martin Heidegger's commentary in *On the Way to Language*, economically expresses a predominant view of language and translation that I think is wrong:

> Wunder von ferne oder traum
> Bracht ich an meines landes saum
>
> Und harrte bis die graue norn
> Den namen fand in ihrem born—
>
> Drauf könnt ich greifen dicht und stark
> Nun blüht und glänzt es durch die mark…
>
> Einst langt ich an nach guter fahrt
> Mit einem kleinod reich und zart
>
> Sie suchte lang und gab mir kund:
> 'So schläft hier nichts auf tiefem grund'
>
> Worauf es meiner hand entrann
> Und nie mein land den schatz gewann…
>
> So lernt ich traurig den verzicht:
> Kein ding sei wo das wort gebricht.[1]

The poem might be rendered thus:

> Some far fetched wonder or a dream
> I carried to my country's seam

And tarried till the Norn obscure
A name would from her well procure—

The better it to grip and hold
Now blooms and glows it through the wold...

Once landed I, fair sailing done,
Possessed of such a rich guerdon

Her search concluded, she made known:
"None such doth this profound earth own."

Whereat it vanished from my hand
No more to ornament my land...

So learnt I to forswear in pain:
Where word fails, shall no thing remain.[2]

George's fable involves lands, shores, travel, and nameless treasures, and has at its center a Norn who pronounces definitive judgment. What is a Norn? Opera-goers will remember the three Norns who sit weaving the rope of Fate in *Götterdämmerung*:

NORNS (O. Norse, *Nornir*), in Northern mythology, the female divinities of fate, somewhat similar to the Gr. Μοῖραι and the Roman *Parcae*. Like them they are generally represented as three in number, and they are said to spin, or weave, the destiny of men. Their dwelling is beside the Spring of fate, beneath the "world-tree," Yggdrasil's ash, which they water with draughts from the spring.[3]

The Norn here has authority to seek a name within her "well" for the object that the speaker has brought from far away: in George's poem it is not only authority over names, such as the French Academy is supposed to wield over the language spoken within the borders of France, but authority over the things represented by names. The traveler brings back to the "seam" or shoreline of his homeland a foreign thing described only in general terms as a "Wunder," "Traum," "Kleinod," or "Schatz" (wonder, dream, jewel, treasure). We will never know what it was. It might have been a cunningly wrought artifact from Byzantium—or a tomato. Yet when the Norn declares (in a more prosaic rendering of George's line) that "no such thing as this sleeps on the deep ground" of her native soil, the object "escaped from my hand, and nevermore did my country claim this treasure." The traveler then "must sadly learn renunciation: / No thing exists where the word is lacking." This is an outcome which Heidegger, forty years later, heartily endorses: "this line makes the word of language, makes language itself bring itself to language, and says something about the relation between word and thing."[4] And that relation is one in which the word dominates: "Only where the word for the thing has been found is the thing a thing. Only thus *is* it....The word alone gives being to the thing."[5] Or, more closely considered, "something *is* only where the appropriate and therefore competent word [*das geeignete und also zuständige Wort*] names a thing as being, and so establishes the given being as a being" (63). The Norn teaches self-denial in the service of the linguistic collectivity. She is not interested in the beauty, utility, or value of the "wunder," but, consulting her lexicon, blocks it at customs, so that "the frail rich prize... does not come to be a treasure, that is, a poetically secured possession of the land [*zu dem dichterisch verwahrten Eigentum des Landes*]."[6] Heidegger represents the dialogue with the Norn as a conversion-event. The speaker might previously have been a collector of exotic words, an amateur of foreign languages,[7] but the guardian of words and things forbids such eclecticism: "What the poet learned to renounce is his formerly cherished view regarding the relation of thing and word.... The poet experiences an authority, a dignity of the word than which nothing vaster and loftier can be thought" (65–6)—the dignity, that is, of the national language. The poet, renouncing, learns that the word is primordial only when the word emanates from the primordial German language; only if the object can be named with a native word will it be rightly named, will it "be."

A counterexample soon follows in Heidegger's discussion: "Take the sputnik. This thing, if such it is, is obviously independent of that name which was later tacked on to it. But perhaps matters are different with such things as rockets, atom bombs, reactors, and the like." *Sputnik* is self-evidently not a German word. Both word and thing wear their alienness on their faces. Its nomination, "tacked on to it" after the object's manufacture, clearly received no Norn's approval; it is so radically ungrounded that it must revolve around the planet forever without a resting place. For Heidegger technological objects like this have no authenticity, but are fabricated and rashly named by the "hurried thinking" of modern technology.[8] If we are to heed the call of thinking, we must learn to renounce that too, and deal only in the things that already "sleep on the deep ground" of a native tongue: rediscovering, for instance, in the words of a Laozi or a Heraclitus the meanings that slumbered in Greek or German. What we should not do is snatch up, with a magpie's appetite, bright terms and treasures from French, say (probably the major danger for George's circle), Italian, Arabic, or Algonquin, and force them into pairings with our ancestral speech.

I have let Heidegger's account of language and naming run on to its logical conclusion, the better to show its unlikeliness. I contend, rather, that languages do not usually have clear bounds, and that no Norn pronounces judgment on the words and things that are to have currency in their porous borders. Sputniks are, rather, the norm, and have always been. In the Book of Genesis, we read, Adam and Eve dwelt in a garden—a what, in the Hebrew text? The Hebrew text calls it a *pardesh*, which is not a Hebrew word at all, but one borrowed from Persian, and transliterated by the Greeks as παράδεισος, whence our word "paradise." The real Adamic language may have been macaronic. As rare as it must be for an authentic word to precede the thing, the new thing that arrives on the horizon of a linguistic community is often accompanied by an exotic word that names it, and how better to name a truly new thing than with a truly new or imported word? Was not Sputnik the first of its kind, a kind that should bear a far-fetched name in consequence? Despite Heidegger's innuendo, "Sputnik" is not actually extraterrestrial, but Russian. Foreign, and a word from enemy territory if you conceive of Germany as the land of thought hemmed in between two empires of technics.[9] Then again, "Sputnik" is not entirely a foreign word, even for the German speaker, because the Slavic root "*put*" that forms its core (*s-* "with" + *put* "path" + *-nik* "agent" = "fellow traveler") derives from the same Indo-European root as German *Pfad*, English *path*, Latin *spatium*, and Greek *pontos*.[10] Boundaries are relative. "Languages" are composed of dialects until a national pedagogical norm elevates one of them to the status of a rule in its particular jurisdiction, and languages are more or less porous, full of traces of contact.

If we consider languages as shading into one another, historically related, or bearing the traces of recent grafts and imprints, what then is translation? What is the knowledge that George's Norn would forbid us? What does the Sputnik have to tell us that is not just a technologically relayed beep?

Friedrich Schleiermacher was more prepared than the Norn to open the German language to foreign echoes:

> Now how shall the translator contrive to disseminate among his readers this sense of encountering the foreign when he presents them with a translation in their own tongue? ... [T]he more precisely the translation adheres to the turns and figures of the original, the more foreign it will seem to its reader.[11]

Antoine Berman calls this the ideal of a "non-ethnocentric translation."[12] It is not ethnocentric so long as it does not take the rules of one tribe's language as definitive, but wavers or travels elliptically between two norms. Yet someone's sense of correctness is bound to be offended. "The cries that translation of this sort must necessarily have a detrimental effect from within on the purity of the language and the peaceful course of its development have often been heard."[13] Schleiermacher is aware that the translator risks condemnation "if, in his attempt to preserve a foreign tone in the language of his translations, he does not observe that finest of lines, and these are dangers and sacrifices he cannot possibly avoid outright, as every person draws this line in a slightly different spot" (54). This amounts to claiming a limited freedom for art, circumscribed by a community of taste consisting of those who share, precisely, a taste for the foreign. Walter Benjamin took as his starting point that "no poem is meant for the reader"—from which one may infer that the success of a translation never has to be conditioned on its acceptability.[14] For the translator of Plato that Schleiermacher was, "the turns and figures of the original" already benefited from unsurpassable prestige and were self-evidently worth emulating; translators from Basque, Chinese, or Yoruba may find the "line" drawn much closer to the bounds of what is normal in the language of arrival. Thus a tension between ethics and aesthetics is set up. Translation can have, among its many purposes, that of challenging ethnocentric illusions of self-sufficiency, but taste is formed on precedents, and it can hardly advance the cause of the translated text for its translation to be found ugly. Yet some kinds of ugliness stretch our capacities for understanding and sympathy, and translators can be an avant-garde, hazarding forms of speech for which the other users of the language are not yet ready.

A tension, however, like an ellipsis, should not be resolved too quickly. It is a mistake to opt for This or That when the to-and-fro of This and That gives both their value. A prescriptive ethics of translation will necessarily find most translations compromised and itself alone pure. Thus the welcome polemic of Lawrence Venuti: translators have long been "complicit in the institutional exploitation of foreign texts and cultures."[15] We are to be on our guard against "domesticating translations that assimilate foreign literary texts too forcefully to dominant values at home, erasing the sense of foreignness that was likely to have invited translation in the first place."[16] More positively:

> insofar as foreignizing translation seeks to restrain the ethnocentric violence of translation, it is highly desirable today, a strategic cultural intervention in the current state of world affairs, pitched against the hegemonic English-language nations and the unequal cultural exchanges in which they engage their global others. Foreignizing translation in English can be a form of resistance against ethnocentrism and racism, cultural narcissism and imperialism, in the interests of democratic geopolitical relations.[17]

But what if we raise our eyes beyond the narrow band of "today" (i.e. 1995)? Is the hegemony of global English the problem of everyone in the world? To some extent, of course, it is, insofar as "the translation practices enlisted by transnational corporations, whether publishers, manufacturers, or advertising agencies, function in the same fundamental ways as those that underwrote European colonialism.... [Their] translations enact a process of identity formation in which colonizer and colonized, transnational corporation and indigenous consumer, are positioned unequally."[18] But the outreach of global capital cannot possibly account for everything that happens when books are translated, adapted, quoted, and read in different regions of the world. "A publishing industry that repeatedly issues fluent, domesticating translations of the latest American bestsellers—written in the standard dialect of the official language—encourages uncritical consumption of hegemonic values while maintaining current asymmetries in cross-cultural exchange."[19] Encourages, perhaps, but does it ensure those results? Is reception so predictable? Identifying the interests served by a book, a translation, or a publishing program (as Venuti often does with no more than a word or two) is not the same thing as examining the document itself, listening for its resonances, reestablishing its context of reception, watching to see what it does. A top-down sociology of reading results in such oddities as the preference for Banana Yoshimoto over Jun'ichirō Tanizaki[20] and the condemnation of Amos Tutuola—in precisely the terms used by upper-crust Nigerians of the 1950s— for his errors and awkwardnesses, his "imperfect schooling, his shaky command of English." Tutuola's novels are hybrid texts, to be sure, "but the calquing isn't intentional. It occurred inadvertently..."[21]—how does Venuti know? The element of the foreign missing from the contemporary, consumer-culture stories of Yoshimoto and foregrounded by every sentence Tutuola wrote matters less for this sociology of international letters than the publishing history of the works: the fact that in the 1950s Tanizaki's novels had the support of high-ranking American academics and élite presses, and that Tutuola was published by Faber and widely misunderstood to be speaking from the mythic core of the African mind, settle their value for Venuti.

There should, there must, be an ethics of translation. But that ethics should not be a truncated model of what ethicists confront and debate in their special domain. Moralizing is not the same thing as ethics. Nor is the domain of the ethical covered by uttering general rules supposed to apply to subsequent practice. Purposes, consequences, circumstances are all part of ethical reflection.

Antoine Berman formulates his ethic of translation as a resistance to the temptation of ethnocentric egotism: "Ethnocentric, here, means that which refers everything back to its own culture, to its norms and values.... Standing over against ethnocentric translation is ethical translation."[22] "Ethical action consists in recognizing and admitting the Other as Other," argues Berman, citing Levinas.[23] Nativizing translation would then be a negation of the otherness of the Other: even in its acts of mediation it is a suppression of whatever in the Other's speech is not already understandable in the terms familiar to the Self.

Does nativization always assimilate so abusively? The historian of Chinese thought Jean-François Billeter protests that the modus operandi of traditional Chinese texts constitutes in itself

> a problem to which translators may not have given sufficient thought, at least those translators who work from Chinese and particularly classical Chinese: how can we avoid letting a text that rumbles with echoes and reminiscences, that speaks to the imagination and to the memory as well as to the intellect, become, in French, even when it is exactly translated, a text that *has nothing to say to us*? The only way is to give it a background resonating, not with the Chinese past, but with our own, in other words, to deliberately introduce it into our literature.... To do this, it is necessary to subject every sentence or unit of utterance to a series of transformations, while strictly respecting the author's thought, and to pursue this series of transformations to the point where a transmutation occurs.[24]

The "series of transformations" turns an argument drawn from a Chinese series of allusions into a series of echoes familiar to the French-speaking reader—familiar one by one, though their concatenation may be unprecedented. The result should be a text that "says something to us" in emulation of the Chinese text's way of "saying something." What Billeter achieves in this way, however, falls under Berman's second interdiction, parallel to his condemnation of ethnocentric translation: the ban on "hypertextual translation." "Hypertextual, here, describes any text generated by imitation, parody, pastiche, adaptation, plagiarism, or any other type of formal transformation that starts from another *pre*-existing text.... *Ethnocentric translation is necessarily hypertextual, and hypertextual translation is necessarily ethnocentric.*"[25] As the opposite of ethnocentric translation, for Berman, is ethical translation (ethics here being construed as consciousness of responsibility toward the Other), so hypertextual translation must be answered with "poetic" translation: rather than being parasitic on some existing object in the universe of the language of the translator, the poetic translation will be original insofar as it speaks for the unassimilated Other.

One limit of the utility of Berman's call for "ethical translation" is its investment in such phantasmic identities as the self, the culture, and the language. This ethics is endangered when we pause to think that texts, cultures, and languages are intrinsically hybrid, traversed by multiple and shifting self/other boundaries, so that ethical responsibility is not clear-cut. Or, similarly, when we consider a case of ethnocentricity that does not derive from our own nation or culture: if ethnocentric translation is the standard in the Other's culture, would it not be ethnocentric of us to denigrate this attribute of the Other's Otherness? Until the way from a relativist to a universal ethics is clear, it will be uncertain how wide a field of applicability can be claimed for this theory of translation.

To return to Billeter's suggestion: if the aim is not to force Frenchness onto the Chinese original but to experiment with the French literary past in such a way as to produce the characteristic echoing effect of Chinese texts recalling their own literary past, the result will be as much a defamiliarization of "la langue de Racine" as it is a rendering-familiar of "la langue de Confucius." There are more than two ways of translating, in short. And translation has faced more than one danger over its history. The conjoined threats of English-language dominance and US-led global capitalism may not be with us forever; indeed, they are not of much use in interpreting most of human history. "The ethnocentric violence of translation" is not a unipolar thing: every empire appropriates, translates, and subordinates, and does not inevitably do so through the erasure of foreignness. Assertions of cultural leadership by translating empires are apt to provoke a counter-assertion on the part of subjected or translated peoples, who are not exempt from propagating appropriative, uniformitizing violences of their own.[26] Faced with any work of literary translation, "Misunderstanding! Distortion! Cultural blinders! Deception!" cries one set of critics, while another set, more optimistic, pleads for "creative adaptation." But no adaptation, however creative, can satisfy the apostles of "foreignization." Translators should be used to the idea that it is impossible to satisfy everyone, and now theorists of translation find that they cannot keep a quiet conscience either. So it would be good if some general lessons could be drawn from the history of cultural exchange and translation—a deeper understanding and a wider perspective on how languages intersect. The project of this book is to move away from the presentism and Anglocentrism that often mark even critical translation studies by examining what translation might be and mean in other attested cultural-historical situations. If such a thing is possible, it would avoid "translat[ing] according to our concept of translation, and *into* our concept of translation."[27] It aims at being descriptive and analytic rather than being led by prescription and short-term advocacy.[28]

Nativization, foreignization, source, target, translatable, untranslatable—the key terms of recent translation study reduce to a single axis, that of self and other, on which are overlaid ethical claims such as resistance, fidelity, and hospitality. At one pole we might situate the Norn, refusing all foreign wares; at the other, Lu Xun with his program of "stiff translation," the use of one's own language to render foreign texts almost illegibly in their literal wording and syntax as a shock treatment for cultural complacency.[29] But—to put it more positively—forms of language hybridity exist that cannot be plotted on the axis of self and other, and therefore cannot easily be called "translation" though translators are often responsible for their occurrence. Such techniques may cut through or leap over the so-called problem of translation.

ASKANCE FROM TRANSLATION

Controversies about translation are usually couched in mimetic terms, as a matter of the accuracy of the reproduction. Thus it is possible for Jacques Derrida to say, quite accurately and without contradiction, that "nothing is translatable" and "everything is translatable."[30] Nothing is translatable if you are looking for a perfect translation; everything is translatable in the sense that nothing is immune to the possibility of being translated (more or less completely, more or less well). But consider this example. In an early chapter of James Joyce's *Ulysses*, the character Stephen Dedalus is remembering his brief spell as a student in Paris. The stream-of-consciousness narration takes us into his thoughts:

> Paris rawly waking, crude sunlight on her lemon streets. Moist pith of farls of bread, the froggreen wormwood, her matin incense, court the air. Belluomo rises from the bed of his wife's lover's wife, the kerchiefed housewife is astir, a saucer of acetic acid in her hands. In Rodot's Yvonne and Madeleine newmake their tumbled beauties, shattering with gold teeth chaussons of pastry, their mouths yellowed with the pus of flan breton. Faces of Paris men go by, their wellpleased pleasers, curled conquistadores.[31]

The technique of showing Stephen's thoughts does not have to respect the difference between English and French, for when he thinks about Paris, it is natural that just as the images, flavors, and associations of the Left Bank come to his mind, so do the French names for these things. It would not do to replace "chausson" with "turnover" and "flan breton" with "custard," because the English foodstuffs are not made in the same way as the French ones and do not have the same taste or texture: the power of the memory, the Proustian memory we could legitimately say, would be lost in such a translation. Now in the French version of *Ulysses*, translated by two close associates of Joyce, we find:

> Paris s'éveille débraillé, une lumière crue dans ses rues citron. La pulpe moite des croissants fumants, l'absinthe couleur de rainette, son encens matinal, flattent l'atmosphère. Belluomo quitte le lit de la femme de l'amant de sa femme, la ménagère s'ébranle, un mouchoir sur sa tête, une soucoupe d'acide acétique à la main. Chez Rodot, Yvonne et Madeleine refont leur beauté fripée, dents aurifiées qui broient des chaussons, bouche jaunie par le pus du flan breton. Des visages de Parisiens passent, leurs charmeurs charmés, conquistadors au petit fer.[32]

In the "English" text, Joyce had written "chausson" and "flan breton," and the translator has apparently given up on translating them, for they appear simply as "chausson" and "flan breton." Though the mimesis between the English and French editions is here perfect, the words are literally untranslatable into French. What is also impossible to render into French is the effect of foreignness that those two French expressions had when appearing in the middle of a paragraph of English prose. The only way to recreate that in French would have been to insert their equivalents in Italian, say, or Spanish, or German— but that would involve reworking the setting of the whole episode to a degree that is out of the question: Paris is not replaceable here by Rome, Madrid, or Berlin, where it happens Stephen never studied.

When foreign words appear in a text, they make it *macaronic*: a patchwork, a hybrid, a graft. The act being performed by the writer is not one of translation, but of *transcription*, inscription, or imposition, much as if the writer were simply inventing a new word ("*impositio nominum*"). The newness of inscription contrasts with the conventional understanding of translation, which seeks to find a correlation between the already existing terms of two languages. The modern poet Hugh MacDiarmid seeks to create an effect of continuous surprise through such inscriptive newness:

> Mony's the auld half-human cry I ken
> Fa's like a revelation on the herts o'men
> As tho' the graves were split and the first man
> Grippit the latest wi' a freendly han'
> ...And there's forgotten shibboleths o' the Scots
> Ha'e keys to senses lockit to us yet
> —Coorse words that shamble thro' oor minds like stots,
> Syne turn on's muckle een wi' doonsin' emerauds lit.
>
> ...
>
> Hee-Haw! Click-Clack! And Cock-a-Doodle-Doo!
> —Wull Gabriel in Esperanto cry

Or a' the world's undeemis jargons try?
It's soon, no' sense, that faddoms the herts o'men,
And by my sangs the rouch auld Scots I ken
E'en herts that hae nae Scots'll dirl richt thro'
As nocht else could—for here's a language rings
Wi' datchie sesames, and names for nameless things.[33]

MacDiarmid's praise of "rough old Scots" with its "datchie [clever] sesames, and names for nameless things" is not exactly written in a Scots that might be heard on the street or in the schools; it is a self-made idiom combining bits of English and various Scottish regional forms, used, as often as not, to paraphrase Pushkin and other great Russians.[34] Jonson complained of Spenser that he "writ no language"; we might modify this to say that what MacDiarmid wrote was, more than his poems, his language.[35] Yet this cut-and-spliced patchwork language may be efficacious: the poet claims for it the apocalyptic power to encompass the past, the future, and the human, animal, and ghostly worlds.

Though MacDiarmid, like Joyce, is capable of translating, translating is not what he principally does. So we can say in answer to Derrida that not everything translates; not everything has to translate; translation is not the necessary channel for every kind of communicative exchange. Aberrant translations, pseudo-translations, interlinguistic puns, macaronics, nonce dubbings, all do violence to the language into which translation is being done—they may even make that language unrecognizable. I might say that they lie in a territory just *askance* of translation.

Askance? "Askance" is a word in English, and I pass for someone who knows English, but this is a word for the use of which I do not have a clear rule. Certainly I have the ability to use it: I can say that theorists of translation look askance at transliteration, but just what kind of relation "askance" denotes is a little vaguer in my mind. As so often happens, "I have only one language, and it's not mine."[36] Trying to lay a firmer hand on that language, I turn to the *Oxford English Dictionary*, where I learn that "askance" is probably an imported word, but no one is sure from where. Although fossilized and appearing now only in the set expression "to look askance at something," i.e. to look on it with disapproval, loathing, or contempt, the word had from the fifteenth to eighteenth centuries the meaning "sidewise, obliquely, askew, asquint." The dictionary's citations from Milton, in *Paradise Lost*, tell the story of the word, which also gives in small compass the story of the world as told by Milton:

iv. 504 The Devil... with jealous leer maligne Ey'd them askance.

vi. 149 Whom the grand foe with scornful eye askance Thus answer'd.

x. 668 He bid his Angels turne ascanse The Poles of Earth.

As for the etymology, it remained unknown for the Oxford lexicographers·

> Wedgwood suggests Italian *a schiancio* "bias, slanting, sloping or slopingly, aslope, across, overthwart"...Koch suggests a formation on Old Norse *á ská*...Diefenbach compares Jutlandish *ad-skands*, West Frisian *skân, schean*, which he connects with Dutch *schuin, schuins*....There is a whole group of words of more or less obscure origin in *ask-*, containing *askance, askant, askew, askie, askile, askoye, askoyne*...which are more or less closely connected in sense, and seem to have influenced one another in form. They appear mostly in the 16th or end of the 15th cent., and none of them can be certainly traced up to Old English; though they can nearly all be paralleled by words in various languages, evidence is wanting as to their actual origin and their relations to one another.[37]

Not passing down the direct line from Old English, but colliding sidewise, or askant, with early-modern English, whether coming from Italy, from the Netherlands, or from the far North, the word "askance" may have received its force of meaning from a "whole group of words of more or less obscure origin" and undefined meaning, continuing to slide along from the point of impact into the domain of the figurative. The dictionary editors continue: "In the fig. phrases *to look, eye, view askance* the idea expressed has varied considerably, different writers using them to indicate disdain, envy, jealousy, and suspicion. The last of these is now the prevalent idea." If the idea expressed has varied so considerably, it may be a fair bet that no one using the word "askance" has had a particularly clear sense of what it means, except that it denotes an orientation somehow distorted, perverted, and devalued, as distinguished from what is direct and upright. The word's history looks to be an example of lexical indiscriminateness: a word of uncertain provenance comes into the language and is used in a number of vague and possibly mutually inconsistent senses by authors who may have had another word in mind. In other words, *askance* exhibits the behavior that I see as running askew to the idea of translation as a substitution of one known meaning for another.

Sometimes substitutes fail us. Let us suppose that we are translating a text from language A to language B—whatever languages you will. Sooner or later a word will come up that refers to a particular circumstance of the climate, flora, fauna, customs, or arts of country A, for which no precise equivalent in country B for the moment suggests itself—and this is the case where one says, "The thing they call *sherbet*, or *amok*, or *kismet*, or *sharawadgi*." Then one goes and explains the thing that has just been named by its foreign name, its name in language A. It is always possible, I hold, to explain sherbet or sharawadgi—that is how we honor the principle of mutual intelligibility—but in doing so we do not single out the foreign thing by a name that comes from language B, the language in which we are doing the explaining, but rather reproduce a name from language A. We thereby transcribe; we become mimics. If the foreign word subsequently takes, if it becomes *the* word in language B for the item we were trying to translate from language A, we speak of it as a "loan word."[38] The term is significant, because it is a lie: a loaned object is one you sooner or later have to give back to the giver, but we have been using *sherbet* since the Middle Ages, *amok* since 1642, *sharawadgi* since 1685, *kaolin* since 1741, and show no signs of returning them to the speakers of Farsi, Malay, or Chinese. The feeling that the word is not completely ours, that it belongs somewhere else, makes us call it, apologetically, a borrowing though in fact we snatched it and intend to keep it.

Loan words are an opposite to translation in the following sense: with translation, interpretation always precedes the restatement; but with loan words, incorporation occurs without interpretation. Translation works out what the meaning of the foreign text is, then elaborates a corresponding set of meanings that will suitably address the speakers of the target language. With transliteration, foreigners are putting words in your mouth: pure mimicry, as when English speakers imitated the sounds of *amok, ketchup, kayak*, or *samurai*. (Not to mention *gavagai*.)[39] The fact that incorporation can be separated from interpretation installs a strangeness in language, a zone of vocabulary where the mouth acts independently of the mind and where the native speaker and native competency are no longer in command.

In such situations, the wholesale use of loan words and alien constructions is sure to provoke anxiety about purity. Speakers of the language as it used to be feel that it is being adulterated. Joining, as he so often does, clarity of insight with dogged defense of dubious principles, Samuel Johnson gave memorable voice to this sentiment in the preface to his 1754 *Dictionary*:

> The great pest of speech is frequency of translation. No book was ever turned from one language into another, without imparting something of its native idiom; this is the most mischievous and comprehensive innovation; single words may enter by thousands, and the fabrick of the tongue continue the same, but new phraseology changes much at once; it alters not the single stones of the building, but the order of the columns. If an academy should be established for the cultivation of our stile…let them, instead of compiling grammars and dictionaries, endeavor, with all their influence, to stop the license of translatours, whose idleness and ignorance, if it be suffered to proceed, will reduce us to babble a dialect of France.[40]

What Johnson is responding to here is the traces of the original signifiers that cling to even the most "domesticating" translations and with the passage of time make themselves at home. He is noticing, that is, a faint trace of transliteration, of direct echo, in translation, and demanding that it be kept out by restricting translations altogether. As if in response to such nativist sentiment, other translations do their best to cover their tracks and replace the obvious foreign loans with back-formations using the native vocabulary.

Indeed, the labeling of loan words as borrowed plumage is complicit with the system of definitions that would center translation on the transfer of meanings from one language to another ("translation" here being a function of the definitions of "meaning" and "language"). Recentering the investigation of language contact on transliteration will involve recognizing that languages are not bounded systems but communicative ones, thriving in contact and exchange with other systems. An example of the more usual contrary way of proceeding will show what is at stake. Emily Apter's *The Translation Zone* turns at one point to Francophone authors from North Africa and the Caribbean who salt their academic or metropolitan French with passages in a hybrid or creole language (Kreyòl, Arabo-French, Arabo-Berber-French, and the like). Apter says: "Insofar as Creole heralds a condition of linguistic postnationalism and denaturalizes monolingualization . . . it may be said to emblematize a new comparative literature based on translation."[41] But in the terms of the distinction I am trying to draw here, this is precisely wrong. To describe Creole as an emblem of translation reasserts the dominance of semantics, of meaning and interpretation. (Haitians would be surprised, additionally, to learn that speaking a Creole language somehow precludes nationalism, or that no Haitians are naturally monolingual.) Creole languages, said to derive their lexical store from one language and their grammatical articulations from another,[42] forcefully remind us that translation is not the only way that two languages can interact. That is, creoles do not translate, but "migrate," their source languages to a new target language; they cite, echo, cut, paste, recombine. As Salikoko Mufwene has argued, there is no structural criterion specific to creoles, despite many attempts over the last 200 years to identify one.[43] What makes a language "creole," if we are to maintain the term, is not its structure but its historical relation to one or more predecessor languages, a relation of incorporation and remotivation. "Creole" expresses not a type but a genealogy. All languages are to some degree creoles (English, with its stores of Anglo-Saxon, Celtic, Norman French, and Latin, being an obvious case). The development of such fusion languages is an extension of the dynamic of "transliteration" (not translation) despite the fact that most creoles, when they first entered the written record, were considered the language of illiterates. If it can be said that languages evolve, then transcription, or the incorporation of foreign verbal matter, must be essential to the process, as translation in the traditional sense would have authority only to rearrange pre-existing elements of the target language. Relying on the model of translation to think about cultural contact and transfer renders creole invisible, secondary, marginal.

Characteristically, it is when the language of omnipotent, omnivalent translation is most emphatic that the indispensability of transliteration comes to the fore. *The Translation Zone* concludes with a fantasia about digital communication as the ultimate extension of translation:

> For it is becoming clear [Apter says] that digital code holds out the prospect, at least, of translating everything into everything else. A kind of universal cipher or default language of information, digital code will potentially function like a catalytic converter, translating beyond the interlingual and among orders of *bios* and *genus*, liquid and solid, music and architecture, natural language and artificial intelligence, language and genes, nature and data, information and capital.[44]

Similar extensions of the term "translation" are also favored by theorists of technology. Lev Manovich remarks of binary code that it serves as a "visual Esperanto" for word, sound, image, movement, money, indeed every kind of data and difference in the world. "In new media lingo, to 'transcode' something is to translate it into another format. The computerization of culture gradually accomplishes similar transcoding in relation to all cultural categories and concepts."[45] Here then is translation carried to an extreme, for Esperanto was supposed to be the universal language, the language for which two-way translatability was always guaranteed. But Manovich's transcoding/translating metaphor, however appealing, is precisely the wrong one, for digital media do not interpret the contents they vehicle in any meaningful way. Your computer does not understand the Word file you type into it, or express its content to another computer's understanding when you email the file to a friend. Rather, it codes the letters and formatting into a sequence of ones and zeroes (i.e. electrical impulses) that are then copied onto the hard disk and recopied, through instructions, onto the other person's computer, then re-represented as letters and formatting. Transliteration again: incorporation without interpretation. Translating, paraphrasing, or summarizing content is something else. Media do not deal with content in that way: they vehicle content, they permit it to be packaged, they subject it to algorithms and encoding, but no more. And when we deal with digital media, as with technological objects generally, we do not "open up the black box," so to speak, and understand its coding from the inside. Rather, our relation with such media is one of quotation, block citation, repetition, and selection. A digitally mediated message is in creole, to the degree that it is complex and multi-medial. I cut and paste; I drop a film clip or a photograph into a slide presentation.

To do this, I do not in the least need to understand the movie camera, the digitization process, the computer program that runs the film clip, or the LCD screen that lights up to display it. Each of these things is for me, practically speaking, a black box with a button on it and a cable that I can use to connect it to another black box. I can make things happen with black boxes regardless of my subjective lack of involvement in the process, but my linking up of my expressive intent with blocked and chunked automatic operations makes me to some degree a post-human person.[46] The "foreignization" involved in the human relation to any technological object (be it a knapped flint) is without return.

Most technology is inscriptional and transcriptional, rather than translational. We use translation to talk to other humans, because humans are keyed to the meaning-based behaviors that translation can address; but machines simply repeat. (This is not to deny sufficiently sophisticated programmed machines a Turing-like level of apparent spontaneity.) When we use loan words, when we devise creoles, we are acknowledging the repetition, the inclusion of otherness, of a machine, in ourselves, transcription as the internal limit of translation.

Transcription, writ large, tells us that we don't express ourselves, rather we discover ourselves, through language. Our cultural forms then become valuable since we no longer see them as mere vehicles for transmitting what is already known. The avant-garde artistic movements of the twentieth century dislocated traditional modes of representation for precisely this reason. What transcription can do, when enlarged to the scope of a method, is teach us new ways of behaving with signs that ought to leave us at odds with—askance from—our former selves. Let us then consider translation as a particular case, a local application, of the transliteration relation, and see what becomes of it.

2

Death and Translation

Traduire, c'est perdre le corps.[1]

MIMESIS

If modernist literary writing and literary theory had a common aim, it was to displace mimesis and authorship—two long-standing doctrines concerning the production and interpretation of texts—in favor of the autonomy of language. "Every text constructs itself as a mosaic of citations, every text is the absorption and transformation of another text."[2] Bold words; but anyone will grant that they hold self-evidently for translations. Perhaps that is why translation has always been so central an agency for reflection on the nature of writing. When translation is being done, "scandals" are never far away: the relation involves trust and speaking on another's behalf, and such intercession raises the prospect of abuse.[3] Translation could even be held to be a perversion of the mimetic theory of art. Rather than imitating human beings or reality (the purpose of poetry according to Plato, Aristotle, and Horace), translation imitates a text. And obedient to that rule of imitation, we readers of translations assume that, if all goes well, we should be having an experience analogous in every point to that of readers of the original text; what a translator has to "say" is, ideally, a trustworthy report on the text being translated, and nothing more. When it departs from the strict program of mimesis, of seconding the primary text, translation speaks in its own right—and thus out of turn. Does a translation ever have the right to contest the translated text's primacy? Perhaps it does, when the "original" incites it to do so. The earliest translation of a Baudelaire poem into Chinese shows how this may happen.

"Une Charogne"
Charles Baudelaire, 1857

Rappelez-vous l'objet que nous vîmes, mon âme,
 Ce beau matin d'été si doux:
Au détour d'un sentier une charogne infâme
 Sur un lit semé de cailloux,

Les jambes en l'air, comme une femme lubrique,
 Brûlante et suant les poisons,
Ouvrait d'une façon nonchalante et cynique
 Son ventre plein d'exhalaisons.

Le soleil rayonnait sur cette pourriture,
 Comme afin de la cuire à point,
Et de rendre au centuple à la grande Nature
 Tout ce qu'ensemble elle avait joint;

Et le ciel regardait la carcasse superbe
 Comme une fleur s'épanouir.
La puanteur était si forte, que sur l'herbe
 Vous crûtes vous évanouir.

Les mouches bourdonnaient sur ce ventre putride,
 D'où sortaient de noirs bataillons
De larves, qui coulaient comme un épais liquide
 Le long de ces vivants haillons.

Tout cela descendait, montait comme une vague
 Ou s'élançait en pétillant;
On eût dit que le corps, enflé d'un souffle vague,
 Vivait en se multipliant.

Et ce monde rendait une étrange musique,
 Comme l'eau courante et le vent,
Ou le grain qu'un vanneur d'un mouvement rythmique
 Agite et tourne dans son van.

Les formes s'effaçaient et n'étaient plus qu'un rêve,
 Une ébauche lente à venir
Sur la toile oubliée, et que l'artiste achève
 Seulement par le souvenir.

Derrière les rochers une chienne inquiète
 Nous regardait d'un oeil fâché,
Épiant le moment de reprendre au squelette
 Le morceau qu'elle avait lâché.

—Et pourtant vous serez semblable à cette ordure,
    À cette horrible infection,
Étoile de mes yeux, soleil de ma nature,
    Vous, mon ange et ma passion!

Oui! telle vous serez, ô la reine des grâces,
    Après les derniers sacrements,
Quand vous irez, sous l'herbe et les floraisons grasses,
    Moisir parmi les ossements.

Alors, ô ma beauté! dites à la vermine
    Qui vous mangera de baisers,
Que j'ai gardé la forme et l'essence divine
    De mes amours décomposés!⁴

"'Une Charogne' [A Carcass] 死屍 by Charles Baudelaire: Preface"
Xu Zhimo 徐志摩, 1924⁵

Among the *Flowers of Evil* of Charles Baudelaire, "Une Charogne" is the rankest, but also the most strangely enticing immortal flower, and a translation can only represent it with "cast-off dregs." The melody and color of Baudelaire's poetry are the vague shadows of the last rays of a setting sun—distant, pallid, sinking rays. Baudelaire is not a night owl, much less a rising lark; his voice is like that of a wounded cuckoo that has coughed up all its blood. His abode is not the green woods, much less the tranquil valleys; he seems to have chosen to dwell in the broken-down tomb of the licentious Greek queen Clytemnestra, with a thistle growing alongside it, and to look from between its spikes at the gloom falling on the Lion Gate of Mycenae. And he seems to be a poisonous plant from the tropics, bearing leaves as long as a crocodile's tail and vast blossoms like embroidered parasols, with a strangely toxic yet attractive perfume, unforgettable even as it numbs you to death. Literary Europe in the second half of the nineteenth century was imbibed with his unique stench. Its power has poisoned not a few, and inebriated even more. Now that the poisoned dead are risen and the inebriates have come back to themselves, they not only have no reproach to make against Baudelaire, but are completely smitten with him and lament to see that strange scent of his overcome by the heavy dust and dirt of time. Today, no matter how desperately they inhale, they are still unable to recover the vanished stench....

I'm just a country bumpkin, and so I can do no more than mouth Baudelaire's poetry, I don't understand it. But genuine music asks only to be listened to. The buzzing of insects by the riverside, the chatter of swallows under the eaves, the sound of water in mountain rivulets, the rustling of pine needles—you have only to use your ears to listen to them, and if you know how to listen, "listening" is "understanding." Those insect calls, swallow cries, water cadences, and pine rustlings will all have a meaning, but their meaning is like the scent on the lips of your beloved—it exists in your imagination. If you don't believe me, go catch an ꞏꞏꞏꞏꞏꞏꞏꞏ ꞏꞏꞏꞏꞏꞏ or a long-tailed swallow, go scoop up a handful of water or snap off a pine branch and ask them what it is they are saying—they will only wriggle their legs or shake their heads at you and curse you for a country bumpkin. And you'll have no one to blame but yourself!

So the secret of Baudelaire's poetry is not in the meaning of his words, but in the intangible syllables he makes; what he penetrates is not your skin (that would be too thick and solid) but that soul that you too are unable to put your hands on. It's like love: the contact of two pairs of lips is just a symbol, and what is really in contact, what really comes together, is your souls. So although I say I'm just a rustic, I do love music, *real* music—by which I don't mean the Salvation Army band with its awful drum or the piano you ladies play. Pardon me if I seem to be speaking too arrogantly—but be that as it may! I can hear not just audible music, but inaudible music too (actually, it has sound but you're incapable of listening to it). I may as well admit it: I must be a total mystic, and why not? I am convinced that the basic constituent of the universe, the stuff of human life, the stuff of both everything that has form and of formless ideas, is nothing but music, a wonderful music. The stars in the sky, the milk-white swans paddling on the water, the mist rising from the forest, a letter from a friend, the cannon on the battlefield, the will o' the wisp floating over the cemetery, the stone lion in the alley, the dream I had last night…every one of these things is made from nothing but music, not a one of them but is music. Send me to the lunatic asylum; I'll grit my teeth and stick to my story. Yes, everything is music—what Zhuangzi calls "the piping of heaven, the piping of earth, and the piping of man."[6] Just music. If you can't hear it, bemoan your own insensitive ears or your thick skin, don't blame me. Maybe you can count one-two-three-four, you can hire a rickshaw, you can write modern free verse, put in order the facts of China's legendary history, or do some other little trick so trivial and limited that it makes one feel sorry for you—nonetheless life is immense, the universe is immense, your spirit is immense.

But coming back to Baudelaire's *Flowers of Evil*: I've bravely reproduced one flower of evil. It's a counterfeit, made out of paper, scrap paper even—made from cloth, or better yet, rags. It's just an outward show: it has no life, no soul, so it doesn't have that unique perfume and poison. Smell and taste it all you like, it's harmless. I looked at two or three English translations and none of them were right—the water of the Jade Spring flows nowhere but in the Jade Spring itself.

The translated poem:

> 我愛，記得那一天好天氣
> 　你我在路旁見著的那東西；
> 橫躺在亂石與薑艸裏，有
> 　一具潰爛的屍體。

牠直開著腿，湯婦似的放肆 (Comme une femme lubrique)
　泄漏著穢氣，沾惡腥的粘味，
牠那癰潰的胸腹也無有遮蓋，
　沒忌憚的淫穢。

火熱的陽光照臨著這腐潰，
　化驗似的蒸發，煎煮，消毀，
解化著原來組成整體的成分，
　重向自然返歸。

青天微粲的俯看著這變態，
　彷彿是眷注一莖向陽的朝卉；
那空氣里卻滿是穢息，難堪，
　多虧你不曾昏醉。

大群的蠅蚋在爛肉間喧鬨，
　醞釀著細蛆，黑水似的沟湧，
牠們吞噬著生命的遺蛻，
　啊，報仇似的兇猛。

那蛆群潮瀾似的起，落，
　無屬的飛蟲倉皇的爭奪：
轉像是無形中有生命的吹息，
　巨萬的微生滋育。

醜惡的屍體。從這繁生的世界，
　彷彿有風與水似的異樂縱瀉。
又像是在風車旋動的和音中，
　穀農急雨似的四射。

眼前的萬象遲早不免消翳，
　夢幻似的，只糊的輪廓存遺，
有時在美術師的腕底，不期的，
　掩映著遙遠的回憶。

在那磐石的後背躲著一隻野狗，
　她那火赤的眼睛向著你我守候，
她也撕下了一塊爛肉，憤憤的，
　等我們過後來享受。

就是我愛你，也不免一般的腐朽，
　這樣惡腥的傳染，誰能忍受——
你，我願望的明星！照我的光明！
　這般的純潔，溫柔！

是呀，便你也難免，艷宛的后！
　等到那最後的祈禱為你誦咒，

這美妙的丰姿也不免到泥草裏，
　　與陳死人共朽。

因此，我愛呀，吩咐那趑趄的蟲蠕，
　　它來親吻你的生命，吞噬你的體膚，
說我的心永遠葆著你的妙影，
　　即使你的肉化群蛆！

My love, do you remember that day of fine weather
　　When you and I saw, by the side of the road, that thing:
Lying on its side among scattered stones and weeds was
　　A swollen dead body.

Legs spread open, it lay loosely like a dissolute woman
(Comme une femme lubrique)
　　Exuding a foul stench, a sticky odor of putrefaction,
Its collapsing breast and belly had nothing to cover them,
　　Shameless in filth.

The fiery sun approached this rottenness,
　　As if in a chemical experiment to transform, roast, and dissolve it,
Separating the elements of the original organism
　　To return them once more to nature.

The blue sky minutely looked down on this perversity,
　　As if gazing towards a heliotrope;
The air was so full of a filthy odor, unbearable,
　　That you all but fainted.

Great hordes of flies were humming and buzzing in the rotten flesh,
　　Bubbling maggots like black water spurted,
They devoured this shell of a living thing,
　　Ah, as fierce as revenge.

The waves of vermin rose and fell,
　　The insatiable flies fought desperately:
As if from shapelessness a breath of life was emerging,
　　Redoubled ten thousand times.

A putrid carcass. From this busy world,
　　A strange music, like wind and water, seemed to escape.
It resembled grain amid the harmonious sounds of a windmill,
　　That a farmer scatters like a sudden shower of rain.

The shapes that meet the eye sooner or later vanish,
　　Like a dream, only a faint outline remains.

Sometimes, under the artist's hand, unexpectedly
    Chiaroscuro evokes a distant memory.

Hiding behind a heap of pebbles was a wild dog
    Whose fiery eyes glared at us as it waited its turn.
It had snatched off a piece of rotten flesh and impatiently
    Waited for us to pass by and let it enjoy more.

As much as I love you, there is no avoiding the universal decay,
    This contagion of corruption, who can bear it?—
You, the bright star of my desire! The sun shining upon me!
    You, so pure, so gentle!

Yes, not even you can avoid it, you, queen of beauty,
    When the last prayers for you have been chanted,
Your wondrous charms must go into the mud and grass,
    To molder among the many dead.

Therefore, my beloved, tell that clumsy worm,
    When he comes to kiss your life and swallow your members,
Tell him my heart will forever preserve your wondrous image,
    Even though your flesh has turned to maggots![7]

ASSIMILATION

The relation between Baudelaire's text and its Chinese translation-with-preface may seem to violate the mimetic norm of translation, until we scrutinize more carefully the notion of mimesis.

Mimesis, a term familiar to readers of Aristotle's *Poetics*, is an instance of a pervasive pattern or model in the philosopher's scientific work—pervasive, that is, if we are willing to recognize a somewhat abstract description of the pattern. In digestion, for example, the mixed substances of food are ground up, separated into various kinds, and then selectively assimilated by the blood, which takes into itself that which, in the food, resembles it and can be used to maintain bodily heat; the leftover is eliminated.[8] Perception, similarly, is accounted for by the sensory organ's being in some way of the same nature as the things it is to perceive. The eye is apt to receive impressions of shape and color because it "is potentially like what the perceived object is actually," that is, it has the ability to be affected by, and to reproduce within itself, the corresponding forms that outer objects possess; the nose and ear and touch likewise receive and reproduce the sensations corresponding to the nature of those organs, but only those.[9] Perception, in its way, digests the object—assimilates it by breaking it down and taking it in, though only formally, not materially. Aristotle extends this pattern of thinking into the linguistic realm by his cognitive redefinition of the older rhetorical term *metaphora*. When he describes the facility with metaphors as a gift for "observing the sameness" (*to to homoion theôrein*) in two unrelated things, he makes metaphor not a relation between words, but a perception and an assimilation.[10] It is an act. If I describe Achilles as a lion, I am not saying that he is made of lion-flesh but that the forms of his activity, of his *energeia*, correspond in me to perceived forms of a lion's activity. Perception involves our organs being affected by the objects of perception, becoming momentarily like them, whereupon the forms of perception are referred to the mind for further distillation and digestion. (At some level, to speak of the mind as a digestive organ is not quite a figure of speech, for what Aristotle calls the *psykhê* runs, like the stomach, on heat.)[11] Presumably when the mind recognizes two different inputs as being similar, as happens in metaphor or mimesis, it creates for the nonce a "form of the forms" of those things, a marker of the respect in which they are the same; and this extraction is what learning and imitating consist of.[12] Not only as thinking beings, but as living creatures we are always engaged in assimilating into ourselves what we need from things and dis-assimilating or rejecting the rest.

Such organic metaphors may seem to have little to offer the Information Age we supposedly inhabit, a time when the body, the self, and matter have ceded control over culture, economy, and politics to instantaneous digital (not analog) communication.[13] Information, one gathers, is not singular but reproducible; it is apt to be realized in an infinity of different codings or formats; it doesn't change when it is transposed from one physical shape to another, or from one medium to another; according to some people, it is morally indifferent; according to others, it is a basic right; still others think it wants to be free. Some people think that our personalities are constellations of information that might be downloaded onto computers and copied into new bodies.[14] As Katherine Hayles puts it, "an ideology of disembodiment" has accompanied cybernetics from its inception in the 1940s onward.[15]

"The fundamental problem of communication," said Claude Shannon in his epochal information-theory paper of 1948, "is that of reproducing at one point either exactly or approximately a message selected at another point."[16] *Reproducing*: representing, re-enacting, miming. "Information" implies the possibility of mimesis and the challenge of a transfer. That which, in an information-bearing object, can be moved to a separate object of similar or different nature (for example, a telephone number being copied from a directory to a scrap of paper, then read aloud to someone who will carry it away in her mind and subsequently enter it on a keypad), is deemed to be the information, and the other properties of any of the objects through which that information transits are merely incidental. Of course, it is possible to be mistaken about where the information lies: supposing that I used black ink for numbers I wanted you to call, and red ink for numbers I wanted to warn you never to call, the numbers alone would not support the information to be conveyed, but a further mark of some kind would be needed. However, that mark would not have to be the same mark as in the original message, so long as some difference could be signaled.

As Shannon discovered, the channels whereby humans receive and transmit information are massively redundant. It would be possible, for example, to remove every other letter of a text, say Baudelaire's poem "Une Charogne," without greatly affecting its legibility.[17] Redundancy guards against loss, for information decays as errors are introduced into the serial "reproduction" of the "message." We might make prefatory declarations about what is and is not information in our messages, but these too might be affected by error or misunderstanding.

Those who deal with literary language can never be sure what is information and what is random noise or mere material support. When Dadaists and Russian avant-garde poets began playing with typefaces, they laid claim to a new dimension of non-negotiable specificity in the reproducible artifacts they were proposing to the attention of readers. Hugo Ball's "Karawane," for example, uses a different typeface in each of its seventeen lines.[18] To translate it into a typographically remote language such as Japanese, or even to read it out loud, one would have to think of equivalent sets of differences to transmit the differences built into the first text. That's assuming the reader had recognized typography as part of the information, not just decoration, of the poem (Ball's poem is in fact often reproduced all in one typeface). To be a reader of literature, you have to leave yourself open to surprises, or as Claude Shannon might have said, to increases in the required carrying capacity of the signal.

And as everyone has heard, poetry is what is lost in translation.[19] Poetry resists paraphrase, its reduction to information-value. To make sense of that assertion with the terminology we've been using just now, we will have to undo some familiar word-associations. Usually we would say that the *form* of the original, namely its meter, rhymes, word order, and so forth, has to be left behind and only its *substance* or *content* (if that!) carries over when it is translated into English or Chinese. But it is truer to the interests of poetry and the kinds of effort involved in writing it, as well as to Aristotle, to say that the form is what is transmitted and the matter is left behind. The word "form" causes confusion, because it appears in two distinctions, that between form and content and that between form and matter, in which it does not have at all the same sense. Let us adjust the terms so as to point up the analogy between Aristotle's hylomorphism (including related processes such as perception, digestion, and mimesis) and contemporary theories of information, including the tacit theory of information (information as meaning) that presides over most translation. Let "form" as in "form/content" henceforth be called "realization," and "content" in that duality be "theme"; let "form" as in "form/matter" remain "form." Thus we shall say that whatever is "reproduc[ed] ... either exactly or approximately" realizes the *form* of the translated poem, and whatever adheres to the wording of one or another version (even be it the original) is the poem's *material*. This will amount to calling "form" what used to be, in literary parlance, called "content"; but the reversal of terms will bring benefits, among them clarity.

More than analogy, Aristotelianism and information-theory exhibit a lineage. Our very word "information" is a medieval invention meant to convey one of Aristotle's theories. See for example Dante, *Purgatorio*, canto 25, where Dante asks the Roman poet Statius why the disembodied souls have faces and expressions and can even appear to grow fat or lean. Statius explains that when the soul makes its leap to the afterlife,

> Tosto che loco lì la circonscrive,
>   la virtù formativa raggia intorno
>   così e quanto ne le membra vive...
> così l'aere vicin quivi si mette
>   e in quella forma chè in lui suggella
>   virtüalmente l'alma che ristette... (88–96)

As soon as space encompasses [the soul] there, the formative virtue radiates around, in form and quality as in the living members...so here the neighboring air shapes itself in that form which is virtually imprinted on it by the soul that stopped there...[20]

Death and translation provide occasions for testing what Statius calls, in a variant phrase, "virtute informativa" (line 41), informative virtue or, we might say, information-value. In Dante's science fiction, the soul makes a body for itself—a virtual body—out of the space it now occupies. No problems with the transmission: the mimesis is perfect, a static-free rendition of identity as appearance. Anyone who has translated between languages will envy this perfection. Wouldn't it be nice if a French poem could automatically "imprint itself on the air" of England or China and virtually reconstitute itself there? If God is doing the translating, and the universe is set up so that an identity can be reconstructed irrespective of place and matter, no Turing test will be needed to check the results. But our usual experience is that the identity of poems, unlike that of telephone numbers, is wrapped up in the material conditions of their realization; to lose those conditions is to lose the poem. Translation is a low-fidelity circuit for high-fidelity information, as careful practitioners will know.

STRANGE MUSIC

Xu Zhimo declares modest ambitions for his translation of Baudelaire's poem "Une Charogne." He describes his version as the "cast-off dregs," the discarded byproduct, of the original. It's a counterfeit flower of evil, "just an outward show.... Smell and taste it all you like, it's harmless." As if to say that translation is impossible, or that style is utterly personal, he ends by conceding that "the water of the Jade Spring flows nowhere but in the Jade Spring itself."

Though these gestures seem to leave a great deal in the translating up to chance, the choice of poem is, again on Xu's declaration, highly determined. "Une Charogne" is "the rankest, but also the most strangely enticing immortal flower" among Baudelaire's flowers of evil, the one that most powerfully transmits "his unique stench." Curiously, the translator ascribes direct acquaintance with that stench to nineteenth-century Europe, and appears to have observed its effects in others rather than to have undergone them himself. This is at least partly a matter of fact. Xu did not read French on his own, but read Baudelaire with the help of dictionaries and previous English translations.[21] "I can do no more than mouth Baudelaire's poetry, I don't understand it," he admits, and then shifts into a different register of justification: "But genuine music asks only to be listened to.... if you know how to listen, 'listening' is 'understanding.'... the secret of Baudelaire's poetry is not in the meaning of his words, but in the intangible syllables he makes; what he penetrates is not your skin (that would be too thick and solid) but [your] soul." This sounds like a desperate compensatory move—for someone unable to access the poet's meaning to claim that meaning is immaterial to what the poet is doing and to put his own experience of Baudelaire, as well as the "secret of Baudelaire's poetry," on the non-linguistic plane of music, exalted by Wagnerians and decadents as the condition to which all other arts aspire. From the way Xu talks about it, an otherwise uninformed Chinese reader might imagine that the so-called translation was his own invention. (In fact it is a fairly close paraphrase, though it omits many conceptual links and misleads the reader to imagine its subject to be a human, rather than animal, cadaver.) Simultaneous with making this claim of direct access to Baudelaire, of a "listening" that is equivalent to "understanding," Xu Zhimo seems constrained to exceed the boundaries of his own language, introducing into written Chinese the English term "mystic" and an unusual Shanghai transliteration for the foreign word "piano" (Mandarin: *pi-xia-na*): words that might well have been inexpressive "music" or mere sound to many of his readers. (The typesetter turned "Mystic" into "Mystu," evidence of difficulty in receiving the signal.) And like a liar compelled to envelop his falsehoods in ever bigger contexts of falsehood, Xu follows his promotion of Baudelaire's poetry to the status of music, which amounts to a denial of its specifically linguistic character—the very character that its translator is unable to appreciate—with the announcement that not only Baudelaire's poetry, but nature, human life, and the entire universe are nothing but music. "The piping of heaven, the piping of earth, and the piping of man," he calls it, using a phrase from the fourth-century BCE philosopher Zhuang Zhou: *tian lai, di lai, ren lai* 天籟地籟人籟. In the context of such an all-encompassing unity, differences like that between French and Chinese appear small. The translator's hyperbolic excuse for his avowed inabilities is, however, the moment at which Xu's preface most closely cites Baudelaire: "étrange musique" (rendered in the Chinese version of the poem as *yiyue* 異樂) is one of the most arresting tropes in "Une Charogne." Thus repeated in various languages and senses, the term "music" connects three texts: Baudelaire's poem, Zhuangzi's parable, and the new text in which Xu combines the first two; its repetition asserts that the two prior texts are in some kind of relationship as well as offering a ground for that assertion in the present text's so-called "mysticism." Is the repetition in any way a mimesis of the first occurrence in the series, the "étrange musique" named by Baudelaire's original?

Like Xu Zhimo's apologetic preface, Baudelaire's poem is concerned with dregs and leftovers. "Rappelez-vous, mon âme," it begins, calling on the poet's beloved to summon up the memory of a grisly sight encountered on a country outing, the decomposing carcass of an unspecified animal (cow? horse?) baking in the sun and bustling with scavenger activity. In a brutal variant on the *carpe diem* theme (for gentler versions, think of Ronsard's "Mignonne, allons voir si la rose" and "Quand vous serez bien vieille, le soir à la chandelle") the narrator reminds the woman that one day, "after the last sacraments,"[22] she will be in the same condition as the carcass, and enjoins her to tell the worms that he, the speaker, has "preserved the form and divine essence / Of my decomposed loves!" The message is a strange one, because it amounts to having the woman say to the worm that she herself, or her body, is a dreg, a cast-off, an incidental support to the "form and essence" ("la forme et l'essence divines") of one of Baudelaire's loves, which is pre-served ("gardé") elsewhere, in Baudelaire, and cannot be "decomposed." Yet short of imagining that Charles Baudelaire is physically immortal, the speaker of the poem must expect to undergo the same fate himself, and thus when he says that he has preserved ("j'ai gardé") the essence of his loves, the "je" must be taken as pure linguistic inscription, the "I" that speaks in every repetition of the poem rather than the "I" that, as biography tells us, died in 1867 during a slow, incomplete recovery from a stroke. "Je" continues to speak to us as the result of an immense series of reproductions that were each, as far as we can tell, deemed successful: transfers from manuscript to print, and from printed edition to printed edition, each successive copyist, editor, typesetter, photo offset machine, translator, and reader recognizing the mimesis of a form and recreating it as the newest link of the ongoing chain. A wonderfully unlikely consistency of forms repeated in the teeth of informational entropy enables us to imagine that Charles Baudelaire is still speaking to us.

The separation of "forme" and "ordure," as a process not a pair of categories, is what the poem lingers over. It is digestive. The stench (like that which Xu ascribes to Baudelaire's enormous "flowers") is impossible to ignore—"la puanteur était si forte, que sur l'herbe / Vous crûtes vous évanouir." The cadaver roasting in the sun ("a god kissing carrion," says Hamlet) is animated with a strange new life as flies and maggots cascade up and down its sides: "on eût dit que le corps... vivait en se multipliant." Its decay is presented on the analogy of information decay, of erasure, forgetting, and fading, through a simile that shows the animal losing all its individual properties and reverting to the state of a rough preliminary sketch. "Les formes s'effaçaient" (note the imperfect tense, for ongoing and incomplete action). But the erasure is, oddly, narrated as a creation in reverse, "une ébauche lente à venir," slow in coming, not going away, "une ébauche... que l'artiste achève / seulement par le souvenir." The counter-natural time sequence (used to powerful effect in "Le Cygne" as well, where a construction site is made to feel like an antique ruin) here makes an argument that the erosion of the animal is the fashioning of an artwork. Is not the speaker's "je," a bare sketch of a person that "lives by multiplying" thanks to the printing press, another such "ébauche"? So the reduction of the animal anticipates, by both analogy and contradiction, the closing injunction to challenge the vermin with the fact of poetry's preservation of essence. Does essence emerge because of, or despite, decay?

It is in the course of this ambivalent description of decay that Baudelaire makes the metaphor that sets off Xu Zhimo's meditation on translation: "Et ce monde [the mob of flies and maggots] rendait une étrange musique, / Comme l'eau courante et le vent, / Ou le grain qu'un vanneur d'un mouvement rythmique / Agite et tourne dans son van." The buzzing and rushing to and fro of decomposition sound like running water and wind, two of the inorganic forces of nature, and also like the sifting of grain. Water and wind are clean and refreshing, and so give the reader relief from the putrid sensory images of the previous stanzas, but the equally wholesome image of wheat being winnowed reminds us, if we stop and think, that carrion is food for the scavenger animals exactly as wheat is food for us, and the scavengers' activity is one of sifting, sorting, and separating, like the removal of edible grain from worthless chaff.[23] The insects do the same work as the harvester, which work parallels the work of the poet in preserving "form" from decomposition. The chain of similes beginning with "strange music" first marks out the polarity between vermin food and human food, then leaves us to relativ-ize it. The music is "strange" in the same way that an artistic process that ends, not begins, with a bare sketch is strange (at least by nineteenth-century standards).[24] Signaling or accompanying the transformation of the animal into food for another, it must certainly be music for some ears, only not for ours, hence "strange."

Xu Zhimo claims to hear in everything, not only in Baudelaire's poetry, a music that he describes in the words of Zhuangzi as "the piping of heaven, the piping of earth, and the piping of man."[25] By inserting the reference to the early Daoist philosophical work, Xu gives Baudelaire a certain Chinese voice; he appropriates "Une Charogne" into an indigenous conversation long since underway. But what is this piping?

One of Zhuangzi's imaginary characters, returning from a trance, gives an account of the mysterious phrase:

Ziqi said:…"You hear the piping of men, but you haven't heard the piping of earth. Or if you've heard the piping of earth, you haven't heard the piping of Heaven.…The Great Clod belches out breath and its name is wind. So long as it doesn't come forth, nothing happens. But when it does, then ten thousand hollows begin crying wildly. Can't you hear them, long drawn out? In the mountain forests that lash and sway, there are huge trees a hundred spans around with hollows and openings like noses, like mouths, like ears, like jugs, like cups, like mortars, like rifts, like ruts. They roar like waves, whistle like arrows, screech, gasp, cry, wail, moan, and howl, those in the lead calling out *yeee*!, those behind calling out *yuuu*! In a gentle breeze they answer faintly, but in a full gale the chorus is gigantic. And when the fierce wind has passed on, then all the hollows are empty again. Have you never seen the tossing and trembling that goes on?"

Ziyou said, "By the piping of earth, then, you mean simply [the sound of] these hollows, and by the piping of man [the sound of] flutes and whistles. But may I ask about the piping of Heaven?"

Ziqi said, "It blows in ten thousand different ways, and each thing remains as it was, all things acting on their own. The Inciter—who is this, if anything?"

子綦曰：...「女聞人籟而未聞地籟，女聞地籟而未聞天籟夫！...
夫大塊噫氣，其名為風。是唯无作，作則萬竅怒呺。而獨不聞之翏翏乎？
山林之畏佳，大木百圍之竅穴，似鼻，似口，似耳，似枅，似圈，似臼，
似洼者，似污者；激者，謞者，叱者，吸者，叫者，譹者，宎者，咬者，
前者唱于而隨者唱喁。泠風則小和，飄風則大和，厲風濟則眾竅為虛。
而獨不見之調調、之刁刁乎？」

子游曰：「地籟則眾竅是已，人籟則比竹是已。敢問天籟」。

子綦曰：「夫吹萬不同，而使其自已也，咸其自取，怒者其誰邪？」[26]

The chapter continues in the narrator's voice: "Joy, anger, grief, delight, worry, regret, fickleness, inflexibility, modesty, willfulness, candor, insolence—music from empty holes, mushrooms springing up in dampness, day and night replacing each other before us, and no one knows where they spring from" 喜怒哀樂，慮嘆變慹，姚佚啟態；樂出虛，蒸成菌。日夜相代乎前，而莫知其所萌. The three kinds of "piping," then, are just sections in the vast, anarchic concert that is Zhuangzi's image for the workings of the different parts of the universe on each other. In human music, someone adjusts and blows the pipes; in the music of earth, the wind that fills the space between earth and sky activates the sound-producing hollows of trees; and the music of heaven is just everything else that goes on, audible or not, with no one to direct or plan it. Someone who can hear this last kind of music, in the thinking of the authors of the *Zhuangzi*, has moved away from judging things in relation to human wishes and desires and has taken a standpoint that is indeed, for the rest of us, "strange." A case study: One of Zhuangzi's imaginary spokesmen, Zilai, lay close to death:

> When Zilai's wife and children began to lament, Zilai's friend Zili reproved them, saying: "Hush! Get back! You have no business mourning transformation!" Then he leaned against the doorway and talked to Zilai. "How marvelous the Maker of Things is! What is he going to make out of you next? Where is he going to send you? Will he make you into a rat's liver? Will he make you into a bug's arm?"[27]

> 其妻子環而泣之。子犁往問之曰：「叱！避！無怛化！」倚其戶與之語曰：「偉哉造物！又將奚以汝為？將奚以汝適？以汝為鼠肝乎？以汝為蟲臂乎？」

Another invented character comes down with a disfiguring disease:

> "Amazing!" said Ziyu. "The Maker of Things is making me all crookedy like this! My back sticks up like a hunchback's and my vital organs are on top of me. My chin is hidden in my navel, my shoulders are up above my head, and my pigtail points at the sky...."
>
> "Do you hate it?" asked Zisu.
>
> "Why no, what would I hate? If the process continues, perhaps in time he'll transform my left arm into a rooster. In that case I'll keep watch on the night. Or perhaps in time he'll transform my right arm into a crossbow pellet and I'll shoot down an owl for roasting. Or perhaps in time he'll transform my buttocks into cartwheels. Then, with my spirit for a horse, I'll climb up and go for a ride. What need will I ever have for a carriage again?"[28]

曰：「偉哉！夫造物者，將以予為此拘拘也！曲僂發背，上有五
管，頤隱於齊，肩高於頂，句贅指天」 . . .

子祀曰：「汝惡之乎？」

曰：「亡，予何惡！浸假而化予之左臂以為雞，予因以求時夜；浸假
而化予之右臂以為彈，予因以求鴞炙；浸假而化予之尻以為輪，以神
為馬，予因以乘之，豈更駕哉！」

For these imaginary Daoist supermen, the right attitude to take before such painful events as death and putrefaction, even one's own death, is one of cheerful, attentive curiosity. "The Perfected Man is without self":[29] the lack of a self is precisely what enables their disinterested contemplation, lets them listen to the "music" of it all, change, as it blows by and through us.

By citing Zhuangzi on music, Xu Zhimo recruits Baudelaire into that company. But what precisely is asserted here? That Zhuangzi is like Baudelaire? That Baudelaire is the French Zhuangzi or that Zhuangzi is the Chinese Baudelaire? Baudelaire's disgust at the rotting animal, his brutality in confronting his companion and his readers with the details of the scene, and his announcement of hard-won verbal victory over the worms have little in common with the aplomb of Zili and Ziyu. The more we try to make an argument out of the parallel, the less it gives back; nor does it seem likely that Xu has in mind any protracted, substantive comparison that would make the Parnassian poets unconscious Daoists, or would fashion some category, such as materialism or naturalism, into which to wedge both writers. Rather, the coincidence of "étrange musique" and *tian lai* is a momentary flash of *Witz*, a case of "seeing the similarity" in unrelated things, an intercultural pun. Accident, collision; nothing to see, no follow-up. On this account Baudelaire and Zhuangzi, having met by coincidence in an elevator, tip their hats and depart.

Fair enough, a fruitless line of inquiry avoided; but is that all? We would still be leaving out of our account the text in which Xu Zhimo does the unlikely translation, pronounces the parallel, joins—for better, for worse, for richer, for poorer—the fates of the two phrases. We would be taking Xu's language as purely constative, his preface as a thinking of thoughts, when it is also, in the way of poets, performative through and through, a doing of deeds (or at least of gestures). Acts, like metaphors, do not reduce to a cognitive content (thus, if I call you an eagle, the act of flattering you remains as a surplus to the meaning of the assertion, even if that assertion turns out to be untrue). The metaphor that unites Zhuangzi with Baudelaire leaves a similar surplus. Probably no one had described the buzzing of flies as "music" before Baudelaire's "Une Charogne." The phrase "strange music" must have been read as irony or sarcasm, and as a condensed version of the whole project of *Fleurs du Mal*: hearing the music in whatever is most degraded. A study of translation as reception might build the case that Baudelaire is translatable only where there is prior knowledge of Plato, Augustine, Dante, Pascal, and their scales of value; only then can Baudelaire antagonize and pervert. But Xu Zhimo does not have to reproduce the conditions for the existence of a "Chinese Baudelaire" in order to perform his translation-cum-appropriation. Back-translating Baudelaire's irony, predicated on the distance between "Spleen" and "Ideal," into Zhuangzi's fable of the "piping of heaven" introduces a supreme indifference to Baudelaire's differences, a transcendence of irony in the image of the "True Man" who is "without self."

By adducing *tian lai* as a possible explanatory gloss on Baudelaire's "étrange musique," Xu does several things at once. As noted, he performs an appropriation: Baudelaire is now grafted onto a Chinese conversation about music, kingship, and cosmology in which the rejection of ritual, aesthetic, or moral distinctions can be a transcendent, not an abasing, move. The ritual specialists who are the objects of Zhuangzi's irony wanted music to be the image of a well-ordered cosmos and thus quasi-magically to set the pattern for a well-ordered society, one in which the keynote was solidly established and the harmonies rang out on schedule, without clashing. For them, the appeal of music was its difference from mere noise. Zhuangzi gives the matter another hearing, and finds that noise, too, is a kind of music; he subsumes the ritualists' vision of order into a vast conception of noise as order, with their version of order a small and unimportant subset of the ontology of sound.

Further, Xu takes Zhuangzi in hand to sketch out a possible response to Baudelaire's poetry: you should approach it in the same way as Zhuangzi's spokesmen approached death, disease, maiming, and other events that usually elicit horror and disgust. The *Flowers of Evil* now take on a Nietzschean profile: they demand a reader who is beyond saying yes and no to parts of experience. The relativist who puts no faith in human points of view will find plenty of nonsense in Baudelaire, beginning with the claim that the poet saves "form and divine essence" from rot, but at least he or she will be a possible Chinese reader for Baudelaire, a role that no one yet had claimed.

Chiefly, though, the model of "étrange musique"/*yiyue*/*tian lai* in combination applies to the verbal act whereby Xu Zhimo proposes it. Like the maggots, the thresher, and the hungry dog, the author of the preface to the translation is appropriating a bit of a pre-existing body, a corpus (whether authorial canon, school tradition, or national literature), assimilating that piece to his need, and discarding the rest. Rather than equivalence, the gesture announces appropriation; rather than asserting new identities between separate and independent things, this translation breaks down and recycles bits of those things. We tend to think of translation on the models of metaphor and of information, as a reconstitution in a different language of what should be an identical complex of meanings. (As a milieu for reconstituting Baudelaire, 1920s Shanghai should have presented ideal conditions.) But translation-as-metaphor disregards, or if very cleverly done takes shameless advantage of, the systematic, organized character of languages: term A in French has its meaning because of its relations to an infinity of other French terms, and it is beyond belief that a term X in Chinese should be found that has all the analogous relations; to translate any A by X is to wound the glorious Saussurian body, the Imaginary, of both languages.[30] Nonetheless, translation happens and it's necessary: the glorious body itself is composed of prior acts of borrowing, glossing, and "abuse" (catachresis), each as patchy and offensive in its way, at its time, as Xu's risky allusion. If we were to think of translating as a process of digestion and decay, we would be faced with having to describe it as a way of dealing not with transportable form but with bits of glutinous linguistic matter, stubbornly adhering to the contexts that gave them their prior meanings, and our own inglorious chewing and assimilation of those bits even as we try to reconstruct the "virtù informativa" that they once had as a complete, articulated set.[31] It is not as if digestion were an alternative to metaphor. Rather, assimilation being the last stage of digestion, biting, digestion, and selective uptake together form a circuit of synecdochic, then metonymic, finally metaphorical appropriation which is the condition of possibility of "seeing the same," of identification in general.[32]

The odd moments of Xu's translation and commentary point to just such a citational, material, or digestive model for translation in a way that retraces the narrative of the Baudelaire poem and makes recognizable a dimension in which it rewrites and inverts one of the major models for metaphor and knowledge, the Aristotelian model in which our traffic with the world is conducted in "forms" that we give and receive. Aristotle described perception and knowledge on the same pattern as digestion. But there is a stage beyond digestion, and for this, let Statius's speech in Dante's *Purgatorio* once more be the reference:

> The perfect blood, [he says,] which never is drunk by the thirsty veins and is left behind as it were food which one removes from the table, acquires in the heart an informing power [*virtute informativa*] for all the bodily members, like that blood which flows through the veins to become those members. Digested yet again, it descends there whereof to be silent is more seemly than to speak; and thence afterwards drops upon other's blood, in natural vessel....[33]

These lines condense a great deal of Aristotelian learning that Dante had gathered from Albertus Magnus, Thomas Aquinas, Avicenna, and Averroes;

they also versify some paragraphs of Dante's prose work *Il Convivio*. "According to the Aristotelian concept, food converts itself into the substance of the body it nourishes only after a series of transformations, or digestions, through which it ceases to be similar and becomes perfectly assimilable."[34] Digestion assimilates food into the blood. In the male, a surplus of the refined food in the blood undergoes a further cooking that turns it into seminal fluid. The semen possesses, in common with the blood but to a higher degree, a "virtù informativa," an informative virtue, that enables it to shape the incoherent matter of female menstrual blood into a new human being.[35] (For Aristotle men supply the form, women merely the matter, of the child to be born.) In the *Convivio* the male contribution to generation is compared to the stamping of a seal on wax or metal, an imposition of form in which no matter is transferred. The womb is a sort of perceptive organ, one might say, that receives forms from outside just like the eye or the ear, and stores them in the form of a child, the mimesis of its father. Aristotle in explaining not only the how but the why of sexual reproduction indicated that "for any living thing that has reached its normal development...the most natural act is the production of another like itself...in order that, as far as its nature allows, it may partake in the eternal and divine. That is the goal towards which all things strive."[36] Statius, in adapting the Aristotelian doctrine to explain the quasi-bodies of the inhabitants of Purgatory, adds that only God can create a soul—a recognizably medieval graft onto Aristotle performed by Aquinas, in order to make philosophical room for the immortality of the soul and the resurrection of the body.[37]

This is medieval information-theory. The relation of the soul to conception and the body is the problem that the word "information" was invented to clarify and a foretaste of such bits of information folklore as teleportation and personality storage. Let us draw together the parallel parts of the theory. The learner or maker of knowledge digests the objects of the understanding, just as his stomach digests the products of the field. Metaphor and digestion are both processes whereby the non-self is assimilated to, that is broken down, sifted, and made a constituent of, the self. Reproduction is normatively (though it never quite works out that way) a process whereby this achieved self "informs" a mass of non-self and stamps it with its own image. The career of metaphor, then, is practically synonymous with the career of normative male selfhood, a process of soul-formation, or identity-formation as we might say in a less overtly (but only less *overtly*) theological manner. The self is the hero of the story of digestion, just as God, together with fathers generally, is the hero of the story of the soul.

Then "Une Charogne," mostly a story of decay, is the story of the process whereby self becomes other: the fully realized creature sinks to the state of a sketch and a stench, the form disappears as its matter is stolen away, identities and metaphorical "samenesses" break down. It is the reverse of the matching of like to like. As the madmen and sages of the *Zhuangzi* remind us, this is nothing other than the process of another's, or of many others', self-formation: one begins to be no longer one's own necessary and permanent frame of reference, and becomes something like a rooster, a crossbow pellet, a rat's liver, or a bug's leg. What occurs in "Une Charogne" is not really a rejection of the metaphorical-digestive model—after all, the "je" of the poem, however materially reduced to an occasion of repeated information, still claims to have "preserved the form and the essence" of his loves, which is more than the animal or the woman can say (another hint that Aristotle has never quite left the premises). It simply changes direction, presenting the process of digestion as it is *undergone*, not as it is *done*,[38] and attempts to translate that process of unselfing into the "ébauche" of a post-mortem "essence." The poem's gamble lies in the link between the two moments. (Xu's translation of the poem, sadly, makes more of the contrast between them, and so it turns toward Poe's mortuary Gothic.)[39] The speaker's patient and detailed study of the "strange music" of putrefaction provokes a compensatory leap to the realm of information, where the self, the "je," does not decay. "L'étude du beau est un duel où l'artiste crie de frayeur avant d'être vaincu."[40] Although saying so involves shelving most of our expectations about the beautiful, we must admit that the last lines of "Une Charogne" are the moment where Baudelaire's artist "screams with fright" and abandons his struggle with the material, maybe just in time. Zhuangzi's Daoist sages, trained to a fine indifference by their long listening to the piping of the heavens, stay the course all the way to the bug's leg—in parable at least. Having no self to defend, they do not adopt a point of view. Baudelaire's poem is all about the possibly hysterical shoring up of a point of view. In this respect at least, Xu's preface confirms its self-diagnosis as "mystical": it seems to want to dissolve any limited point of view with its announcement of a great new understanding that looks like a great new insanity, the empty proclamation that "everything is music" readily paraphrasing itself as "everything is something."[41]

In combining Zhuangzi and Baudelaire as he does, Xu Zhimo makes "strange music" happen. His preface is an example of that whereof it speaks. By breaking loose a little piece of nineteenth-century French Parnassianism and cooking it together with a little piece of fourth-century-BCE Chinese primitivism, Xu makes translation, or comparative literature, or reading, appear as a process of dissolution, of decay, of selective uptake. Baudelaire had done the same thing with Petrarchan lyric conventions to get his poem. Rewriting, translation, or citation use—use up—the materials they digest. Is this perhaps the "afterlife" in translation of which Walter Benjamin spoke?[42] If so, it is not a personal form of immortality, but a process wherein Aristotle, Petrarch, Baudelaire, and Zhuangzi all become to some degree unrecognizable.

Digestion, which undeniably occurs, does not here contribute to the formation of a new self, at least not to a strong one, but to a "monde" (that hardly translatable, and by Xu mistranslated, word; say "crowd") of selves dissimilar to, but fed by, the original carcass: the "everything" of "everything is music." At a point in the creation of the new vernacular literature of twentieth-century China when the rhetoric of the bravest young writers was all about fashioning a new body for the consciousness of the nation,[43] this is a deliberately decadent and possibly counterproductive option. Strange music. Strange too that we should be able to hear music in it—the music of an estrangement.

"WAITING FOR THEIR TRANSLATORS"

While living in Moscow at the time of the first great deportations, Osip Mandel'stam wrote a few lines, perhaps a poem, perhaps just a sketch of a poem:

> Tartars, Uzbeks, and Nenets
> And the whole Ukrainian nation,
> And the Volga Germans
> Are waiting for their translators.
>
> And, it may be, at this minute
> Some Japanese is translating me
> Into Turkish and
> Pierces the depths of my soul.[44]

"Their translators"? That is, the translators who will make those literary treasures previously known only to Tartars, Uzbeks, and Nenets a part of world literature? No; Mandel'stam has something more megalomaniacal in mind, as did Pushkin, whose "Exegi monumentum" Mandel'stam is echoing, and Horace, whose *Odes* III.30 Pushkin was imitating. They are awaiting the translators who will give them Mandel'stam. And one of those potential mediators, a Japanese, is right now translating him into Turkish, perhaps.

The prospect of literary immortality ("Non omnis moriar") assumed, for Horace, the eternity of Rome and the Latin language, and for Pushkin, the vastness of the Russian domains. Mandel'stam proposes to outdo them both in one stroke: he will live on through translations. And what translations! We might expect a Japanese to find it difficult to render a Russian poet in Japanese, but this one is translating him into Turkish, a redoubled astonishment—not only that, but Mandel'stam's non-Russian translator into non-Japanese, non-native Turkish "pierces the depths of my soul."

Our imagination of translating usually assumes a framework of condi-tional solipsism. I alone have privileged access to the contents of my mind; when I voice my thoughts, only people who understand my language are privy to them; a translator's gift is the ability to turn those expressed thoughts into differently expressed thoughts for another linguistic community. And in keeping with this framework, the translator is typically expected to bring the foreign word home—to hear the other's word and translate it "selfwards," so to speak, to make the foreign speech familiar. Mandel'stam imagines his immortality in translation taking an opposite form: the translators send his words "otherwards," into the distant communities of Nenets, Uzbeks, and so forth; and in the possible world here imagined, the Japanese other is conveying them into still another region of otherness, Turkey. Yet despite, or because of, these concentrically expanding circles of distance, this is the translator who can drive right at the poet's soul. The best response to house arrest is to broadcast one's subjectivity as if on radio waves, going ever out-ward from whatever one has been and known—a weirdly ecstatic response to what Mandel'stam must have felt was his personal peril.

"Traduire, c'est perdre le corps." But not to exchange it for a bodiless spiritual form. One gains in translation a different body, a different series of bodies. The language of the other breaks up the language of the initial utterance, cannibalizes it in a strange music of mimesis. One sees, I hope, why with their polarization around self and other, major and minor, dominant and subordinate, and their ethical anxiety (itself framed by ideas of ownership), the current theories of translation were not of much help to me in trying to understand the sort of translation Xu Zhimo's Baudelaire represents. By suspending those assumed orientations I found that the translation's canni-balization of the poem was a precise response to the poem, an extension of its poetics, and nowhere more so than where its gloss on the poet's probable intent made the least sense, was most irresponsible. Is the "ethics of transla-tion" a cannibal ethics? Translation itself had a lot to tell me, if I could learn to read it as something other than translation as we usually know it.

3

MATTEO RICCI THE DAOIST

The great obstacle to understanding Matteo Ricci (Li Madou 利瑪竇, 1552–1610) is that we know too much about him. We have a clear, detailed idea of what Counter-Reformation Roman Catholicism was all about, and we have Ricci's journals and his letters to his superiors, sometimes rich with the wisdom of hindsight, not to mention the pamphlets and archives of the Rites Controversy that erupted some seventy years after his death. All this makes his background and mental world less remote from us than it might seem.[1] We look on his life in China as a translation of which we already possess the original.[2] So we tend to follow that course, and ask such questions as: How did Ricci present the content of Tridentine Catholic doctrine (a content which is no special mystery to us twenty-first-century people) in the new and not necessarily receptive context of late-Ming China? What sacrifices and accommodations did he make to his hearers? Did he concede too much? Did he achieve genuine conversions?[3] We know so much, in fact, that the discussion can easily slip into a prescriptive tone, describing not only what Ricci did but also what he should have done. Shouldn't he have told his interlocutors about the darker side of Christianity, the wars of religion, the corruptions of the instituted churches? Shouldn't he have made distinctions where he assimilated diverse things, or analogized where he drew a differentiating line? Was he sufficiently respectful (or on the contrary too respectful) of native practices? These questions matter, because, at least as far as seventeenth-century Chinese were concerned, "The Western countries are situated some hundred thousand *li* away from China... and their mutual communication began with Ricci" 西國去中州十萬里...通之自利子始.[4]

As we ask what Ricci should have done, we fail to ask ourselves if we know what he actually did, or we neglect the contexts in which that question can be most profitably asked. That is, what did the people who did not already know what we know—who knew about Christianity and the West only as much as Ricci told them—make of his activity? Who was Ricci, after all, in a Chinese context? What was his Chinese career, if described in terms other than those he brought with him from Italy and Goa?

In other words, the question still before us is that asked by Li Zhi 李贄 around 1599, in a letter to a friend describing his encounters with this curious character:

> Now he is perfectly able to speak our language, he can write our characters, he follows the customs and ceremonies in use here, he is an unusually accomplished man....But I don't know what he has come here for. I have already met him three times, and I still don't know what he is here to do.[5]
> 今盡能言我此間之言，作此間之文字，行此間之儀禮，是一極標致人也....但不知到此何為，我已經三度相會，畢竟不知道此何幹也.

If we rule as inadmissible the evidence provided in exotic languages like Latin, Italian, Spanish, Portuguese, and French (not to mention English), and restrict ourselves to Chinese sources close in time to Ricci's lifespan, answering Li Zhi's question becomes harder, but also more intriguing. Li Zhi's bafflement becomes our own.

Which is not to say that "the Chinese Ricci," as we may call him, is a perfect enigma. The language used by contemporary and near-contemporary Chinese to describe Ricci has definite patterns of its own, to which nothing on the European side corresponds. Discovering these patterns—and coming to see that there is more to the dialogue than is visible from the standpoint of what we usually assume is the "content to be transmitted" of Ricci's career—will be our reward for momentarily suppressing the alphabetic languages and their archives.

A FISH, A BIRD, A MAN

Li Zhi furnishes an apt starting-place. Ricci was a social man; he enjoyed his conversations with Chinese intellectuals, and discreetly boasted in his journals of the "sonnetti" or poems dedicated to him by his learned friends. One such piece of occasional verse has been preserved in Li's *Fen shu*:

"To Li of the Far Occident"
Descending in *xiao-yao* fashion from the Northern darkness,

Through long and twisted wanderings marching toward the south:
Like the Kshatriya you announce your [new] clan and personal names,
And like a visitor from the Immortals' island you record the watery stages.
Behind you is a hundred-thousand-*li* voyage,
And now you raise your eyes upon the nine-walled capital.
Have you seen the glory of our country yet, or not?
From the middle of heaven the sun shines directly down.[6]

　　贈利西泰
逍遙下北溟，迤邐向南征.
剎利標名姓，仙山紀水程.
回頭十萬里，舉目九重城.
觀國之光未？中天日正明.

As if led on by the unanswered question of his letter (at present, we have no way of knowing which came first, poem or letter, but it is likely that the poem figured in the social exchanges on which the letter reports), Li Zhi construes Matteo Ricci's inexplicable presence in a series of alternative ways, each supported (as you would expect in Ming social verse) by a textual reference. The first line gives us the most to chew on—it may, in fact, be too great a piece of poetic license for us to swallow. The thing that, in *xiaoyao* fashion, descends from the Northern Darkness is none other than the huge fish Kun named in the opening lines of the first chapter of the *Zhuangzi*：北冥有魚，其名為鯤 . . . 化而為鳥，其名為鵬. . . . 是鳥也，海運則將徒於南冥 ("In the Northern Darkness there is a fish, its name is called Kun. . . . It changes into a bird, and its name is called Peng. . . . This bird, when the seas shift, makes ready to migrate to the Southern Darkness").[7] That chapter bears the name "Xiaoyao you," usually translated as "Free and Easy Wandering."[8] So the allusion, first of all, indicates that Ricci is someone whose journeys parallel those of the giant fish/bird that regularly travels from one end of the world to the opposite, a course, as Zhuangzi tells us, of 90,000 *li*—a comparison that makes Ricci, with his 100,000 *li* of travel, a rather extraordinary person. And it appears that Ricci confronted those distances in an untroubled, "free and easy" manner. In the second half of the couplet, Li tells us that Ricci's travels were in fact long, meandering, and difficult, *yili* 迤邐, like the marching of the soldiers described in frontier ballads.[9] The parallelism with *yili* makes the term *xiaoyao* in the first couplet seem, retrospectively, inappropriate; this is a problem to be tackled later.

"A Kshatriya, you announce your new clan and personal names": the term *chali* 剎利, the Chinese rendering of the title of the warrior caste of India, allows Li Zhi to work in some hopeful stories about foreign relations. The royal families of Zhenlaguo 真臘國 (Chenla), Shiziguo 師子國 (Sinhala), and Poliguo 婆利國 (Borobudur, in Java), small Buddhist kingdoms far off in the southern seas, all bore the clan name Kshatriya/Chali. The Zhenla kings began offering tribute to the Chinese emperor in Tang times; the Ming reopened relations at the founding of their dynasty, and habitually sent a Chinese official as an advisor to the Zhenla court.[10] Ricci's Italian name would have meant nothing at all to Li Zhi, but his adoption of the Chinese surname Li 利 evoked, punningly, the willingness of the Chali 剎利 to become part of the Chinese cultural orbit, and so made him "speakable" in the language of poetic-historical allusion.

The Chali of South Asia are remote, exotic, but part of Ming political reality; Li Zhi, still reaching for the right analogy, goes a step farther and describes Ricci as being like someone who has seen the mythical Island of the Immortals and can draw you a nautical chart for getting there. The Island of the Immortals, Xianshan or Penglai, is supposed to be out in the Eastern Sea (it has been at times identified with Japan) and invisible to most travelers. One of Ricci's most famous productions was his world map containing several new continents and dozens of strange-sounding place names. The effect of this new depiction of the globe on his visitors can be imagined.[11] In a preface Li Zhizao 李之藻, editor of the anthology of Chinese Catholic writings *Tianxue chuhan* 天學初函 (A First Collection of Celestial Studies, 1628), wrote about a guided tour of Ricci's map room:

> In the *xingchou* year of the Wanli emperor [1601] Mr. Ricci came to reside in the capital. I went with several friends to visit him. On his walls were hanging great maps of the whole world. With longitudinal and latitudinal lines, they were extremely detailed. Mr. Ricci used to say, "This is the path of my travels coming from the West," and comment minutely on the mountains and rivers, continents, sites, and customs. He also had a printed volume of maps made which he took with him to his audience in the Forbidden City. Using these maps, Mr. Ricci explained to me that the earth was represented as a round spot and the heavens as a larger circle around it.[12]

Hence the cartographic theme, almost obligatory in Chinese writing about the early missionaries. And so now, in line 5, the traveler has reached his destination: the imperial palace surrounded by its nine-layered wall. "Have you seen the glory of the country yet?" asks Li Zhi, voicing his perplexity about the stranger through a quotation from the *Book of Changes* (*Yijing* 易經). Under the hexagram "Guan" 觀, the oracle-interpretation says: 六四．觀國之光．利用賓于王 ("A broken line in the fourth place: Observe the country's glory. It will be advantageous to become the guest of a king"). Wang Bi's 王弼 commentary, expanded on by Kong Yingda 孔穎達, paraphrases this as: 居在親近而得其位，明習國之禮儀，故曰利用賓于王庭也 ("By staying in the intimacy [of the court] one may obtain an appropriate position; one becomes familiar with the rituals of the country. Therefore it says: there is advantage in being the guest of a royal court").[13] The quotation is apt for, as everyone knew, Ricci's purpose in coming to Beijing and, in fact, his design ever since arriving in China in 1583 was to seek an audience with the emperor. He was the "guest" of high-ranking officials such as Li Zhizao and Xu Guangqi 徐光啟, and had certainly learned the rituals of the country (行此間之儀禮, to quote Li Zhi's letter to a friend again). The "glory" of a country is simply, as in the *Yijing* text and its commentaries, the behavioral evidence of virtue that can be seen in customs and manners. The glory of the Ming Empire, says Li Zhi's concluding line, is all around Ricci, whether or not he will ever win his way into the palace; like the sun, that traditional emblem for the power and uniqueness of the monarch, it shines on everyone. And the verb for the sun's action, nicely, is *ming*: the word-choice here may be a subtle response to what some felt was Ricci's presumptuous habit of naming his country of origin the *Da Xi* 大西 (Great West), a title close enough to that of the "Great Ming" (*Da Ming* 大明) to seem to challenge it.[14]

Li Zhi's poem asks repeatedly: Who or what is Matteo Ricci? It runs through a series of tentative answers. Perhaps he is an extraordinary creature fit to be told about in *Zhuangzi* or a *zhiguai* 志怪 tale of the strange; perhaps he is a laborious and not entirely carefree traveler; perhaps he is an exotic noble with a vaguely Sanskrit name, come from some land of snakes and elephants to present his gifts of regional produce; perhaps he is one of those mysterious voyagers who have seen the land of the fairies and may possess the secret of immortality.[15] The poem shifts then and closes with a stab at contextualizing Ricci and expressing the point of his travels for him. Li Zhi will now describe Ricci's voyage as a pilgrimage to the capital, a situation for which there are ample expressive resources in Chinese poetic language. But the rather prosaic and obvious, though patriotic, ending does not quite correspond to the more exuberant tropes of the first four lines.

The real logical problem of the poem is the standout epithet, *xiaoyao*, in the first line. It is not strictly necessary as a part of the allusion to the Peng bird and its enormous migrations between the Northern and Southern Darknesses. Although the fable of Kun and Peng occurs in the chapter "Xiaoyao you" of the *Zhuangzi*, the compound *xiaoyao* occurs only in the last words of that chapter, as part of a different parable. There Zhuangzi says to his teacher Huizi, "So I see you have a huge tree and you're bothered by the fact that it's useless [as timber]. Why not plant it in No-Such-Village, or in No-Man's Wilderness, where you can linger in non-action by its side, or lie *free and easy* in sleep underneath it?" 今子有大樹，患其无用。何不樹之於无何有之鄉，廣莫之野，徬徨乎无為其側，逍遙乎寢臥其下？[16] The commentaries by Xiang Xiu 向秀 (*fl.* 263) and Guo Xiang 郭向 (*c.*252–312) take the fable of the useless tree to be the lesson of the chapter as a whole, and read that lesson back into the story of the Peng. For while the Peng is engaged on its vast migrations, a little sparrow is hopping from branch to branch and laughs at it for wasting its effort: sparrow-like hopping is already "the ultimate in flying, so where does that guy think he's off to?" 此亦飛之至也，而彼且奚 適也？[17] Although the narrator of the *Zhuangzi* text says, "This shows the difference between the small and the great" 此小大之辯也，Guo Xiang contradicts that verdict: "The 90,000-li flight of the great Peng, or the foot-long hop of the sparrow into the neighboring hedge—although one is large and the other is small, each is true to its own nature. And if each fulfills its lot, the *freedom and ease* [of the two creatures] is identical" 夫大鵬之上 九萬，尺鷃之起榆枋，小大雖差，各任其性，苟當其分，逍遙一也.[18] Since every edition of the *Zhuangzi* opens with an explanation of the first chapter's title phrase, incorporating the seeming disagreement between text and commentary, the evaluation of *xiaoyao* is apt to be bipolar: perhaps the advice given to Huizi, to abandon limited perspectives on "usefulness" and let his mind wander in the shade of his monstrous tree, speaks through the image of the vast Peng bird (the person who has left petty interests behind is therefore great), or perhaps it speaks for the chittering sparrow who sees nothing great about even so vast a bird as the Peng; rather, greatness and smallness are relative to achieving one's purpose in life, and no one else can or should set your purpose. Li Zhi is expressing ambivalence about this visitor from abroad: is he as awe-inspiring as the Peng, or is he no more of a big deal than the sparrows and Chinese officeholders who have never left their country? Applied to Matteo Ricci, *xiaoyao* can be either a magnifying, heroic epithet or a "perspective by incongruity" (as Kenneth Burke might have called it). This man, "extremely refined [or: complex] inwardly, and extremely austere in outward appearance" (中極玲瓏，外極樸實) according to Li Zhi,[19] becomes enigmatic when evaluated in a relativistic framework.

But that relativistic framework is certainly not one that we would ever hear Matteo Ricci applying to his own mission. The relativity of categories to the narrowness of the uses for which people employ them, the idea that ease and freedom are the highest values, and the method of achieving them by refusing to play the games of conventional language and morality—these sound like positions Ricci argues *against* in his book of dialogues *Jiren shipian* 畸人十篇 (Ten Chapters from an Extraordinary Man), but in no case views that he would have adopted or even seen as promising first stages on the way to Christian truth.

Xiaoyao, then, does not directly describe Ricci himself, it describes the way Chinese observers felt about him; it expresses the effect he had on people who were otherwise at a loss to account for him. Ricci, like the *peng* bird, comes from unimaginably far away, and makes us feel like little birds that have never flown farther than the next hedge; he brings us news of fantastic worlds that we have never seen or read about, and legends and histories unrecorded in any of the libraries of our empire; he startles us out of our habitual weights and measures and scales of value. He is both a fabulous beast, like the animals Zhuangzi writes about, and a modern-day Zhuangzi, come to enlighten and disturb. Perhaps, too, he is not so different from us. However, the phrase describes him differently for readers who identify it with a quick glance at the *Zhuangzi* (or the dictionary) and for those who remember the text and its commentaries. He will be a wonder for the former, a puzzle for the latter, but either way, an embodiment of the uncanny.

And that is how, somewhat coincidentally, Matteo Ricci became a Daoist.[20]

PRONOUNCING PARADOXES

Ricci a Daoist? But isn't it well known that Ricci sought to present himself as a Confucian scholar in high cap and broad belt, after an initial period of experiment with a quasi-Buddhist identity?[21] The claim is certainly not that Ricci adhered to the philosophy or religion of Daoism, rather that Chinese contemporaries described him in terms taken from the traditional language used to talk about Daoist sages and wonder-workers, and that he found strategic and publicity value in allowing them to do so. It was a matter of intercultural role-playing, then; but as always with role-playing, it is not a completely simple matter for observers to separate the disguise from the reality. Ricci accepts his Daoist identity or mask in the title of one of his most popular works, the *Jiren shipian* of 1607–8.[22] Ricci's Italian journals call this "his book of *Paradoxes*"; Pasquale d'Elia translates the title more literally as "Ten Chapters of a Strange Man," and points out the source of the phrase *jiren* in a passage of *Zhuangzi* translated by d'Elia to read: "The strange man is strange to other men, but similar to heaven."[23] Let us use "exceptional" and "extraordinary" as nonce equivalents.

The title is a mixture of humility and astute publicity. Li Zhi's letter on Ricci, written to satisfy the curiosity of an unnamed friend, as well as his poem and many documents by others show that Ricci had long since acquired a reputation in China as an unusual person whom one would want to meet, and the printed dialogues give the Chinese reader a vicarious opportunity to "converse" with him. The narrator and main speaker in these dialogues only refers to himself as "I," 余, but the first page of the book is labeled: "Narrated by Li Madou" 利瑪竇述. The character *shu* 述 may indicate Ricci's indirect contribution to the writing, somewhat as if it were subtitled "As told by Matteo Ricci." Without the narrator ever naming himself the "exceptional man," much less the "man similar to heaven," the dialogues are plainly centered on Ricci as "exceptional man": each chapter opens with a question or a comment by a Chinese scholar, answered with an intentionally provoking speech by the first-person narrator. The book "is called *Paradoxes*," says Ricci, using the passive voice (*chiamossi così*)

> for the many opinions treated there which are extremely commonplace among Christians, but for the Chinese are unheard-of paradoxes. Such as: time is impermanent and passes by easily; for a good life, it is useful to be ever meditating on the hour of death; this life of ours is a continual death and misery; the reward of our works is not to be found in this world, but in the life to come; it is difficult, though useful, to keep silence and speak little; each of us must examine his sins and chastise himself; and other similar topics.[24]

Thus the "strange" or "extraordinary" character of the book: an effect of context. The phrase *jiren* 畸人 never appears in the dialogues, although the title including it appears at the head of every chapter and on the edge of every page; it is as if the "I," in accepting the name of *jiren* bestowed on him by his friends, were simply bowing to necessity—an impression confirmed by the numerous prefaces contributed by readers and admirers of Ricci, in every one of which "exceptionality" or "strangeness" is a leading topic.

But the meaning of *jiren* is not as vague as d'Elia and many others have made it—it is not just an homage to the unusual origins and amazing mental powers of this visitor from the other end of the world. As Ricci knew, it carries the sense of a person who is *paradoxical*, that is, who runs counter to generally received opinion (*para tên doxan*); and the author who has done the most to carve out a place for the antinomian, antisocial, "oddball" (as Victor Mair translates *jiren*) role in Chinese history is, once more, Zhuangzi.[25] The *Zhuangzi* passage in which *jiren* occurs and acquires its canonical meaning fits too tightly with the topics of Ricci's dialogues for the reference in the title to have been anything but specifically intended:

> Master Sanghu, Meng Zifan, and Master Qinzhang were three friends...and one day Master Sanghu died. He had not yet been buried. Confucius heard of this, and sent [his disciple] Zigong to assist at the funeral. Zigong arrived and found one of them weaving mats, the other strumming on the zither, and they sang in harmony: "Ah, Sanghu! Ah, Sanghu! You have returned to your genuine form, and we remain here as men!" Zigong rushed in and said: "May I ask what you are doing, singing in the presence of a corpse? Is this the correct way to behave?" The two men looked at each other and laughed....
>
> Zigong then reported back to Confucius: "What manner of men are these?"...Confucius said: "They are wanderers beyond the bounds, and I am a

wanderer within the bounds....They look upon living as an execrescence, a protruding wen, and look upon death as the draining of a sore or the bursting of a boil. This being so, how could they possibly draw a line between life and death, before and after?"

子桑戶，孟子反，子琴張三人與友 . . . 而子桑戶死．未葬．孔子聞之，使子貢往侍事焉．或編曲，或鼓琴，相和而歌，曰 ：「嗟來桑戶乎！嗟來 桑戶乎! 而已反其真，而我猶為人猗!」子貢趨而進曰 ：「敢問臨尸而歌，禮乎?」二人相視而笑 . . .

子貢反，以告孔子曰：「彼何人者邪?」 . . . 孔子曰：「彼遊方之外者也，而丘，遊方之內者也 . . . 彼以生為附贅縣疣，以死為決癈疽潰癰，夫若然，又惡知死生先後之所在!」[26]

Here, as in many other places in the *Zhuangzi*, indifference toward death and the consequent disregard for the polarities of pleasure and pain, good and evil, that structure ordinary living are signs of transcendence.[27] The shocking behavior, in Zigong's eyes, of the two surviving friends no doubt parallels the repelled fascination many normal Chinese felt on learning of Ricci's beliefs that "for a good life, it is useful to be ever meditating on the hour of death; this life of ours is a continual death and misery," and so forth. When Zigong reports his indignation back to his master, however, Confucius only regrets having sent his disciple on such a useless errand, for men such as Meng Zifan and Master Qinzhang do not need condolences. Because they "wander beyond the bounds," *you fang zhi wai* 遊方之外, conventional distinctions such as life and death and the conventional behavior that follows therefrom—mourning a death, clinging to life—have no meaning for them. They are "free and at ease in the realm of non-action," 逍遙乎無為之業, as the story goes on to say. Zigong thought that they were inept at ritual, thoughtless, careless, or callous; Confucius explains that they belong to an alien form of existence with its own set of values, and that what makes sense for the *fangnei* (those within the bounds) does not make sense for the *fangwai* (those without the bounds). Indeed Confucius describes himself, in comparison to those eccentrics, as "one of Heaven's condemned" 丘天之戮民也, an unfree person.

Having had his values re-valued by this explanation, Zigong says, "I should like to ask about the *jiren*, the odd man." (*Ji* is etymologically the "oddness" of odd numbers, the remainder in dividing up land or objects.) Confucius's answer: "The *jiren* is odd as regards men, but of a pair with heaven" 畸人者, 畸於人而侔於天. "Of a pair," *mou* 侔 or *ou* 偶, is the opposite of *ji*, "odd": in the perspective of heaven or nature, *tian*, 天, the *ji* is not *ji* at all. The *jiren* is not just a "strange man," but some sort of holy fool whose nature corresponds with that of the universe. So with this context re-established, we can see more fully what the point of naming Ricci's dialogues *Jiren shipian* was. The phrase *Jiren* tells Ricci's reader to expect to relive the anecdote from *Zhuangzi*—to anticipate a movement from shock and disbelief to a new form of awareness which will be *fangwai*.

Evaluating irony, after a lapse of 400 years, is not easy; in a context of mutual interpretations between two cultures just beginning to establish their relations, it may be impossible. But we must try. Although the phrase *jiren* is important for naming and situating the Ricci effect, its connotations are not to be taken "straight," any more than the fact that Li Zhi mentioned Penglai in a poem about Ricci means that he believed Ricci was an immortal. Ricci must have determined that the echo of *Zhuangzi* would be strategic—it would help to establish him in the world of Chinese letters. It was, for Chinese readers, a familiar sign of unfamiliarity. But as for the phrase guaranteeing a substantive, consistent similarity of aims between Zhuangzi's eccentrics and Ricci's teachings, that, clearly, would be impossible (and Ricci, with all his reading, would have known that). The title is ironic both as a title (it promises something it doesn't quite deliver) and as a quotation: although Ricci must have hoped that people would say of him that he was "odd as regards men but of a pair with heaven," he would not have wanted them to mean it in the way that Zhuangzi's Confucius did, primarily because the meaning of "heaven" in the two contexts was so different. Using the strategic phrase *jiren* to nominate himself, then, involves Ricci in a revisionist stance toward the Chinese tradition, and particularly that part of the tradition that we call Daoism, a part for which generally Ricci had very little use.[28] In one respect at least, however, Ricci found himself having to occupy the same corner of the Chinese intellectual landscape as Daoist writers like Zhuangzi. Like them, he was something new and strange, not only outside the mainstream but in many ways counter to it. And perhaps only a Daoistic guise would afford so strange an author, so strange a teaching, a position from which to address the Chinese public. As often in Chinese history, and particularly in the late years of the Ming, a fantastic, fabulous, or supernatural imagination and a willful rejection of conventional values and public life answered a real need. (As literary versions of the fantastic in the late Ming, consider such phenomena as the runaway success of *Mudan ting* 牡丹亭 [The Peony Pavilion (1598), by Tang Xianzu 湯顯祖]; the writings of Li Zhi; and the sudden emergence of many female writers and their championing by established male writers.) We tend to see Ricci in his mandarin's robes, quoting from the *Shi jing* 詩經 and *Shang shu* 尚書, brushing aside Buddhism and Daoism as impure superstitions, standing next to his altar with the highly respectable Xu Guangqi 徐光啓—in other words, as the Confucian–Catholic hybrid impressed on our minds by both sides in the Rites Controversy. But that Ricci could only emerge in the context of an already established Tianzhu

天主 church in China, with its audience ready-made and eager to find ways of serving Kongzi 孔子 (Confucius) and Yesu 耶穌 (Jesus) simultaneously. To catch the attention of those not yet converted, Ricci had to put on more arresting guise, even if it went no farther than the titles of his books. An accidental Daoist he may have been, but not an entirely innocent one.

THE MOUNTAIN MAN

In any case, Ming people loved writing about this bearded Italian as a Daoist. His books often list him as Li Madou *shanren* 山人 (Li Madou the mountain recluse), a title that Ming cognoscenti found overused by literary pseudo-hermits.[29] The prefaces contributed to editions of the work printed in Ricci's lifetime make considerable play with the designation *jiren*, mostly in predictable ways (using it as a hyperbolic term of praise for Ricci the man).

The preface by Zhou Bingmou 周炳謨, the longest of the set, asks what makes Ricci an "extraordinary man," and answers: "Chiefly, it is his not fearing death" 求所為畸人者何在, 其大者在不怖死.[30] The reason is that Ricci is confident in Heaven's reward for good deeds (信以天也…天所佑者善也).[31] Strengthened by that belief, says Zhou, "one can exist on the border of going and coming [another *Zhuangzi* tag], entirely free of care" 去來之際, 自無 弗灑然也. The Buddhists and Daoists make similar claims, but in grossly exaggerated and unbelievable form; the Western doctrine, says Zhou, has "mysterious principles but practical consequences" 其指玄, 其功實. (One such consequence presumably was the feeling of having been freed from mortality.) Ricci's teaching resembles that of our Chinese sages, but with a difference. The original charge of the sages and worthies was to perfect the worldly realm, "so," says Zhou in a sentence florid with *Yijing* allusions, "when the Sage appeared as if yoking dragons to mount the heavens, bringing by his very emergence order into the world, the [basis?] on which he pronounced his commands could not neglect the consideration of the length and shortness of life" 以故御天之聖首出庶物, 而立命之[基]亦無膩於妖壽之數.[32] In other words, the purposes of the early sages were confined within a rational calculus of maximum benefit to mankind, and in accomplishing those goals they could not afford to look indifferently on early death. The sages were decidedly *fangnei* (within the bounds). "But theirs is a Dao that the people use daily and cannot know" 彼百姓特日用不知耳,[33] while the Western schools make special efforts to transform people through education and reform the foolish. This is why the spread of Ricci's religion can become something known in every house and courtyard, with everyone exerting him- or herself to perform the services Heaven commands (是以其教之行能使家喻戶曉,

人人修事天之節), rather than a specially selected class of officials. This book can thus help to repair the decrepit customs of our age (此刻之裨世道非小也), when so many who start to recite the Classics in childhood are still repeating them in old age without any understanding of how to put them into action. In sum, Ricci may be considered one of those whom the ancients called a Perfect Man (蓋庶乎古所稱至人也)—this last epithet being drawn from the first chapter of *Zhuangzi*.[34]

Zhou Bingmou's preface rather loosely echoes some of the themes already associated, through the *Zhuangzi*, with the idea of the "odd man" who is not as other men are, and ties them in with other strands of late-Ming cultural dissatisfaction. The strange, *fangwai* man who does not fear death and promises release from anxiety about dying is not opposed to "the teachings of our sages" 吾聖學, but transcends and complements them. The sages of China, it is argued, limited their efforts to happiness in this world, and kept the thought of a future world to themselves; now Ricci comes to breach those limits, and concurrently to spread to the many what had been the special knowledge of a few. Ricci appears here as an oppositional figure—multiply and vaguely oppositional. The mixture of aspirations that we can credit to Zhou Bingmou (in the absence of more definite biographical information about the man) are characteristic of many streams of late-Ming heterodoxy, including the grassroots, practical Confucianism of the Taizhou 泰州 school with its projects for turning everyone into a sage, the Buddhist–Daoist–Confucian syncretism of Jiao Hong 焦竑, the antinomian philosophical essays of Li Zhi, and even the conservative reformism of the scholars who some years later were to constitute the Donglin 東林 party.[35] All these and more, despite their mutually antagonistic programs for change, could find something of themselves reflected in the figure of the *jiren*.

The prefaces to *Jiren shipian* have been the object of a study by Pasquale d'Elia, SJ, the tireless editor of the *Fonti Ricciane*. D'Elia's essay bears out the point made earlier about the need to forget what we know, or think we know, about Ricci: its translations of Chinese texts are marred by an over-insistent Christianizing. The language used by Zhou Bingmou to talk about "the reward of Heaven" or the liberated attitude of the person who no longer fears death is not far from that used by Chinese moralists long before Ricci ever came to China; the words would not be out of place in a commentary on the *Daode jing* or *Zhuangzi*. But d'Elia's determination to force onto Zhou Bingmou an acknowledgment of a paradise after death, a personal, intelligent God, and a strict accounting of sins and good actions, causes him to misconstrue words and sentences, to throw statements out of their proper context, and to ignore Zhou's transparent allusions to *Zhuangzi*, *Daode jing*, *Yijing*, and other texts.[36] Those allusions, of course, allow Zhou to construe Matteo Ricci in a context that escapes d'Elia entirely—the context, that is, of what we could call with some slight exaggeration the late-Ming counter-culture. Now d'Elia was far too good a scholar of Chinese to get grammar, lexicon, and context wrong unless something particular was blocking his view, and the obstacle must have been the later institutional myopia of the Catholic Church in China that reduces Chinese intellectual life to the Cheng-Zhu orthodoxy of the later imperial examination syllabus, sees nothing in Buddhism and Daoism but superstitions to be combated, and no longer recruits its allies in the literary *bohème* that would have stopped and looked eagerly at any book with a phrase like *jiren* or *fangwai* in the title.

SOMETHING NEW AND STRANGE

The identification of Ricci as some sort of Daoist—and a heterodox one at that—came naturally not only to his partisans, but also to his opponents. Jacques Gernet has shown that the measures of repression declared against Christianity in the last years of the Ming strictly paralleled those applied to the "White Lotus" and "Non-Action" sects, with which Ricci's sect could easily be confused from an official point of view.[37] Like other Chinese minority religions, *Tianzhu jiao* was loosely based on a textual revelation but chiefly on the words and actions of its charismatic leaders; it called assemblies or conclaves, mixing men and women and people of diverse social status; it promised benefits in this life and the next to the faithful, and was rumored to assure them of their personal immortality in case they were subjected to a martyr's death (a belief which threatened to detract from the magistrate's power to intimidate). And like many secret cults, it arrogated to itself imperial prerogatives (that of sacrificing to Heaven, normally the right of the monarch alone). So it is no wonder, and not necessarily the sign of a particular animus against Christianity, that the *Ming History* should present Ricci as a decidedly marginal figure, ending by comparing him with the chiefs of recent peasant rebellions:

> In the ninth year of Wanli, Ricci began sailing, and after nine years of travel he arrived in Canton and Macao. From then on his religion began to seep into the middle country 中土. In the twenty-ninth year he came to the capital, and went to the Board of Rites to present his foreign tribute gifts, saying that he was a subject of the Great Western Ocean [Kingdom]. The Board of Rites replied that in the statute books there was no such thing as the Great Western Ocean Kingdom; under "Western Ocean" there was only the kingdom of Suoli 瑣里國 (Coromandel). There was no way of knowing if he was telling the truth. But since he had been in China for twenty years, his case did not fall

under the Regulation for those who "come from afar with gifts to express their zeal for loyalty"; moreover, the gifts were trifling (viz., one picture of the Tianzhu and the Tianzhu's mother). He also had with him a piece of an immortal's bone, and other such things. (Now if they have already turned into gods or immortals, they should be able to fly, so why would they need bones?) It is truly as Han Yu of the Tang said: such inauspicious and filthy objects are not meant to be brought into palaces.[38] Moreover, these "local products" were not submitted through the proper official channels for translation and inspection, as Ricci found an official of the inner palace to carry them in by a side path—a dereliction on the official's part, and a lapse in the Bureau's duties. He additionally failed to report to the Bureau for translation and verification of his tribute articles, but instead privately took a lodging in a monastery. The officials of the Bureau could not understand what he had in mind. But every presentation of tribute must be followed by a bestowal [from the Board], and every diplomat from abroad must be gratified with a meal. The officials of the Bureau presented him a hat and belt to take home to his country, and ordered him no longer to live concealed in the two capitals, lest he continue to have relations with the people there and create new scandals....

From Matteo Ricci's entrance into China, the number of Europeans here has not ceased to grow. A certain Wang Fengsu 王豐蕭 [Alfonso Vagnoni], living in Nanjing, did nothing but stir up the populace with the religion of the Lord of Heaven. From gentlemen and officials down to the common people of the lanes and alleys, many were attracted to follow him.... Vice-Minister of Rites Shen Que 沈㴤 and Supervising Secretary Yan Wenhui 晏文輝 wrote a joint memorial accusing them of professing heterodox opinions and misleading the masses. It is likely that they are the cat's paw of the Franks [Portuguese].... They hold nighttime meetings and disperse at dawn. Their religion is no different from the White Lotus and Non-Action sects.

The people who come from Italy are particularly clever, accomplished scholars. Their only intent is to spread their religion; they do not seek salary or advantage. In their books are many things that the Chinese have never encountered before, and so, for a time, those desirous of strange and new things (*hao yi zhe* 好異者) gave them their approval.[39]

The *Ming shi*, written in the last decades of the seventeenth century, narrates the Jesuits as one small element of the general collapse that would usher in the Qing—the failure of authority to command the loyalties and aspirations of people, the emergence of rival centers of power such as messianic sects. A small stroke in that picture is to specify Ricci's readership: "those desirous of strange and new things."

It would not be hard to manufacture an addendum to the *Daode jing* 道德經 by stringing together well-chosen phrases from the Gospels and Epistles: "Blessed are the meek; for they shall inherit the earth" (cf. 柔弱勝剛強); "Love your enemies, bless them that curse you, do good to them that hate you" (cf. 殺人之眾，以哀悲泣之); "So the last shall be first, and the first last" (cf.聖人後其身而身先，外其身而身存 and 反者道之動，弱者道之用); "But God hath chosen the foolish things of the world to confound the wise...and things which are not, to bring to nought things that are" (cf. 天下萬物生於有，有生於無); and so on.[40] Of course, hunting up parallels proves nothing; what makes a religion go is its purchase on a situation, and so what really ought to be compared are perhaps the situations in which the writings we categorize as Daoist had their most powerful appeal, at one or another time in Chinese history, and the situation of people in European late antiquity, when out of a motley collection of proverbs, parables, and mira-cle-tales emerged a social formation that ended by displacing, indeed almost thoroughly overpowering, the epics, philosophies, law digests, sciences, and official constitutions built up over the previous millennium.[41] By presenting himself as some sort of Daoist, or a figure from a Daoist book, Matteo Ricci was, in an unanticipated way, returning to Christianity's much earlier strug-gle with pagan rhetoric and imperial ideology: for that religion was once a counter-culture too. His self-translation coincided with the self-positioning of Paul more closely than might seem possible for a follower of developed Catholic institutions.[42]

The task of this chapter has been to fill in the meaning of the exorbitant claim in its title. Of course Ricci never presented himself as a "Daoist" in so many words; he had nothing to say in favor of the established Daoist religion in his Italian journals.[43] He named himself a "Western scholar" *xishi* 西士, a "European" *Ouluoba ren* 歐羅巴人, or "a member of the Society of Jesus" (*Yesu hui zhong ren* 耶穌會中人), and signed his texts using a ring with the cipher IHS where a Chinese literatus would use an inked seal.[44] But the lan-guage whereby he described himself and let himself be described in Chinese affiliates him with the sort of people in his world who framed their lives and personalities in terms drawn from the *Daode jing*, the more mysterious interpretations of the *Yijing*, and above all the *Zhuangzi*. The specificity of the *Zhuangzi* needs to be brought out. The "Daoism" of Ricci's Chinese persona is definitely not that of Laozi, the advocate of silence who wants to avoid the glare of publicity and stay close to nature, "the mother."[45] Nor has it anything to do with the established Daoist religion, chartered by the state to issue pardons and letters patent in the name of the Jade Emperor On High.[46] It is rather the disputatious, paradoxical, countercultural persona of Zhuang Zhou in the *Zhuangzi*, who may call on Laozi as an example of the incorruptibly autonomous sage, but does not imitate Laozi's behavior.

What did Matteo Ricci come to China intending to do? That is the question we think we can answer. But the question most worth exploring is: How might his intentions at the outset have been affected by the encounters he made and the negotiations in which he found himself over the years of his residence there? What happens to an intention that must translate itself into alien and perhaps even antagonistic terms in order to be realized? How was he found, not lost, in translation? The arc of his translation does not only go in one direction, from Rome to Beijing. A return shock of translation occurs simultaneously from China toward Europe, if our ability to see it in Ricci's Chinese texts is not obscured by the egocentricity of the "source."[47]

Ricci's "Daoism," if we can call it that, was a performance shaped by the codes of Ming literary life, an "otherward" translation of the self. This case makes such alternatives as "nativizing vs. foreignizing translation" seem unpromising, except as a starting point for more finely drawn distinctions. Or definitions capable of including their opposites: for what we have here is a thoroughly "nativizing" translation of Ricci's personality into Chinese, with the exception that Ricci was no native and that he surely was not solely responsible for his choice of persona. Rather, he reproduced, transcriptively, his Others' view of him as Other. "Nativizing" himself into the alien character of a prodigy, monster, or transcendent allowed Ricci a native kind of foreignness. Taking clues about how to be Chinese from the *Zhuangzi* gives the foreigner expression in a time-honored Chinese idiom—the idiom of strangeness, for the *Zhuangzi* is full of strange characters, talking animals, science fiction, infinities, impossibilities, and logical knots. Indeed the *Zhuangzi* provides a prime native resource for describing the foreign without leaving Chinese cultural terrain, as it did for Xu Zhimo attempting to translate Baudelaire in 1924 and as it had done in such consequential "trials of the foreign" as the introduction of Buddhism to China. That persona, we could say, represents a Chinese way of being strange.

And a strange way of being Chinese, for through the centuries, the *Zhuangzi* has been the bible of eccentrics, the roadmap leading away from the highways of worldly success, the classic of anti-classicism, the norm of abnormality.

4

The "First Age" of Translation

"RECEPTIVITY"

Liang Qichao's 梁啟超 1920 essay "The Literature of Translation and the Buddhist Canon" 翻譯文學與佛典 concentrated on the period 400–700 CE, when teams of translators brought thousands of Pali and Sanskrit originals into Chinese, using standardized lexical equivalents, transliterations, and a new system of genres to create a Sino-Buddhist literature. The essay closed with a clear indication of its intended relevance to the contemporary situation:

> Although for lack of time and space I have been unable to address this topic as exhaustively as I had wished, the reader of these pages should be able to judge of the importance of the literature of translation for a nation's culture. We are today in a second age of translation, and those who are engaged in that work should aspire to look to the ancients without shame!
> 吾對此問題，所欲論者猶未能盡，為篇幅及時日所限，姑止於此。讀斯篇者，當已能略察翻譯事業與異國文化關係之重大。今第二度之翻譯時期至矣，從事於此者，宜思如何無愧古人也！[1]

The "second age of translation" of which Liang spoke might also be called modern Chinese literature. It already included such hybrid works as Yan Fu's translations/adaptations of Darwin and John Stuart Mill, Lin Shu's classical-Chinese paraphrase of *La Dame aux camélias*, Hu Shi's "experiments" in vernacular free verse, Lu Xun's "Diary of a Madman" (based on Gogol'), and countless other cultural forms pervading daily life and communications, making contact with foreignness more or less the hallmark of modernity as experienced by Chinese.[2] Foreignness had been similarly pervasive and valued in China only once before:

> In ancient times our nation was often in contact with alien races. But the foreigners' culture was always treated as lower than our own, and the relationship was always conducted using our language and characters. The dragoman was not worth mentioning. As for a warm reception given to foreign cultures, an open-minded receptivity toward them, and the sense that translating was an honorable endeavor—all that came only with the introduction of Buddhism.
>
> 然我國古代與異族之接觸雖多，其文化皆出我下；凡交際皆以我族語言文字為主，故「象鞮」之業，無足稱焉，其對於外來文化，為熱情的歡迎，為虛心的領受，而認翻譯為一種崇高事業者，則自佛教輸入以後也。[3]

A cultural nationalist might see this as a lamentable concession. (Indeed Hu Shi would a few years later complain bitterly about the "humiliating domination of the whole nation by a foreign religion which was opposed to all the best traditions of the native civilization.")[4] But Liang Qichao put forward a different argument about the grounds of cultural vitality:

> The stronger the receptivity of a nation's culture, the greater its power of growth: this is a constant principle. Our nation's receptivity to cultures outside it was exhibited principally in the epoch of the introduction of Buddhist teachings. Thus not only the world of ideas underwent an unprecedentedly vast transformation; the world of letters did as well...
>
> 凡一民族之文化，其容納性愈富者，其增展力愈強，此定理也。我民族對於外來文化之容納性，惟佛學輸入時代最能發揮。故不惟思想界生莫大之變化，即文學界亦然 . . .

And so, Liang tried to argue, the overwhelmingly powerful current in twentieth-century Chinese letters, the vernacular movement with its upending of the traditional hierarchy of genres and styles, was a delayed outgrowth of the Buddhist translation movement of the fourth and fifth centuries:

> The *Flower Sutra*, the *Nirvana Sutra*, the *Prajñaparamita Sutra*... Texts like these, so rich in literary value, and translated by masters of the art into the most beautiful Chinese, were enjoyed by people of every stratum of society....Their influence was transmitted directly to ordinary literary works....And in more recent eras, great works [of vernacular fiction] on the order of *Shuihu zhuan* [The Water Margin] or *Honglou meng* [Dream of the Red Chamber] show, in many points of their style and structure, their debt to the *Flower* and *Nirvana* Sutras.

若華嚴，涅槃，般若等 . . . 此等富裕文學性的經典，復經譯家宗匠以
極優美之國語為之逐寫，社會上人人嗜讀 . . . 其影響乃直接表見於一
般文藝 . . . . 而近代一二鉅製水滸紅樓之流，其結體運筆，受華嚴，
涅槃之影響者實甚多。[5]

These premodern novels, along with play-scripts and ballads, were just emerging from the netherworld of popular entertainment to occupy the top ranks of the modern Chinese literary canon. Once again, Liang's fourth-century Buddhists are pointing at the contemporary. And on this, Hu Shi and Liang Qichao were in agreement: two chapters of Hu's 1928 *History of Chinese Vernacular Literature* are devoted to Buddhist translations and their influence on the written language, making them precursors of twentieth-century *baihua*.[6]

Liang had always been willing to learn from other cultures and to recommend products drawn from them (like the social novel) as models to be followed in China, but "The Literature of Translation and the Buddhist Canon" is something of a manifesto.[7] Under the cover of recounting a history, it argues that foreign influence in literature is not something to which one submits helplessly, as one surrenders to a powerful master, but that it testifies to the strength of the receiving culture. It came at a particular juncture in Liang's career, his intended shift from public affairs to scholarship. In 1917 Liang retired from his job at the Ministry of Finance; in 1919–20 he took a long trip to Europe. His first writing project after his retirement was to be a history of Buddhism in China, of which the essay on translated literature is one rounded-off fragment. The choice of topic addresses contemporary anxieties. Was Chinese culture dying out? Was the whole civilization losing its way? Certainly the nation was in trouble, with the provinces dominated by warlords and the port cities sliced up for foreign concessions. Liang's praise of the long-past outward-looking moment of Chinese culture under Buddhist influence asserts that receptivity is not an index of weakness, but of strength. By invoking this longer perspective Liang wants to assert that the hybrid culture, wrought through and in translations, of the late Qing and early Republic is no anomaly. It does not represent a break in the continuity of Chinese identity, but belongs rather to the regular and attested processes of cultural growth.

But on what terms are foreign texts to be naturalized? Liang's judgment of the quality of translations follows a "golden mean" pattern: translations should be faithful but not too literal, legible but not too free. The translations of An Shigao 安世高 (active 148–80 CE) were praised by Dao'an (312–85) as "well-argued but not over-elaborate, straightforward but not crude" 辯而不華，質而不野 and "wondrous in thought and delicate in reasoning, impossible to put down" 義妙理婉，每覽其文，欲罷不能.[8] Liang seconds Dao'an's praise for An Shigao's translation style. Some translations, on the other hand, "dilute the wine with water" and "equip Hundun with holes, killing him in the process"—two extremely telling analogies for translators' failures.⁹ There is no greater flaw than introducing a subjective ideal that surreptitiously puts itself in the place of the spirit of the original. [The editor of the *Sanguo zhi* 三國志] Chen Shou said [of such translators]: "What the Buddha transmitted, they weave and mingle with the Chinese *Laozi*." For the translators of the early period were steeped in Laozi and Zhuangzi, and plucked out expressions from them to adorn the Buddha's words. For example, the *Forty-Two Section Sutra*: not only is the writing style imitated from Laozi, but the teaching follows him as well. Sutras of this sort adulterate Buddhist teaching with the pre-existing Chinese philosophy of non-existence: just what is meant by "wine diluted with water."

「葡萄酒被水」，「鑿成混沌終」之兩喻，可謂痛切．蓋譯家之大患，莫過於羼雜主觀的理想，潛易原著之精神．陳壽謂：「浮屠所載，與中國老子經而相出入」．蓋彼時譯家，大率漸染老莊，采其說以文飾佛言，例如四十二章經非惟文體類老子，教理亦多沿襲．此類經典，攙雜我國固有之虛無思想，致佛教變質，正所謂被水之葡萄酒也。¹⁰

A closer look at the *Sutra in Forty-Two Sections* will show what kinds of "adulteration" Liang has in mind. Traditionally held to be the earliest Buddhist scripture circulated in China (a view that is, like much about the text, far from certain), the so-called *Sutra* (more precisely a florilegium or sampler) is made up of a prologue and forty-two paragraphs, each delivering an aphorism, comparison, or anecdote. A person schooled in the Chinese classics who encountered Buddhism for the first time through this composition would have found it alternately familiar and disorienting. Here are a few sections retranslated with emphasis on the salient terms:

[Prologue] When the World-Honored One had realized the Way (*chengdao* 成道), he had this thought: "To forsake desires and [attain] tranquility: this is the greatest triumph." He dwelt in great meditative fixity and subdued all demonic ways. In the garden of the Deer Park he rotated the dharma-wheel of the Four Noble Truths. He converted Jiaochenru and four others and demonstrated the fruits of the Way. Later, there were many doubts voiced by *biqiu* who begged the Buddha to resolve them. The World-Honored One taught and commanded, and on each point they were enlightened. They brought their palms together and bowed in assent, and followed the honored commands.

世尊成道已，作是思惟：離欲寂靜是最為勝；住大禪定降諸魔道。於鹿野苑中轉四諦法輪，度憍陳如等五人而證道果。複有比丘所言說諸疑，求佛進止；世尊教敕一一開悟，合掌敬諾而順尊敕。

[1] The Buddha said: Those who leave their families and go forth from their homes, who know their minds and attain the root, and have understood the dharma of non-action (*wuweifa* 無為法), are called *shamen*. Those who constantly observe the 250 precepts and maintain purity in order to instantiate the Four Noble Truths through their actions shall become *aluohan*. An *aluohan* can fly and transform. He lives an extremely long life and can move heaven and earth. Next in order are the *anahan*, who at the end of their lives become spiritual beings and rise to the nineteen heavens to be confirmed as *aluohan*. Next after them are the *situohan*. A *situohan* ascends once and returns once, attaining thereby the state of *aluohan*. Next come the *shuntuohuan*. A *shuntuohuan* dies seven times and is born seven times before being confirmed as *aluohan*. Cutting off attachment and desires is like cutting off the four limbs: one will not use them again.[11]

佛言：辭親出家，識心達本，解無為法，名曰沙門。常行二百五十戒、進止清淨，為四真道行成阿羅漢。阿羅漢者，能飛行變化，曠劫壽命，住動天地。次為阿那含，阿那含者，壽終靈神上十九天證阿羅漢。次為斯陀含，斯陀含者，一上一還即得阿羅漢。次為須陀洹，須陀洹者，七死七生便證阿羅漢。愛欲斷者，如四肢斷，不複用之。

[11] A *shamen* asked the Buddha: "Through what causal factors does one attain knowledge of one's previous lives and reach the supreme Way?" The Buddha said: "By purifying one's mind and guarding one's intent, one can reach the supreme Way. It is like polishing a mirror: when the dust is removed the luminosity is revealed. Cut off desires and be without demands, and then you will attain [knowledge of] past lives."[12]

沙門問佛。以何因緣得知宿命。會其至道。佛言。淨心守志。可會至道。譬如磨鏡。垢去明存。斷欲無求。當得宿命。

The *Sutra in Forty-Two Sections* does not much resemble the sutras later translated from Sanskrit. Whereas the great sermon-sutras such as the *Diamond Sutra* or the *Lotus Sutra* systematically develop specific points of doctrine within a frame-story of ceremony, dialogue, and assent by the internal audience, this propaganda document is pithy, disconnected, and modular in structure. Its format cannot possibly represent that of a hypothetical Indic original, but an adaptation to the context of reception. Through its organization, the text makes a tacit claim of comparability with the existing scriptures around which interpretive communities had already grown up in China. In it the Buddha occupies the same speaking role as Confucius in the *Lunyu* ("the Master said" followed by an aphorism or vignette), and its short paragraphs have been described as "stylistically probably modelled upon the *Xiaojing* [Classic of Filial Piety] or the *Daode jing* [Book of the Way and its Power]."[13] The reader, then, is encouraged to behave toward this text as he would behave toward those better-known texts, recognizing the voice of authority, the command to practice, and the promise of wonder-working effects. The *Classic of Filial Piety*, made an elementary manual of ethics and politics by the Han Dynasty on account of its brevity and clarity, articulated its vision of world-transformation similarly:

> The Master said, "For teaching the people to be affectionate and loving, there is nothing better than filial piety.... For securing the repose of superiors and the good order of the people, there is nothing better than the rules of propriety. The rules of propriety are simply (the development of) the principle of reverence. Therefore the reverence paid to a father makes (all) sons pleased. The reverence paid to an elder brother makes (all) younger brothers pleased. The reverence paid to a ruler makes (all) subjects pleased. The reverence paid to the One man makes thousands and myriads of men pleased. The reverence is paid to a few, and the pleasure extends to many. This is what is meant by an 'All-embracing Dao.'"
>
> 子曰：「教民親愛，莫善於孝。. . . 安上治民，莫善於禮。禮者，敬而已矣。 故敬其父，則子悅；敬其兄，則弟悅；敬其君，則臣悅；敬一人，而千萬人悅。所敬者寡，而悅者眾，此之謂要道也」。¹⁴

As if offering an instruction manual for first-time users, the *Sutra in Forty-Two Sections* presents a series of "ipse dixit" definitions of the Buddhist Way. Although many readers would have found terms like *aluohan, biqiu*, and *shuntuohan* mysterious, the text offers many signals keying its promises to long-familiar aspirations. The Buddha's Way is a *wuweifa*, a "pattern of non-action" like those put forth by countless adepts of the *Daode jing*. Those who follow him can hope to live immeasurably long lives and to fly in the air like the supermen of the *Zhuangzi*. "Moving heaven and earth," "guarding one's intent," and making the mind tranquil and smooth like a reflecting surface are operations familiar to readers of such basic texts as the *Xiaojing*, the "Great Preface" to the *Shi jing*, the *Yijing, Zuo zhuan*, and *Xunzi*.¹⁵ Even the great problem of filial piety (that a monk would leave his ancestors without descendants) is briefly addressed.¹⁶

The doctrine of the *Sutra in Forty-Two Sections* would then seem to be compromised, impure, "diluted." Is this an instance of surreptitious translation, deceptively grafting a new teaching onto old phrases? In Liang's view, it was a happy day when "the honest and loyal Dao'an" 忠實之道安 saw the error of the earlier translators and raised up a cry against it.¹⁷ Liang's examples are meant to lay out a typology and history of translation. The typology first: translations can show the degree of "receptivity" of the cultures that produce them. Translations that accept the foreign culture only conditionally, on the basis of its resemblance to the home culture, are at the low and primitive end of translation. Then the history: the earliest translations were crude gestures at approximating Buddhist ideas, barely distinct from pre-existing Chinese ideas found in Daoist or Confucian texts; progress was made with An Shigao's versions, which adhered to both the values of faithfulness ("substance," *zhi* 質) and of elegance ("form," *wen* 文).[18] Finally, a high degree of "receptivity" produces translations that are faithful enough to substitute for the original, as the massive influence of Buddhism in China after the fifth century attests. Dao'an, surveying the field in the late fourth century with hundreds of examples of translation from Sanskrit before him, could offer authoritative judgment on the virtues and failings of translators in his *Inventory of the Many Sutras, Ordered and Classified* of 374 CE. For the "literature of translation" to take its first hesitant steps away from the home culture, it must renounce its "subjective ideal" and hew to the "spirit of the original." Only in a transitional period, quickly to be left behind, did the Buddha's words need to be "adorned" or disguised with those of Laozi and Zhuangzi. What Berman would call "the test of the foreign," if passed, confirms a culture's "receptivity."

But what was there to receive? The authors/translators/adapters of such hybrid texts as *The Sutra in Forty-Two Sections* may not have known the contours of the Buddhist concepts to be conveyed, or the extent of their correspondence to such Chinese terms as *dao* and *wuwei*, clearly enough to perform a conscious act of deception. Rather than reject the "watered wine" of the *Sutra in Forty-Two Sections* and similar texts, we should see them as advancing into a linguistic territory without known landmarks, adapting, not only Buddhist ideas to Chinese audiences, but the Chinese language to new uses. Now that we have thousands of comprehensive, authenticated presentations of the Vedic and Buddhist principle of *ahimsa*, to present it as equivalent to the Daoist ideal of *wuwei* seems false and clumsy; but for non-native speakers and their Han-dynasty associates feeling their way through the Chinese language for new possibilities of utterance, it may have been the best option available, not to mention one that had a ready-made local following. Arhats may fly and transform, though not in precisely the same way or for the same reasons as the "True Men" imagined by Zhuangzi; but the differences were incidental to getting the point across. Translation needed to nativize the foreign concepts, but as it did so, it began to foreignize the native ones: for example, by considering the feeding of one's parents in a hierarchy of acts of generosity finely differentiated as to their worth, or by using the term "non-action" to designate a specific set of refrainings from harmful action. Only debate and experiment could reveal what the barriers to equivalence were. Like Dao'an, we can measure the potential for misunderstanding, but on a basis of information that could not have been available to the original participants. Liang's history of translation sets self-abnegating fidelity as the endpoint, but what, at the outset, was there to be faithful to?

The early Chinese monks, forced to be eclectics by the circumstances under which the doctrine was presented to them, had to base their opinions [of Buddhism] on a bewildering variety of Mahayana and Hinayana sutras, monastic rules, spells and charms, legends and scholastic treatises of different epochs and schools....One of the most serious problems was of a linguistic nature: only a few foreign [instructors] could freely express themselves in Chinese, whereas before the late fourth century no Chinese seems to have had any knowledge of Sanskrit.[19]

The great translator An Shigao, a hostage from Parthia, is described in his biography as a speaker of *hu* 胡, "barbarian language"; he was also able to understand the languages of birds and beasts. In his home country he had already gained "comprehensive knowledge of the foreign classics" 外國典籍 莫不該貫 and was known for his unusual intelligence; thus when he arrived in Luoyang around 148, "in short order he became familiar with the Chinese language, and set about expounding the various sutras and changing [their language] from barbarian into Chinese" 至止未久，即通習華語，於是宣 釋眾經，改胡為漢.[20] "Expounding" the scriptures barely preceded "changing" their language, for the teacher brought the text with him, possibly in memory. To his audiences, the teacher and the scripture were in effect one.[21] The vague designation of the language of the scriptures as *hu* ("foreign" or "Western; Central Asian") indicates the degree to which an original text was unimportant for the act of "expounding" and rewriting. Indeed the "texts" An Shigao taught may have been nothing but a pattern in his well-stocked mind. The basis of his teaching, it is said, consisted of meditation exercises and numbered lists. A mnemonic catalogue of points of doctrine, each one susceptible of expansion into sentences and paragraphs of commentary, might well appear to its possessor indifferent to its linguistic garb, and thus easy to improvise around, "change," or "correct" into Chinese wording.[22]

Two centuries later, and despite a great expansion in Buddhist institutions, the translation effort was still dependent on foreigners from Kashmir and Central Asia, "acting as informants 'producing' 出 (i.e. reciting or writing out) the original texts." "Most of these masters knew little or no Chinese when they arrived; they merely recited the Sanskrit text of the scriptures which they knew by heart or of which they possessed manuscripts."[23] "The first Chinese who is known to have mastered Sanskrit is the late fourth-century translator Zhu Fonian."[24] Moreover, "Buddhist scriptures arriving in China in the early centuries of the Common Era were composed not just in one Indian dialect but several," so that "the possibilities for ambiguity, or of outright misunderstanding, were rife....Barring strong evidence of another kind, we should assume that any text translated in the second or third century CE was *not* based on Sanskrit, but rather on one or another of the many Prakrit vernaculars."[25] Dao'an himself, despite his assertion of qualifications to judge the merits of translations, was what we might call "a 'general manager' and adviser" to the translation workshop that produced the Chinese sutras:

> He asked the foreign masters to recite whatever they could "produce," discussed translation problems with his collaborators, disapproved some obviously faulty translations, revised the Chinese versions after they had been "noted down" (筆受), and wrote the prefaces.... Although Dao'an did not and could not take part in the work of translation itself, he appears to have been well aware of the problems connected with rendering the Sanskrit texts into Chinese.[26]

Who was responsible for discovering such "problems"? The typical scenario of translation involved an informant (possibly flanked by an interpreter), transcribers into Chinese, specialists charged with polishing that content into literary-Chinese form, and an editor to review the whole. The informant, in the early centuries, was a Central Asian immigrant such as Zhi Qian 支謙 or An Shigao; later, he might be one of the rare Indian Buddhist scholars to cross over into China, such as Vighna (Weiqinan 維祇難) in 274. We know little about the transcribers and polishers; some of the editors, like Dao'an, have left eloquent testimonies to the process, but these may mislead if we take them to be descriptions of the kind of language-to-language operation we usually call translation:[27]

> The bulk of the translation work was done by the Chinese participants—the bilingual interpreters who "transmitted the language," *chuanyu* 傳語 (i.e., made an oral translation), someone who "received (the oral translation) by the brush," *bishou* 筆受 (i.e., wrote down a draft Chinese text), and others who "polished" [*runse* 潤色] and edited the text. As we shall see, this considerably reduced the part played by the foreign monks in the translation process, and placed the full burden of interpretation upon the shoulders of their collaborators; in many cases the foreigner would not even be able to check the correctness of the translation.[28]

Correspondence with an original then could not have provided the standard against which to evaluate these early translations, even for a strict judge like Dao'an, since the original was inaccessible to most of the parties to the translating process and the final product could not be read by the bringers of the originals. How then could a translation be vetted for what we might call, loosely, its "accuracy"?

Imagine that I am asked to evaluate the translation of an Egyptian novel into English, and I do not know Egyptian Arabic. I could perhaps judge it by how "well it reads," how accurately it fulfills the expectation I would have of a novel in English, but this is obviously a poor criterion and plays into the norms of "nativization" excoriated by theorists of translation. I could compare it with other novels already translated from Arabic, assuming that they have sufficient features in common that the English versions of novels A, B, and C should resemble that of novel D—another imperfect method, but slightly more relevant. That criteria of this second sort were not absurd in the case of Buddhist Chinese "translation" is arguable on the grounds that the source texts were, or were supposed to be, highly uniform in style, organization, and doctrine, and that the goal of the translation workshops was to create a standardized Buddhistic Chinese with systematically plotted lexical fields. Histories of Buddhist translation often remark on the development of a specialized, somewhat arcane religious idiom: "As early as the third century CE, a distinctly Chinese Buddhist 'scriptural style' had developed, as different from Chinese secular literature as from its Indian prototypes; in its turn it became frozen into a kind of canonical language and divorced from the living language."[29] "Kumārajīva [鳩摩羅什, 334–413] created a very fluent, eminently readable, and yet reasonably accurate translation idiom which, together with its hundreds of new Chinese readings of Sanskrit terms, was soon taken over by subsequent translators."[30] But rather than features of autonomously developing language or individual style, these properties of the specialized target language must have been developed in order to compensate for the unavailability of the "original." Editors such as Dao'an and Kumārajīva had the social function of unifying Chinese Buddhism's originally diverse "rhetorical communities."[31] A large comparison-set and a standardized terminology allowed translations to be checked, in a certain sense, from the receiving end. Moreover, like an engineering manual and unlike most novels, the Buddhist sutra could be judged by how well it *worked*—by how it performed the tasks expected of a sutra, one of which was to extend previous doctrine rather than contradicting it. Translation workshops and the understanding of translation that grounds them imply criteria of success and failure, of idiomatic fluency and exotic accuracy, specific to their milieu. What only seems to relate to the poles of literal and free translation in such remarks as Dao'an's appreciation of An Shigao really has more to do with the establishment of generic codes and the perception of compatibility.

In short, this is a translation situation in which reception dominates. Translation is mostly rewriting, adaptation of new content to the body of texts already produced, circulated, and accepted by the textual community. But Dao'an acted within a monastic environment, surrounded by people who had already "taken refuge in the sangha" and its textual community. The obstacles to the acceptance of Buddhism in China did not concern his public. These included "the essentially pragmatic and secular world-view of the Confucian tradition; the 'political theology' of the Mandate of Heaven; a totalistic conception of imperial authority, also in the religious sphere...and an outspoken Sinocentric attitude towards anything foreign or 'barbaric.'"[32] To confront those obstacles, other translators had to use different means, also oriented toward reception, but aiming at the conversion of different publics: in one set of cases, this was "a public of Chinese lay devotees with rudimentary schooling, standing outside the élite of scholar-officials, but sufficiently literate to read these texts with their limited vocabulary and their unadorned style...a sub-élite of clerics and copyists, the lowest fringes of the bureaucracy, and traders and artisans."[33] For them, the message could pass adequately through a linguistic vehicle that was "erratic, crude, full of vulgarisms, often chaotic to the point of unintelligibility....The style," says Zürcher, "is strikingly 'un-Chinese.' There is no trace of any concession to Chinese literary taste (or of any familiarity with it)."[34] The truly difficult public, the one whose attention was most selective but also most valuable, was that which had already given its youth over to the study of the Classics and the philosophical Masters: the gentry and scholar-official élite. What Liang Qichao, in a teleological mood, framed as the progress of Chinese translation from crude hybrids of self and other toward a fully realized mimesis of Sanskrit sacred literature may best be seen as a difference of audiences, addressed one after another as Buddhism gradually found its heterogeneous public.

ALIGNED MEANINGS?

The biography of Zhu Faya 竺法雅 (an older contemporary of Dao'an, thus active in the early 300s) in the *Lives of Eminent Monks* depicts him as a cultural boundary-crosser:

> Faya was from Hejian [in Hebei, north China]. Serious, upright, and imposing, from his youth he delighted in external [i.e., non-Buddhist] learning 外學, and once he reached maturity he came to understand Buddhist teachings. The sons of scholars in robe and cap [i.e., sons of the gentry] came to him for instruction. Faya's students at the time were proficient in the secular classics 世典, but not yet skilled in Buddhist reasoning. So Faya, together with Kang Falang and some others, excerpted numbered items from the sutras and matched them with external [i.e., secular] books 外書. He made these his examples in oral explanation, calling them *geyi* [aligned meanings]. Consequently, Pifu, Tanxiang, and others also debated [these] *geyi*, in order to instruct their followers. Faya was clever, spontaneous, and good at getting to the pivotal issues; he combined external classics 外典 and Buddhist sutras in

his expositions. Whenever he went over the texts with Dao'an and Fatai, looking for doubtful passages, together they brought out the essence of the sutras entire. Later he established a temple in Gaoyi with more than a hundred monks in residence, glossing and explicating without a pause. Faya's disciple Tanxi emulated his master's eloquence and was honored by the crown prince of Zhao, Shi Xuan [d. 348].

法雅，河間人。凝正有器度，少喜外學，長通佛義。衣冠士子，咸附諮稟。時依雅門徒，並世典有功，未善佛理。雅乃與康法朗等，以經中事數，擬配外書，為生解之例，謂之格義。及毘浮、曇相等，亦辯格義，以訓門徒。雅風彩灑落，善於樞機，外典、佛經，遞互講說。與道安、法汰，每披釋 湊疑，共盡經要。後立寺於高邑，僧眾百餘，訓誘無懈。雅弟子曇習，祖述先師，善於言論，為趙太子石宣所敬云。35

This passage, explicated by Chen Yinke in a pair of influential essays, launched the fortunes of the term "geyi," broadly used to indicate a syncretic philosophy integrating native Chinese Daoist ideas with those coming from India in the wake of Buddhism.36 But the crucial sentence (以經中事數，擬配外書，為生解之例，謂之格義) is interpreted diversely. Tang Yongtong, in a 1968 essay following Chen Yinke's hypothesis, translates the sentence thus: "taking the 事數 (categories) which were within the scriptures, [Zhu Faya] compared and paired them with the outer books [i.e. non-Buddhist writings], thus making instances (examples) to promote understanding: this he called *geyi*."37 In Victor Mair's reading, the sentence should be translated as follows: "Consequently, [Zhu Faya]…correlated the enumerations of items in the sutras with non-Buddhist writings as instances of lively explication; this was called 'categorizing concepts.'"38 At stake here are the meaning of the phrase "geyi" in this passage and the extension of the term to cover a range of interpretive practices. Chen's sense of the term, like Tang's, is broad, Mair's narrow, and the difference between them is important for our understanding of the way early Buddhism participated in Chinese intellectual life.

The introduction of "geyi" into modern Chinese historical vocabulary by Chen Yinke occurred casually, almost as an aside. Noticing an apparent absurdity in a Six Dynasties text, Chen accounts for it as strategic or devious quotation:

But what we see here is not just a misunderstanding; in fact, it can be explained by the intellectual temper of the times. For those scholars who participated in "pure conversations" during the Jin often enjoyed bringing Buddhist canonical texts and secular writings into forced combinations. Among monks and their followers there was, moreover, a specific method known as "*geyi*."

Although *geyi* is rarely mentioned, it flourished for a time, and its influence on the thinkers of the period was extremely deep, so it cannot go without a discussion here.

但此不僅由於誤解，實當日學術風氣有以致之。蓋晉世清談之士，多喜以內典與外書互相比附。僧徒之間復有一種具體之方法，名曰格義。格義之名雖罕見載記，然曾盛行一時，影響於當日之思想者甚深，固不可以不論也。[39]

Chen then goes on to cite the biography of Zhu Faya and similar texts to demonstrate that the pedagogy of early Buddhist teachers often relied on citing more familiar non-Buddhist writings as analogies and exempla. Allowing "outer" or non-Buddhist books to be used as glosses and peda-gogical helps was a strategy designed to enable potential converts to enter the Buddhist way of thinking. The strategy could go too far: Chen cites the case of one sutra (known as the *Tiwei jing* 提謂經) that had been expanded with references to Chinese classical texts, and was therefore rejected as corrupt.[40] Tang Yongtong's 1968 article makes an even stronger claim for the importance of "geyi" already in its title: "On 'Ko-yi,' The Earliest Method by Which Indian Buddhism and Chinese Thought Were Synthesized." Tang elaborates:

> The term *geyi*... very seldom appears in Chinese Buddhist books; it desig-nates the method used by the Chinese devotees of Buddhism prior to the Western Chin Dynasty; with the advent of the Eastern Chin, learned Buddhists discovered its defects and discarded it. Therefore there were very few men who knew it....
>
> In *geyi*, ideas originally Chinese are made use of; they are compared with those of Buddhism, in order to enable a student familiar with Chinese concepts to come to a full understanding of the doctrines in India.... Probably Faya had originally arrived at his understanding of the Buddhist works from the standpoint of comparison with Chinese thought.
>
> Of precisely what does the *geyi* method consist? It is not simply a broad, general comparison of Chinese and Indian thought; rather it is a very detailed process by which each of the ideas or terms of the respective terms are individually compared and equated. *Ge*, in this context, has the meaning of "to match" or "to measure"; *yi* means "name," "term," or "concept"; *geyi* is (the method or scheme of) matching ideas (or terms), or "the equation of ideas."...
>
> Just how Faya worked [the correspondences] out is not known.... However, we can be sure that Faya and his colleagues, in their oral expositions of the scriptures, had a detailed and definite method of comparative procedure, as a

result of which, moreover, they gave numerous instances for the purpose of promoting the full understanding of their students. Such, in general, was the method of *geyi*.[41]

Similarly, Ge Zhaoguang's intellectual history of China exploits the concept of *geyi* to account for change and persistence in patterns of thought:

> In the second decade of the fourth century, after the Jin court fled south in 317, the fundamental situation of the elite intellectual world...finally underwent a great change. "When [the Jin] crossed the Yangzi...Buddhism flourished greatly."...[C]elebrated scholars highly knowledgeable about philosophy...were ardently discussing Buddhist ideas. Precisely because these men were deeply steeped in traditional Chinese knowledge, their discussions of Buddhism went beyond the ordinary concerns about redemption, offerings to the Buddhas, charitable donations and retribution to explore the profound theories of the Buddhist religion. As a result they very soon arrived at quite a few doubts and questions....All these doubts required realistic explanations, and understandable terms were needed to make these explanations, but such understandable terms could only come from the Chinese cultural context. Therefore early translation of Buddhist ideas relied on traditional Chinese terms, especially Daoist terms that seemed to have similar meanings. This gave rise to the practice of *geyi* or "matching the meanings." As Chen Yinque astutely pointed out, the *geyi* method represented the first step in the beginning of the Chinese understanding of Buddhism, and Tang Yongtong's research also shows that it was perhaps used very early on....The *geyi* method had to be used because the ancient Chinese language simply did not contain terms that corresponded to all those complicated Buddhist concepts....Although this method of *geyi* was later criticized and abandoned by genuine theoreticians of Buddhism, still at the time it served both a bridging and an enlightening function and facilitated the emergence of the meanings of Buddhist thought in the Chinese linguistic context.[42]

This scenario accounts for the adoption of a foreign ideology by educated Chinese through a process of cultural hybridization in which Chinese ideas and thinkers play an active role, using their inherited terms and frames of reference to arrive at their own understanding of Buddhism: an understanding which later Buddhists would discard as being inaccurate and obsolete. Like Liang's history of translation, going from mixed beginnings to a full acknowledgment of the other's otherness, this narrative allows for mediating stages in a merging of intellectual streams otherwise difficult to imagine. It has thus become part of the accepted historiography of Chinese Buddhism.

To this scenario, however, an article by Victor Mair proposes radical limitations. Mair's investigation re-examines the key source text referred to by every discussion of *geyi*, scours the whole body of Chinese literature (secular, Daoist, and Buddhist) for occurrences of the term, which are surprisingly rare, and traces the proliferating concept of *geyi* in twentieth-century scholarship back to Chen Yinke's writings.[43] Mair announces that "*geyi* had nothing whatsoever to do with translation, but that it was instead a highly ephemeral and not-very-successful attempt on the part of a small number of Chinese teachers to cope with the flood of numbered lists...that came to China in the wake of Buddhism."[44] *Geyi* was in Mair's view merely "an exegetical technique of circumscribed application and limited duration," namely "the correlation of lists of enumerated Buddhist concepts with presumably comparable lists of notions extracted from non-Buddhist works."[45] The subsequent history of the term has gone off on a tangent, according to Mair:

> After the meager series of texts cited above [i.e. Zhu Faya's biography and a similar passage from the biography of Dao'an, to be discussed below], there is no significant mention of *geyi* until the twentieth century, when it is miraculously revived by modern historians and made to play a key role in the early development of Buddhism in China.
>
> The overwhelming majority of the modern translations and interpretations of *geyi* are partially or totally false.... [M]ost of what Chen [Yinke] has to say about *geyi* is sheer speculation....
>
> Among the many bizarre twists in the saga of *geyi* is the development of what Japanese specialists refer to as *kakugi Bukkyō* 格義佛教 ("*geyi* Buddhism"). Here we have the reification of a hypothetical construct that never existed in historical reality, but one that—once born—takes on a life of its own...with countless disquisitions being written on the nature and impact of what is essentially an imaginary phenomenon.[46]

Mair cites Tsukamoto Zenryū, Feng Youlan, Xiao Gongquan, Arthur Link, Arthur Wright, Wing-tsit Chan, Kenneth Chen, Whalen Lai, Leon Hurvitz, Erik Zürcher, Ren Jiyu, and others as "*geyi* enthusiasts" "ensnarled in the labyrinthine coils of the *geyi* trap" and prone to "confusion and imprecision" in their "sweeping assertions...unsupported by the actual textual evidence."[47] But is their error simply one of having misunderstood the term "geyi"? In rejecting the term "geyi" as it has been commonly understood since Chen Yinke, Mair also means to reject the claim that there existed "a method of comparing and matching with Chinese thought to cause people to understand Buddhist writing easily," a method relying chiefly on a vocabulary taken from Daoist texts. But his own argument should lead us to treat the term "geyi" and the practice formerly known as *geyi* as two separate things.

It does not follow from the statement "Scholars have been mistaken about the meaning of the term geyi" that "the practices scholars have mistakenly called geyi never occurred," unless there is an essential link between the term "geyi" and those practices. If indeed the practice of citing pre-Buddhist Chinese texts, usually but not exclusively the Laozi and Zhuangzi, in support of Buddhist argument, never, or rarely, or only trivially, occurred, then that should be shown through a discussion that does not depend on the meaning assigned to the term "geyi."[48] Mair attempts to rebut the scenario of a syncretic "Daoistic Buddhism" (Dōkyōteki Bukkyō 道教佛教, Tsukamoto's coinage) in the Eastern Jin by asserting that "Daoist religion was hardly enough well established [then...] to have subsumed or significantly colored Buddhism."[49] But the examples of cross-cultural glossing given by Chen Yinke have nothing to do with the Daoist religion, which, as is widely recognized, developed in China partly as a rival cult to expanding Buddhism; they refer only to adaptive use of the Daoist philosophical texts that were in favor among the disaffected intelligentsia of the Six Dynasties.[50]

The lexicographical cast of Mair's corrective leaves it wanting in another regard. Mair speaks as if attributing a meaning to "geyi" were simply a matter of getting it right or wrong—mostly wrong, of course: "erroneous understanding...wildly imaginative articles...overblown theses...empty and ahistorical...a colossal, chimerical congeries..."[51] What was Chen Yinke's motive for calling attention to the phenomenon of intercultural glossing, even if he erred in giving it the name "geyi"? Why did the term appeal to other scholars, not only historians of early Buddhism but those working in religion more generally, the history of ideas, and the theory of translation, for example? What new perceptions did it make possible? To what thoughts did it give an outlet? What, in a word, was at stake?

By retrieving "geyi" from the stockpile of seldom-used hermeneutic terms, Chen Yinke may have wanted to propose a solution to the dilemma of cultural identity in the twentieth century's "age of translation." Where Liang Qichao, like Lu Xun twenty years later, championed translation as an art of self-abnegation, and where Hu Shi called for a reversal of translation's effects by a "de-Indianization" of Chinese culture, Chen sought to show how inherited concepts could find new uses in building a context for imported arguments.[52] And contra Tang Yongtong, Chen did not insert geyi into the history of translation as a preliminary phase, "The Earliest Method" of Sino-Indian philosophical synthesis; he knew quite well that Buddhism had had over 200 years of history in China by the time of Zhu Faya. His investigations bore on a specific kind of ideological transformation, the adoption of Buddhism by educated aristocrats against a background of war, exile, and cultural collapse.[53]

Chen Yinke may have erred in calling it "geyi," but numerous biographies, letters, and polemical writings show the importance of the practice of translation-as-citation for the Buddhist apostolate to the literati. Returning to the biography of Zhu Faya: the account of Faya's early education is written, unsurprisingly, from a Buddhist point of view in which all non-Buddhist learning is designated "external" (*waixue* 外學): at most there is a slight distinction between the "books" and "canons" of the secular world (*wai shu* 外書, *shi dian* 世典, *wai dian* 外典), the "canons" being, presumably, the works considered necessary for scholarly advancement and office-holding. Unlike many earlier monks, Faya began his life as a member of the literati, was first trained in the books and methods of that social group, and only later "understood the Buddhist doctrine." It was in mediating the Buddhist writings for his literati students that he conceived the operation he called "geyi," whatever that was: perhaps, indeed, it started from the numbered lists that occur in both Buddhist and pre-Buddhist Chinese canonical texts. Given its Buddhist standpoint, the biography of Zhu Faya is not interested in what the "external works" that formed the basis of his *geyi* were. Nor does it tell us how they were interpreted. For his biographer, *geyi* is simply a pedagogical tool useful when speaking to the uninitiated. But Chen Yinke, wanting to understand this mediation process, relates the story of Faya's discovery to that of another renegade literatus, the founder of the Pure Land sect, Huiyuan. Huiyuan's biography begins similarly with a story of early secular accomplishment, unanticipated conversion, and clever deployment of non-Buddhistic learning for Buddhistic ends:

Shi Huiyuan, whose original surname was Jia, was a man from Loufan in the commandery of Yanmen. In his early youth he loved to study, and the prominent qualities of his intellect became abundantly manifested. At the age of thirteen he accompanied his maternal uncle, a member of the Linghu family, to study at Xuchang and Luoyang, so that he became a student at the [Imperial] Academy at an early age. There he gained a comprehensive knowledge of the Six Classics, and especially excelled in the study of *Laozi* and *Zhuangzi*. As his natural capacities were very great and his insight was brilliant and extraordinary, even the most prominent among the experienced literati all stood in awe of him.

At the age of twenty-one, he wanted to go over to Jiangdong to join Master Fan Xuan[54] in order to live in retirement together with him. But it happened that, after Shi Hu had died [349 CE], the Central Plain was ravaged by banditry and chaos, and the roads to the South were obstructed, so that his desire could not be fulfilled.

At that time, the *sramana* Shi Dao'an had founded a monastery at the Heng Shan in the Taihang mountains; he widely preached and extolled the formal doctrine, and enjoyed great fame. For this reason Huiyuan went to join him, and as soon as he had seen him, he was all filled with reverence and thought, "This is truly my master." Later, when he heard [Dao'an] explain the *Prajñāpāramitā*, he became suddenly awakened [to the Truth] and said with a sigh, "Confucianism, Daoism and the [other] Nine Schools of philosophy are all no more than chaff!" Then he…entrusted his life [to the Buddha] and became a disciple….

[Observing Huiyuan's intelligence,] Dao'an often sighed [in admiration] and said, "Should Huiyuan not be the one who will cause the Way to spread over the Eastern country?"

When he was twenty-four [357 CE], he was already giving sermons. Once a guest who listened to the explanation [of the scripture] raised objections against the concept of transcendent Truth [as explained by Dao'an].[55] The debate lasted some time, but the [opponent's] doubt and lack of understanding still increased. Then Huiyuan mentioned a [corresponding] concept taken from the *Zhuangzi* by way of analogy, whereupon the deluded [opponent] reached a clear understanding [of the truth]. From then on Dao'an made an exception and allowed Huiyuan to refrain from discarding secular literature.

釋慧遠，本姓賈氏，雁門婁煩人也。弱而好書，珪璋秀發。年十三隨舅令狐氏遊學許洛。故少為諸生。博綜六經，尤善莊老。性度弘博，風鑒朗拔。雖宿儒英達，莫不服其深致。年二十一欲渡江東就范宣子，共契嘉遁。值石虎已死，中原寇亂，南路阻塞。志不獲從。

時沙門釋道安立寺於太行恆山，弘贊像法，聲甚著聞。遠遂往歸之。一面盡敬，以為真吾師也。後聞安講波若經，豁然而悟，乃歎曰：儒道九流皆糠粃耳。便...委命受業。....

安公常歎曰。使道流東國其在遠乎。

年二十四便就講說。嘗有客聽講難實相義。往復移時，彌增疑昧。遠乃引莊子義為連類。於是惑者曉然。是後安公特聽慧遠不廢俗書。[56]

Huiyuan's early career mirrors Faya's: studies of the Confucian canon, together with the extracanonical works *Laozi* and *Zhuangzi*. The young Huiyuan makes a name for himself through his brilliance and learning, and is even admitted into the most prestigious academic institution in the realm, but this *succès d'estime* is not followed by any administrative career. At the age of twenty or so, he is already contemplating retiring from worldly life. When one avenue of retirement is closed to him, he follows another, attracted by the reputation of Dao'an without, apparently, knowing much about the content of his teaching. Instant conversion follows. The books he had been studying now appear to him as no more than "chaff": the word connoting trash to be discarded, but also mere outer husks, implying that somewhere may be found a seed of greater value. His teacher sees in him a future emissary to the "East" (that is, the southeast regions of China, where the Jin dynasty still reigned and some degree of law and order prevailed). The version of Buddhism taught by Dao'an and other masters from the North was somewhat at odds with the emphases then current in the "East":

> an amalgamation of Northern Buddhism with its stress on devotional practices, trance and thaumaturgy and based upon the translated scriptures of the archaic period of which it is a direct continuation, and the more intellectualized Southern gentry Buddhism with its peculiar mixture of Dark Learning and Mahāyāna notions and its ontological speculations based upon the *Prajñāpāramitā* and the *Vimalakīrtinirdesa*.[57]

Huiyuan, like Faya, was known for his expertise in, precisely, the texts of the "Dark Learning" (*xuanxue* 玄學): *Laozi, Zhuangzi,* and the *Yijing* as revived by the commentaries they had recently received, the work of Wang Bi 王弼, Xiang Xiu 向秀, and Guo Xiang 郭象.[58] And Huiyuan's competence rises to the occasion when an uncomprehending hearer "rebuts" or "raises difficulties about" (難) his exposition of the difference between appearance and reality: when the *Zhuangzi* resolves the guest's confusion, Dao'an "exceptionally" (特) allows him "to refrain from discarding" (不廢) the worldly learning that, presumably, other monks would be expected to leave behind them on entering the Buddhist life.

After quoting from the biography, Chen Yinque adds: "The introduction of analogies and examples by citing the *Zhuangzi* is similar to [the above-mentioned] '*geyi*.'"[59] The main concern here is not the term "geyi" (which appears nowhere in the account of Huiyuan's life), but the relations established between two bodies of texts and their habitual publics. In the Buddhist sources, these relations are exploited in a single direction (from "secular" to Buddhist) by members of a particular population (former literati now converted to Buddhism, speaking to other literati). But these sources are naturally biased in favor of their own textual community. For the Buddhist sources, allowing "outer" or non-Buddhist books to be used as glosses and pedagogical helps falls under the category of "skillful means" (*upaya*); it is only a strategy used to enable potential converts to enter the Buddhist way of thinking. On the showing of the *Gaoseng zhuan* biographies, such uses of analogy are exceptional, both because the circumstance is rare and because the aim of Buddhist translation and pedagogy was to create a self-sufficient canon of writings that would not need to be accredited by means of Confucius or Laozi.

The sources, then, allow us to clear up the problems surrounding *geyi*. The term itself may have a narrower meaning, but the phenomenon of illustrative citation from an alternative canon is well-attested. Appropriative citation of Daoist texts for Buddhist aims is not a massive phenomenon characterizing, en bloc, a whole age of Chinese Buddhism, but it enabled and symbolized conversions among the intellectual gentry. That these moments of contact between the sutras and the Dark Learning are exceptional does not mean that they were trivial. Not many young men renowned for their secular learning became monks, but among those who did were some of the great intellects of their time. The moments of encounter between the two textual traditions testify to the wit and insight of singular individuals. Perhaps then it is not surprising that they can be both rare and influential.

The influence of *geyi* seemingly comes to an end in another *Gaoseng zhuan* passage, this time from the biography of Sengxian 僧先, Dao'an's contemporary and inspirer:

> At the time of the Shi clan's disorder, [Sengxian] retreated to Mount Feilong, where he wandered in thought among the peaks and valleys and set his mind on meditation. Afterward his old friend Dao'an followed him.... Because they read texts and discussed ideas together, new realizations came to them quite frequently. Dao'an said: "The *geyi* [interpretations] of the former time often run contrary to doctrine." Sengxian said: "Well, we should analyze them in a *xiaoyao* spirit; what business do we have judging the former sages as right or wrong?" Dao'an said, "If we are to promulgate and illustrate philosophical teachings, it must be with absolute propriety. When the dharma-drums are beating in measure, who is first and who is later?" Thereupon Sengxian, Dao'an, Fatai, and others went south to the Jin territory, where they preached and accomplished vast transformations.
>
> 值石氏之亂，隱於飛龍山，遊想巖壑，得志禪慧。道安後復從之....
> 因共披屬思，新悟尤多。安曰：「先舊格義，於理多違」。先曰：「且
> 當分析逍遙，何容是非先達?」安曰：「宏贊理教，宜令允愜。法鼓競
> 鳴，何先何後?」先乃與安、汰等南遊晉平，講道宏化。[60]

The exchange of Sengxian and Dao'an on interpretation figures another stage in the accommodation of *xuanxue* to Buddhist learning. Dao'an finds contradictions between the old-style *geyi* (the correlations between numbered lists) and the *li* 理, the systematic totality of the doctrine as it has begun to appear to him. Sengxian's response invokes the *Zhuangzi*: we should approach different interpretations in the spirit of *xiaoyao*, meaning by that, as Guo Xiang's commentary puts it, that "although [the Peng bird] is large and [the sparrow] is small, each is true to its own nature. And if each fulfills its lot, the *xiaoyao*, the freedom and ease, [of the two creatures] is identical."[61] *Xiaoyao*, thus understood, stands for the casual syncretism of gentry Buddhism, seeking not a comprehensive system but flashes of insight when one text is struck against another by an exceptional mind. But Dao'an insists on correctness (using a term, *yunqie* 允愜, with Confucian ritual associations). He has already moved on to a different vision of the Buddhist rhetorical community as a *lijiao* 理教, one in which consistency is prized, not variety, in which the drums will follow a single rhythm and the earlier and later sages are to be held to the same standard. As a result of their conversation, Sengxian must have acknowledged Dao'an's vision. The "vast transformations" in the Buddhist institutions of the south that follow their exchange include the establishment of the monasteries and translation workshops that make Dao'an a pivotal figure in the history of Buddhism.

The stories about *geyi* all have Dao'an as their pivotal character. Zhu Faya, who names the technique, shares it with Dao'an; Dao'an strikes it down as a possible way of entering the *li* or rationality of Buddhism; nevertheless Dao'an permits Huiyuan, whose analogical use (*lianlei* 連類) of *Zhuangzi* seems to have something in common with *geyi* correlations, to go on citing the *Zhuangzi* in extramural teaching. And Dao'an, in the history of Chinese Buddhism, represents a different form of textuality and interpretation, one that will resolve difficulties not by appealing to texts outside the Buddhist canon but by collating analogous passages within it.[62] Though he could not read a Sanskrit or Pali original, Dao'an was perfectly able to detect differences among the Chinese translations and thus to attempt correction of their "losses" and "difficulties." In human terms, Dao'an's solution presupposes the monastery as a set-apart domain of reading, writing, translation, and teaching; his enterprise could not have been supported by the occasional leisured gatherings characteristic of *qingtan* and *xuanxue* syncretism. In hermeneutic terms, Dao'an looks forward to a condition in which Buddhist texts are sufficient unto themselves and their readers are drawn from a population that has already opted to make those texts their universe.

Permissible hybridity, for Dao'an, happens only at the meeting-points of textual universes, and for the sake of drawing members of the "outside" world into the circle of Buddhist belief. Once the moment of conversion is past, correlations between the worlds only "run counter to reason." Dao'an recognizes, that is, that different canons and different communities exist. Within canon A and within canon B, set protocols of reading permit sense to be made. The zone of purported equivalences, where A = B, is always suspect, conditional, contingent, like a figure of speech. It can only be fleeting.

But strategic reading that breaks through the envelope of one's own textual community is exactly what Chen Yinke found valuable in what he called *geyi* and what we may call citation-as-translation. Let us leave Dao'an to his triumphs and remain on the threshold. The phenomenon of translation through citation, a subversive mixture of old and new, is both undeniable and complex. In a far higher and subtler measure than the mixing of vocabulary and genres in the *Sutra in Forty-Two Sections*, these practices of interpretation hybridize and transculturate.[63] Analogy and citation supplement the blocked understanding of alien texts. More pertinently, they offer to solve the problem that arises where the value of the content or message of the texts to be transmitted is uncertain. Value will come, in such a situation, from attaching the non-valued content to content that is valued—in this instance, the texts of the Confucian and Daoist movements better appreciated by the not-yet-converted. What arises is not equivalence (for that might seem to devalue, by putting them on the same plane, texts already highly valued by one side or the other) but coincidence, a clash of perspectives: the familiar (e.g. *Zhuangzi*) is read as an allegorical equivalent or pathway to the unfamiliar (Sanskrit learning). In that process, the unfamiliar becomes knowable and the familiar is defamiliarized.[64] Understandably, such negotiations had no more place for someone like Dao'an, who knew what to value.

ZHUANGZI SOUNDS A MYSTERIOUS NOTE AND HUIYUAN ANSWERS IT

Although the hagiographical sources make room for citation-as-translation only where it leads to conversion, the construction of a pidgin language is never one-directional. Enabling communication, a shared language allows meanings to come in and to go out. Terms in such a language are "boundary-objects," in Star and Griesemer's sense, that is:

> scientific objects which both inhabit several intersecting social worlds . . . and satisfy the informational requirements of each of them. Boundary objects are objects which are both plastic enough to adapt to local needs and the constraints of the several parties employing them, yet robust enough to maintain a common identity across sites. They are weakly structured in common use, and become strongly structured in individual-site use. . . . They have different meanings in different social worlds but their structure is common enough to more than one world to make them recognizable, a means of translation.[65]

When the object of the discussion is the drawing of a boundary or the subordination of one domain to another, the terms serving as "boundary-objects" take on a new dimension: they can no longer be one-dimensional lines, but become elastic, opening into spaces that different participants seek to occupy, with the result that no commonly agreed-upon insides and outsides can be defined. A joke from the Six Dynasties milieu that gave rise to literati Buddhism may serve as an illustration:

> Liu Ling often got drunk to the point of being completely unrestrained. Sometimes he would remove his clothes and go naked in his rooms. People upbraided him on seeing this. Ling said: "I take Heaven and Earth as the pillars and roof of my house, and take my house for underwear. What are you good people doing in my underwear?" 劉伶恆縱酒放達，或脫衣裸形在屋中，人見譏之。伶曰：「我以天地為 棟宇，屋室為幝衣，諸君何為入我幝中？」[66]

Liu Ling, a disaffected gentry scholar living in a period of violence and collapse, is famous for his use of alcohol as a means of "inner emigration." In the story, the people who are blaming Liu Ling accuse him of behaving in a way that is improper, inappropriate for his situation in life. They are invoking a rule, a norm. He answers them by describing his place in the universe in a way that makes his accusers intruders, voyeurs, fleas in his underwear. A boundary is proposed and then redrawn; those who thought themselves outside are now inside. But this is not actually the cleverest thing about the joke. Liu Ling's retort to the busybody neighbors echoes the *Zhuangzi*:

> When Zhuangzi was on the point of death, his disciples desired to give him a deluxe burial. Zhuangzi said, "I [will] take heaven and earth for my coffin and vault; I [will] take the sun and moon to be my funerary ornaments and the stars and planets for my grave-gifts. The whole of nature can be my catafalque. How then would my funeral preparations leave anything to be desired? Why add anything more?"
> 莊子將死，弟子欲厚葬之。莊子曰：「吾以天地為棺槨，以日月為連璧，星辰為珠璣，萬物為齎送。吾葬具豈不備邪？何以加此！」[67]

Like Liu Ling's intruders, Zhuangzi's disciples get it all wrong. In a Confucian family environment, one should buy stout boards for the parent's coffin because one cannot bear the idea of the parent's body coming to harm. One should supply exquisite grave-goods because one cannot bear the thought that the parent will not continue to live and be active.[68] But the right thing as understood by conventional morality is usually the wrong thing to do in Zhuangzi's world. To the protestation that, if he is left unburied, birds of prey will pick his flesh apart, Zhuangzi responds in the spirit of "Making Things Equal" (chapter 2 of the *Zhuangzi* book): "Above, to be eaten by birds and kites; below, to be eaten by ants and mole-crickets—if it comes to a contest between them, why be partial to one or the other?" 在上 為 烏鳶食 , 在下 為螻蟻良 , 專彼與此 , 何其偏也！ Zhuangzi's sublime indifference, like Liu Ling's nakedness, proves their membership in the *fangwai* (those who wander outside the bounds).

No one would say that Liu Ling offers an interpretation of the *Zhuangzi* passage, except in the trivial sense that to quote something ascribes to it a possible meaning. It is rather an application, a mapping of the citation onto a new occasion. Much of the unclarity surrounding *geyi*, Buddho-Taoism, and the status of translation in China would be resolved if we adopted application and rewriting as our models for cultural transfer. What must happen for such transfers to occur is not that an identity, relative or absolute, be discovered between ideas from two mutually alien discourses, but only that a mapping of one on the other occur, like the momentary confusion of meanings in a pun:

> If, therefore, we derive unmistakable enjoyment in jokes from being trans-ported by the use of the same or a similar word from one circle of ideas to another, remote one…this enjoyment is no doubt correctly to be attributed to economy in psychical expenditure. The pleasure in a joke arising from a "short-circuit" like this seems to be the greater the more alien the two circles of ideas that are brought together by the same word—the further apart they are….We may notice, too, that here jokes are making use of a method of linking things up which is rejected and studiously avoided by serious thought.[69]

Dao'an would here occupy the role of "serious thinker." This is not to say, however, that the model of citation-as-translation occurs only in unserious contexts. Few matters could have been more serious for the Buddhist church than its relation to the Chinese state. A periodic crisis in the early centuries of Buddhist institutions concerned the precedence of authority between the empire and the *sangha*.[70] The Classics appointed for the imperial curriculum were categorical: "under the whole sky, no land that is not the king's land; to the very shores of the land, no man but is the king's servant" 普天之下 , 莫非王土 ; 率土之濱 , 莫非王臣.[71] But monastic communities claimed an exemption from the duty to pay obeisance to the emperor, and from various consequent obligations (taxes, military service, corvée labor). Over the period 402–4 the warlord Huan Xuan 桓玄 compelled the last Jin emperor to abdicate and then set himself up as emperor of the short-lived Chu dynasty. Justifiably suspicious of potential traitors, Huan Xuan seems to have wanted to settle this pending question even before taking the throne. Discussion with court officials led nowhere, and Huan Xuan invited Huiyuan to give his opinion.[72] Huiyuan's answer, "That The Monk Does Not Bow Before the Ruler" (*Shamen bujing wangzhe lun* 沙門不敬王者論), addresses the boundary question in part through a mosaic of Zhuangzi quotations—a series of "boundary objects" in their own right.

"That The Monk Does Not Bow Before the Ruler" begins by describing life in the family and in the monastery—two radically different ways of being. "The monk who has left the family behind becomes a sojourner outside the bounds [*fangwai zhi bin* 方外之賓], whose traces are effaced [*jijue* 迹絕] from among physical things."[73] The king's power is limited to protecting life and inflicting death, but beyond both is Nirvana (*nihuan* 泥洹).[74] "Although heaven and earth are revered for their production of life, they have never been able to exempt a living thing from change; although kings and nobles are honored for safeguarding their subjects, they have never been able to guard those subjects from misfortune." Nature and the state belong to one realm, the enlightened person to another. The king's power goes no farther than compelling "universal acquiescence" 順通; the monk's resides in a "unique and absolute teaching, an unchanging principle" 獨絕之教，不變之宗.[75] "Thus the *sramana* can face the Lord of ten thousand chariots as an equal" 斯沙門之所以抗禮萬乘高尚其事.[76]

If Huiyuan were content to leave the discussion at this, it would be a claim of superiority founded on the texts and reasonings current in his own community, which necessarily (that is, self-evidently) give that community a rank above the king's. But he knows that this is not enough, and might amount to conferring an outlaw, seditious status on Buddhism. There must be a common ground for arguing, an authority to which both sides can appeal. His opponent has already voiced the claim that the Chinese Classics are patterned on Heaven and contain all necessary knowledge. Huiyuan will play with this, as if confident that he can show that the official understanding of indigenous Chinese philosophy (let alone that of the mysteries of Buddhism) is incomplete:

> It has always seemed to me that the Buddhist Law and the Doctrine of Names [i.e. Confucianism]—respectively, the Buddha's way and that of Yao and Confucius—respond to one another at a profound level, though they have different starting-points; that though monastic life and secular life are obviously different, their endpoint is one.... Thus if one starts by admitting their differences and seeks their unity, one sees that they will necessarily meet in reason; if one starts by postulating their unity and seeks their differences, one will realize the incompatibility of their ways of embodying the Ultimate.
>
> 常以為道法之與名教。如來之與堯孔。發致雖殊潛相影響。．．．．是故自乖而求其合。則知理會之必同；自合而求其乖。則悟體極之多方。[77]

The opponent notes Huiyuan's facility at "citing the lords and kings of all the ages and making them appear to be in agreement with Buddhism, and taking

the system of your maxims to an extreme in order to dispute the authority of
the ruler: for such is your imputation 引歷代君土使同之佛教，今體極之
至以權君統，此雅論之所託.[78] But Huiyuan's argument for priority depends
on there being something beyond life and death, and that the opponent will
not admit:

> [Opponent:] The endowment of spirit is limited to one life. When the life is
> exhausted the breath evaporates, and it is the same as nothing....The spirit
> resides in the body as fire resides in wood....Even supposing that the identity
> or difference [of spirit and matter] were an inextricable mystery, the theory of
> existence and non-existence [of living beings] depends on agglomeration and
> dispersion. The coming-to-be and passing-away of all things in the world is
> simply what is known as the agglomeration and dispersal of vital breath.
> Therefore Zhuangzi says: "Man's life is the agglomeration of breath. When it
> agglomerates there is life, when it disperses there is death. If life and death
> follow from that, there is no point in troubling about it; why indeed should
> I suffer anxiety?" An ancient thinker who gave voice to the Way so aptly must
> have understood something of it. If matters indeed stand so, then the horizon
> of reasoning must be this one life. When this life is exhausted, change is at an
> end. The point of our discussion is to be sought here.[79]
>
> 稟氣極於一生。生盡則消液而同無。...猶火之在木。...假使同異之分
> 昧而難明。有無之說必存乎聚散。聚散氣變之總名萬化之生滅。故莊
> 子曰。人之生氣之聚。聚則為生。散則為死。若死生為彼徒苦。吾又
> 何患。古之善言道者。必有以得之。若果然耶。至理極於一生。生盡
> 不化。義可尋也。

By restricting the context of argument to this one life, and by appealing to
the authority of Zhuangzi (the indigenous Chinese philosopher thought
to be most compatible with Buddhism), the spokesman for royal power no
doubt thinks that the debate is now located in a jurisdiction where he is sure
to win: the limits of "this one life," where the joining and separation of vital
breaths mark the horizon of the knowable. A *Zhuangzi* citation drives home
the point: "The spirit resides in the body as fire resides in wood": when the
wood is gone the fire ceases to be. There can be no outer realm beyond
change.

But the *Zhuangzi* allusion—extended perhaps as a diplomatic courtesy by
the king's spokesman?—is one the Buddhist can turn to his advantage:

> The ancients who spoke of the Way were not always in agreement, so allow
> me to cite and explain them. Zhuangzi sounds a mysterious note in the "Da
> zongshi" chapter, saying that "the Great Clod burdens me with life and rests

me with death." Elsewhere he treats life as a bridle upon men and death as a return to genuineness. This is what he calls "knowing that life is a great affliction and considering that the absence of life is a return to the origin." ... Zhuangzi also says, "If someone is afflicted with a human shape, one especially rejoices in the fact; but a human shape goes through ten thousand changes, and never even begins to reach the ultimate." For this reason, what is called "knowing life" is not exhausted by one transformation. If you merely "chase after things" you will be "unable to return to the origin"....

You have not sought deeply to know what is meant by "the simultaneity of life and death," and misunderstand "agglomeration and dispersal" to apply to one existence only.... The analogy of the fire and the wood originates in the Sacred Canons. If you lose track of its path of development, you will never understand its mysterious suggestion. Thus its subtle words are submerged in your commonplace teaching, which causes you, my worthy opponent, to be confused. Imagine that our time had never had a Master enlightened as to the source [of being]. Then we would not know that anyone had had this fore-knowledge; the marvels of mysterious transmission would be lost to the age and never heard from.... Indeed, were it not for those who achieved such vision, who would be able to assess these transformations? Allow me to prove this with a substantial example. When fire is transmitted to firewood, it is like the spirit being transmitted to a bodily form. When fire is transmitted to a different piece of wood, it is like the spirit being transmitted to a different body. The former wood is not the latter wood: thus we can know [by ordinary reason] the marvelous art of the "finger" [despite what is] "exhausted." The former bodily form is not the later bodily form: thus we can know [by enlightenment, *wu* 悟] the profundity of resonance between attributes[80] and fate. The person who is confused sees [only] the body that decays in one life, and supposes that the spirit and its attributes vanish together. It is like someone who, seeing a fire go out on a single piece of wood, says that fire is now completely gone forever. This is what comes from being confined to a narrow notion of "caring for life," without seeking to extend its implications more widely.[81]

古之論道者。亦未有所同,請引而明之。莊子發玄音於大宗曰。大塊勞我以 生息我以死。又以生為人鞿羈,死為反真。此所謂知生為大患。以無生 為反 本者也。...莊子亦云。特犯人之形而猶喜之。若人之形萬化而未始有極。此所謂知生不盡於一化,方逐物而不反者也。...

論者不尋方生方死之說。而惑聚散於一化。...火木之喻原自聖典。失其流統。故幽興莫尋。微言遂淪於常教。令談者資之以成疑。向使時無悟宗之匠。則不知有先覺之明。冥傳之巧沒世靡聞。...自非達觀孰識其變。請為論者驗之以實。火之傳於薪。猶神之傳於形。火之傳 異薪。猶神之傳異形。前薪非後薪。則知指窮之術妙。前形非後形。則

悟情數之感深。惑者見形朽於一生。便以為神情俱喪。猶覩火窮於一
木。謂終期都盡耳。此曲從養生之談。非遠尋其類者也。

Huiyuan concludes his disquisition by affirming that the mystery of
reincarnation, knowledge of which sets the Buddhist sangha apart, confirms
the non-subordinated status of the clergy, and thereupon invites the king to
recognize the Great Way. The king's advisors then agree that the monastic
condition should be grounds for exemption from ordinary service. But how
should the honors paid by kings and princes to the Buddhist religion
be viewed? As a favor? Can a monk receive a gift without thereby entering
a circuit of exchange in which he is once more relegated to the position of a
subordinate? The king's reply comes

> after a long pause: "Let me offer you worthies an example that is close at hand.
> If there is someone in this land who can preach the doctrines of time and
> fate and who can penetrate the customs of remote regions, even those where
> ninefold translation is required, I ask you, should the king offer him sustenance,
> official conveyance, and robes?" They answered, "Yes."
>
> 主人良久乃應曰。請為諸賢近取其類。有人於此奉宣時命遠通殊方九
> 譯之俗。問王當資以糇糧錫以輿服不。答曰然。[82]

A graceful concession, at least: he recognizes the outcome of the debate by
making an indirect homage to Huiyuan and to all the translators who had
brought the Buddhist gospel to China—indeed to translation itself.

If the king's representatives made a single error in this hard-fought
disputation, it was in citing the *Zhuangzi* as an authority. Huiyuan shows
in his reply that he has lost none of his early training. The last sections of
the debate, in particular, are a mosaic of *Zhuangzi* quotations, trimmed
and put end to end so as to suggest that Zhuangzi, the early Daoist sage,
was a believer in reincarnation and that he too was conscious of something beyond this life—life after death being the postulate that more
than anything else grounds Huiyuan's arguments for the autonomy of the
Buddhist church. With a certain ambiguity, Huiyuan refers to the example
of the fire and the wood as "originating in the Sacred Canon," a passage
which the court has failed to "trace in its development." The phrase "Sacred
Canon" (*shengdian*) has something of a deictic quality. Like such designa-
tions as "the Holy Bible" or "the Glorious Quran," it indicates the speaker's
belonging to a community that holds the one to be holy or the other glorious. It ordinarily refers to the Confucian Classics, and could be stretched,
under a Buddhist's brush, to cover the sutras (as if to say: "*our* Sacred
Classics"), but it is rather a surprise to see Zhuangzi appearing under that
heading. (If Huiyuan meant that the Buddhist sutras invoked the analogy

before Zhuangzi did, he did not here give a clear hint of that intention.)[83] In the following paragraphs, however, we see *Zhuangzi* being treated as a "Sacred Canon" or prooftext.

That book "sounds a mysterious note," says Huiyuan, in its sixth chapter, "The Great Ancestral Teacher": "the Great Clod burdens me with life and rests me with death." *In extenso*, the passages quoted from read:

> *The Great Clod* supports me with a body, *burdens me with life*, deprives me with old age, *rests me with death*. Thus that which makes my life good is, by the same reason, that which makes my death good.
>
> 夫大塊載我以形，勞我以生，佚我以老，息我以死。故善吾生者，乃所以善吾死也。[84]

> If you hide a boat in a cove or conceal a mountain in a marsh, you can call that secure, but if in the middle of the night a strong man lifts them up and runs away, the sleepers will be none the wiser. When hiding things, their bigness or smallness shows what is appropriate, and yet something can escape. But as for hiding the world in the world, there would be no place to escape to. This is the general condition of all things. *If, by chance, we happen into the human form, we are delighted that this is so; but the human form, for example, is one of ten thousand transformations and has not even begun to reach their limit:* is this not a joy that exceeds all expectations? So the Sage wanders in the [aspect] of things that cannot vanish, and all are preserved. Early death is good, living to a great age is good, the beginning and the end are both good. If people would emulate such a one, how much more should they [try to be like] the binding knot of the ten thousand things, that on which the one transformation [of things] depends![85]
>
> 夫大塊載我以形，勞我以生，佚我以老，息我以死。故善吾生者，乃所以善吾死也。夫藏舟於壑，藏山於澤，謂之固矣。然而夜半有力者負之而走，昧者不知也。藏大小有宜，猶有所遯。若夫藏天下於天下，而不得所遯，是恆物之大情也。特犯人之形而猶喜之，若人之形者，萬化而未始有極也，其為樂可勝計邪！故聖人將遊於物之所不得遯而皆存。善妖善老，善始善終，人猶效之，又況萬物之所係，而一化之所待乎！

Reading the passage without a predetermined agenda, we might think that the core sentence is "Early death is good, living to a great age is good, the beginning and the end are both good"—in other words, the very fact of our existence is so surprising and improbable that we should receive whatever fortune we get with amazement and gratitude rather than trying to adjust it to the narrow expectations of our present desire. The "ten thousand changes" are, in such a reading, the potential different existences that we might have had, not a series of lives lived by the same soul as determined by its karmic valences. For the following claims—that Zhuangzi "treats life as a bridle upon men and death as a return to genuineness" and calls life "a great affliction" and death a "return to the origin"—textual loci are easily found:

> Ziqi, Ziyu, Zili, and Zilai talked together and said: "Who can take non-exist-ence as the head, life as the backbone, and death as the tailbone? Who is aware that *life and death, survival and destruction, are the same thing*? I will be that person's friend."[86]
>
> 子祀、子輿、子犁、子來四人相與語曰：「孰能以無為首，以生為脊，以死為尻，孰知生死存亡之一體者，吾與之友矣」。...
>
> [After Zi Sanghu died, his friends] sang together: "Oh, Sanghu, come back!, Oh, Sanghu, come back! You have *returned* to your *genuine* [form], leaving us behind as humans!"[87]
>
> 相和而歌曰：「嗟來桑戶乎！嗟來桑戶乎！而已反其真，而我猶為人猗！」
>
> The ancients reached perfection in some matters. How so? There were some who thought that when nothing yet existed, perfection and achievement were reached, and nothing could be added. The next category thought that once things existed, one had only to consider *life a loss and death a return*, but in this they were still making a distinction.[88]
>
> 古之人，其知有所至矣。惡乎至？有以為未始有物者，至矣盡矣，弗可以 加矣。其次以為有物矣，將以生為喪也，以死為反也，是以分已。

"The simultaneity of life and death," another name for the wheel of reincar-nation, appears both in chapter 2, "A Discourse on Making Things Equal" and in chapter 33, "In the World":

> Nothing but is a "that," nothing but is a "this." ... Thus it is said: "Thatness arises from thisness, thisness is the cause of thatness." This-and-that are simul-taneously generated designations. And yet, *what is born is simultaneously what dies, what dies is simultaneously what lives*; what is true is simultaneously what is untrue, what is untrue is simultaneously what is true; the basis of right is the basis of wrong, the basis of wrong is the basis of right.[89]
>
> 物無非彼，物無非是。... 故曰：彼出於是，是亦因彼。彼是，方生之說也。雖然，方生方死，方死方生；方可方不可，方不可方可；因是因非，因非 因是。是以聖人不由，而照之于天，亦因是也。
>
> [Zhuangzi's teacher] Hui Shi had many topics. His books could fill five carts. ... He said: ... "Heaven is on the same level as earth. Mountains are even

with marshes. The sun is at its apex and sets simultaneously. *Whatever is born dies simultaneously.*"[90]

惠施多方，其書五車 . . . 曰： . . . 「天與地卑，山與澤平。日方中方睨，物方生方死」。

Even where Huiyuan is not bent on showing that Zhuangzi had advance knowledge of the theory of reincarnation, his language is peppered with *Zhuangzi* citations. For example, the dismissal of the king's hasty efforts at philosophy as "chasing after things" echoes Zhuangzi's rueful verdict on his teacher Hui Shi: "What a pity! Hui Shi's talent raced here and there without achieving success; he *chased after* ten thousand *things* and *never returned* [to the essentials]. He was like a man trying to shout down an echo, like a man running races with his shadow. How sad!" 惜乎！惠施之才，駘蕩而不得，逐萬物而不反，是窮響以聲，形與影競走也。悲夫！[91] Phrases drawn from *Zhuangzi* orient the discussion: *zhi sheng* 知生, "knowing life," *yang sheng* 養生, "caring for life." Huiyuan nearly makes Zhuangzi a co-author of his discourse.

Huiyuan's main *Zhuangzi* example is itself a fragment and has excited the imaginations of many readers. It occurs at the very end of chapter 3, "The Importance of Caring for Life" (*Yang sheng zhu* 養生主) and just after a paragraph describing the mourning for Laozi as unnecessary: "When the Master arrived, it was his time; when he left, the Master did so compliantly. Dwelling in timeliness and located in compliance, he could not be penetrated by sadness or joy. The ancients used to call this 'unleashing by the gods'" 適來，夫子時也；適去，夫子順也。安時而處順，哀樂不能入也，古者謂是帝之縣解. Then follows the puzzling statement: 指窮於為薪，火傳也，不知其盡也。 In an over-literal rendering: "Fingers emptied in doing firewood. Fire, transmitted. Unknown its ending."[92] According to Guo Xiang's commentary, "The firewood is brought forth by the fingers, and the fingers exhaust the purpose of bringing firewood, thus the fire is transmitted and does not sputter out; the mind subsists, surrounded by care-for-life, lifespans continue and are not broken off" 前薪以指，指盡前薪之理，故火傳而不滅。心得納養之中，故命續而不絕.[93] So then: the funeral of Laozi is completed by a short metaphorical send-off, forbidding mourning and promising that life or the Way will continue without him. The fragment is then glued to the previous episode by commentary, rather than figuring as an unrelated passage that merely chanced to be copied here. In a more fluent wording based on Guo's understanding, it would read: "The finger [analogous to the Sage?] completes its purpose in making firewood; fire is what is transmitted; no one knows when it will ever end."

Guo Xiang's comments continue, now encompassing the chapter's main topic: "Thus the lifespan continues and does not end; thus we see that 'caring for life' is the giving of life to life.... The fire is transmitted and lifespans continue, and this is the ultimate realization of 'caring'; how do we know that our age will not end and a new life begin?" This rendering, compatible with Huiyuan's intention of asserting reincarnation through the voices of ancient Chinese, is reproduced in Huiyuan's argument. Even more than the *Zhuangzi* text itself, it may have led Huiyuan to read the fragment as confirming that life or spirit is transmitted from one body to another, with some "wonderful art" of karma and fate accomplishing the work done by the "fingers" in the *Zhuangzi* fragment. As the upshot of Huiyuan's exegesis of this comparison, the king's narrow-mindedness makes him "care" for only this piece of wood, not for the fire—foolishly in comparison with the Buddhist community, bound together by lines of causality crossing vast numbers of lifetimes. Once again, Zhuangzi has delivered Huiyuan's most telling point. Has Zhuangzi become a Buddhist, in the same way that Matteo Ricci would find himself becoming a Daoist?

TESSELLATION

In excerpting the passages that Huiyuan used to build his mosaic, I have found that to cite existing translations of the *Zhuangzi* would have made for nonsensical or at least awkward pairings with the Huiyuan text. A translation of a philosophical book, of course, tries to respect its coherence, to represent, as far as possible, "what Zhuangzi meant." The kind of translation needed here, however, would have to represent "what Huiyuan meant to have Zhuangzi mean," often quite a different matter. The pieces of the mosaic, we might say, show the grain and markings of the rock from which they were taken, but they have been reshaped for their intended use and can no longer fit back in the quarry. Retranslating those passages requires us to keep their meaning suspended in ambiguity, so that they can serve Huiyuan's purposes as well as some of Zhuangzi's purposes. The shorter the citation, of course, the less chance the original context can have of commanding interpretation and ruling out rival understandings, so it serves Huiyuan's allegorical purposes to cite briefly and cut out the larger framework. Just as in the acts of appropriation designated *geyi* by Chen Yinke, Huiyuan is moving *xuanxue* phrases and terms into a Buddhist discourse, claiming mutual translatability of the terms thus used in order to address an audience of outsiders in the language they know best.

As with the naked Liu Ling's witty allusion, we could not call this an interpretation, rather an application or an appropriation. Huiyuan selects widely and capriciously from the *Zhuangzi* text, building his argument from the pieces he has knocked loose from the earlier edifice. Huiyuan's tessellation of the *Zhuangzi* has all the ambivalence of the "revisionary ratio" Harold Bloom calls "tessera," wherein "the later [author] provides what his imagination tells him would complete the otherwise 'truncated' precursor [work] and [author], a 'completion' that is as much misprision as a revisionary swerve is."[94] Did Huiyuan misunderstand Zhuangzi? Did he distort the earlier thinker's meaning? Although he seems to assert that Zhuangzi, as a Sage of former times, must have had some revelation of the truths that would enter China only 500 years after his death, very little of Huiyuan's argument depends on this pleasant imagination: the *Zhuangzi* serves him as material for a new-style pagoda. Citation translates Zhuangzi's very words into a new idiom, a new era, a new cosmology.

Huiyuan's success, like Liu Ling's, results in the redrawing of the boundary from which the contest of languages and rhetorics began. As a result of gambling his sovereignty over a *Zhuangzi* quotation, the king finds himself not the sole master over the peasants, officials, and monks on his territory, but the tolerated local administrator of a corner and a moment of a much vaster realm of space, time, and fate—this reversal being the result of citation-as-translation, the semantic conversion of statements valid in a Confucian/Daoist world to statements valid in a Buddhist one. Huiyuan has used the citation method not, as in Chen Yinke's examples, to facilitate conversions, but to claim authority over languages: his own language (the language of translated Buddhism) and the adversary's language (the Classics, *Zhuangzi*, and other "external works"). The *Zhuangzi* itself, like the piece of wood in the crucial analogy, seems to be used up in the process, rather than being identified with the transmitted fire. But it is hard to imagine Zhuangzi complaining about that.

How marvelous the Creator is! What is he going to make of you next? Where is he going to send you? Will he make you into a rat's liver? Will he make you into a bug's arm? ... If the process continues, in time perhaps he'll change my left arm into a rooster. In that case I'll keep watch on the night. Or perhaps in time he'll transform my right arm into a crossbow pellet and shoot down an owl for roasting. Or perhaps in time he'll transform my buttocks into cartwheels. Then, with my spirit for a horse, I'll climb up and go for a ride.[95]

偉哉造物！又將奚以汝為？將奚以汝適？以汝為鼠肝乎？以汝為蟲臂乎？ ... 浸假而化予之左臂以為雞，予因以求時夜；浸假而化予之右臂

以為彈，予因以求鴞炙；浸假而化予之尻以為輪，以神為馬，予因以
乘之，豈更駕哉！

Incidentally, Huiyuan's use of the wood and fire analogy led to problems of
its own. In his zeal to proclaim a realm outside change and spiritual realities
that outlasted material things, he seemed to assert the individuality and
immortality of the soul, two fundamental causes of attachment and delusion
according to Indian Buddhist teaching.[96] Shall we blame the translators?
That much at least is not Zhuangzi's problem.

5

THE EXTRAVAGANT ZHUANGZI

THE GOOSE THAT DIDN'T CACKLE AND THE DOG THAT DIDN'T BARK

The foregoing chapters have not been framed as a comprehensive history of translation in China, still less as the "Chinese theory" of translation or "Chinese approach" to it. Rather, as a chain of examples organized around pivotal moments in the annals of translating in China, they are meant to draw out some of the features of that tradition that instructively contrast with assumptions about translation common in other parts of the world.[1] The most obvious feature is the importance of mediation. A work's translation into Chinese had to integrate it into the existing body of Chinese literature, even if that meant transforming it in many respects. Translating could not be (as are many translations done today) a substitution of the words of the original with equivalent terms from the Chinese dictionary; it had to be rewriting, adaptation, the creation of plausible "backstories" for the text. The reason for this, in turn, lies in the vast prestige and horizon-blocking bulk of Chinese literature. A text had to resemble other works in that corpus to get any sort of audience among educated people. Furthermore, literary writing, in premodern China, was recognizable through its high degree of intertextuality: a text constitutes itself as literary through perpetual dialogue with predecessor texts, reminiscences of their wording, emulations of their form, and in some cases repetition of their rhymes. A text that came into the world without this tissue of connection would give an impression of entire forgetfulness and utter nakedness; for the sake of its reception, it had to come trailing clouds of allusion. The translator provided these, as mediator and naturalizer.

In due course, a distinct group of texts within the Chinese language could form, as did Buddhist literature, a sufficient intertextual corpus of its own. But the initial moments of a translation-tradition—moments like the introductions to China of poetic Modernism, Counter-Reformation Christianity, and Mahayana Buddhism—needed to find an anchor in existing traditions outside themselves.

And in each of these events, a single text plays a vital role in the mediation: the *Zhuangzi*, a collection of essays, arguments, and fables usually taken as the apex of philosophical Daoism and ascribed to an author of the fourth century BCE. For an exotic type of text to find a place in the Chinese textual tree, it had to be grafted onto a particular branch of Chinese literature, and time and again it was the *Zhuangzi* that provided the most hospitable milieu. This type of relationship has not, to my notice, received attention in theories of translation: let us call it *textual sponsorship*. The naturalization of new texts and types of writing in China regularly occurred with the *Zhuangzi* as sponsor.

A sponsor, etymologically, is a person who "answers" for another, as in the Christian ritual of baptism.[2] "Wilt thou be baptized in this faith?" asks the officiant, and the godparent, acting as sponsor for an infant (*in-fans*, one incapable of speech), answers: "That is my desire."[3] Absurd though it may seem, this is a form of valid engagement, a performative contract predicated on certain conditions. (Moreover, it was a necessary precaution among people who feared the consequences of going unbaptized in a period of high infant mortality.) Where cash supplies were shallow, as often in the ancient economy of the Mediterranean, large purchases were made possible by promises, that is, through networks. Even in so personal a matter as marriage, what we might call the principals were "the ones spoken for" (*sponsa, sponsus*). The promise made by a suitable sponsor was sufficient for conveyance.[4] Sponsorship establishes a certain relation among the parties. So too with translation. The foreign text is of course *in-fans* until a translator makes it speak. But for most of Chinese history, translators were nobodies, their work hardly valued. The translator needs an intercessor with the receiving community. The more powerful that intercessor within the community of destination, the better the chances that the sponsorship relation will take hold and have effect. I would not be able to sponsor anyone for Chilean citizenship or Coptic baptism, for example, because I lack standing in those communities. Analogously, a text by Baudelaire, Matteo Ricci, or the Buddha needed sponsors, mediators having standing in the Chinese literary tradition, before they could be accepted as having something to say.

Why then should this role have so often fallen to the *Zhuangzi*, among all possible Chinese literary texts? The *Zhuangzi* is notable for being one of the few books in ancient China to have made much of cultural difference. In its first chapter we read:

> A man from the state of Song took some ceremonial bonnets to Yue, intending to sell them there. But the people of Yue were accustomed to shave their heads and tattoo their bodies; they had no use for such objects.[5]
> 宋人資章甫而適諸越，越人斷髮文身，無所用之 。

The merchant comes from the small principality of Song, founded by surviving members of the Shang royal house after the founding of the Zhou dynasty in around 1100 BCE. The hats that he wants to sell are of a particular, refined, archaic kind (the erudite reader of *Zhuangzi* will recall that one of Confucius's disciples preferred the Song style of ceremonial cap).[6] As he travels into the far south, he enters the territory of Yue (probably not yet "the state of Yue," an entity that would only later emerge in response to the Central States' political and military organization, but a confederation of Yue tribes). Ceremonial bonnets are a sign of integration into the Chinese order of ritual, gift exchange, sacrifice, and family lines: a cosmological and political token. And as the merchant is disappointed to discover, the men of Yue shave their heads, so they lack the capillary infrastructure to maintain the Chinese ceremonial cap (held in place by a long pin: word for word, "they lacked a place to use them"). Worse yet, they tattoo their bodies—"in order to ward off the danger of serpents and dragons," says the commentary, giving us to understand that the Yue go naked and swim, using tattoos as camouflage or magical defense. These naked men lack the very possibility of joining the Chinese symbolic order, but they are not, for Zhuangzi, deprived of anything on this account: they simply "have no use for" it. They are free of the object the man from Song sells, and from the need it satisfies.

Cultural difference is just one of the forms of difference that the *Zhuangzi* stages—the anecdote about the merchant from Song is inserted into a longer argument about the difference between ordinary people, even the sages who founded the Chinese cosmos, and the True Men, the transcendent supermen, whom the *Zhuangzi* presents as the only models worth following:

> Atop faraway Mount Gushe, there lives a spirit-man whose flesh and skin are like ice and snow; he is pure and delicate like a virgin, eats not the five grains but sucks the wind and drinks the dew; he rides on flying dragons and wanders beyond the four seas. His spiritual concentration is such that things are preserved from sickness and the yearly crops mature.... [Here occurs the story about the merchant from Song.] [The sage] Yao brought order to the people of the world and governed the land within the seas peaceably. But when he went

out and saw the four [spirit-]men on the distant Mount Gushe, on the south side of the Fen River, his sight failed him and he forgot all about his empire."

藐姑射之山，有神人居焉，肌膚若冰雪，淖約若處子，不食五穀，吸風飲露。乘雲氣，御飛龍，而遊乎四海之外。其神凝，使物不疵癘而年穀熟。....堯治天下之民，平海內之政，往見四子藐姑射之山，汾水之陽，窅然喪其天下焉。

The observation about cultural difference and the uselessness, to others, of what we may find supremely useful, is an analogy for the "transvaluation of all values" that many chapters of the *Zhuangzi* seek to accomplish.[8] Frequently, the book tries to shock with tales of bizarre creatures, aberrant behavior, and grotesque transformations, all of which it pronounces normal and good, while it also stages the self-critique of such an incarnation of the normal and the good as Confucius (" 'I am one of heaven's condemned,' said Confucius").[9] There is nothing so strange in foreign literature that something stranger cannot be found in the *Zhuangzi*. Flowers of evil? A man who rises from the dead? A philosopher who is able, through the exercise of negation, to transcend space, time, and mortality? The attentive reader of the *Zhuangzi*, ready to exercise the privilege of selective quotation, can find all these and more anticipated there.

The *Zhuangzi* is largely written in the mode of parody. Like the stories of Borges, it drapes its improbable anecdotes in a fantastic bibliography; it revisits people and incidents already famous in Chinese literature, only to give them an unexpected turn; it puts speeches in the mouths of imaginary people, or imaginary speeches in the mouths of historically attested people. Parody is rewriting; perhaps the *Zhuangzi*'s constant use of writing at a remove from immediacy gave it the profile most suitable for sponsoring the rewritings of translators.

Far from expressing the core values of the Chinese tradition, the *Zhuangzi* expresses a persistent form of marginality within it. When, at the end of the Han Dynasty, the promises of the Kingly Way had failed and the cycle of rebellions, conquests, and short-lived successor dynasties that followed showed the price of political engagement to be unacceptably high, the *Zhuangzi*'s "transvaluation" found a ready audience among disappointed, embittered, or simply fearful gentry intellectuals. For them, the question of how to "hide the world within the world" was a real and pressing one. In the late Eastern Han, Wei, Jin, and Northern-and-Southern Dynasties, the *Zhuangzi* re-emerged, was brought up to date by new editions and commentaries, and formed the basis of conversation and study ("pure conversation," *qingtan*; "mysterious learning," *xuanxue*) among the free-spirited seekers who populate Liu Yiqing's miscellany *Shishuo xinyu* (A New Account of Tales of the

World).[10] The socially secure have never had a good word to say for these disaffected bohemians. "The Jin people were so contemptuous and unrestrained that they were accustomed to self-aggrandizement. The so-called 'refined reasoning and abstruse words' that they bragged about were only something plagiarized from the Buddhist sutras and the *Laozi*. With such pretentious prattle, they confused and cheated ignorant people."[11] But despite or because of such disapproval, the *Zhuangzi* has always had a public—of marginal people or of non-marginal people in marginal moods. It is the outside of the inside of the Chinese tradition, the work best placed, it may be, to serve as intermediary between the outside and the inside of the tradition. And thus, appropriately, the sponsor for incoming translations.

But translations not only took the *Zhuangzi* as a model for imitation. They also mined it for materials. In this, too, the *Zhuangzi* stood ready to serve: composed of hundreds of loosely connected parables, imaginary dialogues, illustrations, and debates, it contains a whole storehouse of styles. Its pithy phrases easily rise from their contexts and walk to new purposes. A work more uniform in style or systematic in presentation would have resisted such reuse.

The need for a sponsoring work was most acute in China because the indigenous literary tradition was so powerful, tightly woven, and obligatory. Even where the specific reference to such a sponsor as the *Zhuangzi* is not apparent, the fact that so much of the work loosely called "translation" in China was closer to rewriting or adaptation by monolinguals should call us to focus on the receiving "literary system." In other, more porous literary traditions, a translation may not stand in such obvious need of sponsor works before it can attain legitimacy—but this does not mean that sponsorship is not a factor. It may be that the conditions specific to Chinese translation over most of its history operate in every tradition, though in a manner more widely dispersed and discreet in its effects.

EXTRAVAGANT AUTHORSHIP

Thus: marginality, fragmentariness, awareness of cultural limits, transvaluation, parody—these all predisposed the *Zhuangzi* to stand as model and sponsor for unclaimed spiritual ragamuffins wandering into China and needing a translator. By naming the *Zhuangzi* as the sponsor-figure for some of the most influential acts of translation in premodern China, it may seem that we are crediting the author of that work with an extraordinary form of prescience, the ability to see beyond his cultural confines and make room for the world. Who is this "dangerous man," as Oscar Wilde called him, this Zhuangzi who "may be said to have summed up in himself" (among much else) "almost every mood of European metaphysical or mystical thought, from Heraclitus down to Hegel"?[12] To whom do we owe the sponsorship of so much newness in Chinese culture?

In other words, "How Much of *Chuang-tzu* Did Chuang-tzu Write?," as Angus Graham, translator of the seven "Inner Chapters" of the *Zhuangzi*, asked.[13] Sima Qian ascribed to the historical Zhuang Zhou a corpus of some 100,000 words. Three hundred and fifty years later, Guo Xiang's edition, at approximately 80,000 words, seems to have been the first to divide the text into "inner," "outer," and "miscellaneous" chapters, reflecting Guo's sense of their probable genuineness. The *Han shu* records a text of *Zhuangzi* in fifty-two chapters; our present text contains thirty-three, probably reflecting Guo Xiang's editorial trimming. Although "from earliest times the [Inner Chapters] have been considered to be the actual work of Zhuang Zhou ... contain[ing] all the major themes,"[14] the remaining chapters have not benefited from such credit. Graham divides those chapters thematically into material of a "Primitivist" cast, "Individualist" sections indebted to Yang Zhu, the writings of Zhuangzi's imitators, and content supplied by "Syncretic" Daoists who were probably responsible for the compilation of an early complete *Zhuangzi* text. Other scholars apply their own filters to separate the text into as many "streams" or "layers" as they find necessary to account for the composition of the whole. (Like Moses, Zhuang Zhou is credited with the authorship of chapters that depict him as already dead.) Readers who apply a protocol of reading derived from philosophy tend to seek consistency across the chapters and arguments, exerting themselves to work up a system of doctrine (Is Zhuangzi a skeptic, a relativist, or a relativist skeptic? Is he a conventionalist? and the like), often at the price of considerable selectivity.[15] Those whose aims are philological seek parallel passages and quotations that might authenticate or disauthenticate segments of the present text. Those who chart the influence of the text are vigilant to distinguish the *Zhuangzi* as Zhuangzi might have written it from the ideologically mutable *Zhuangzi* commentaries and paraphrases that shape the work's changing reception from time to time under the leadership of Xiang Xiu, Guo Xiang, Cheng Xuanying 成玄英, and other powerful readers. Each of these modes of reading establishes, for its distinct purposes, zones of core and periphery. At the core would stand Zhuang Zhou's original *Zhuangzi*, no longer accessible to us except by inference; radiating away from it in successive zones we might have the work of Zhuang Zhou's disciples, then that of his imitators, his editors, his readers, the forgers who circulated work of dubious value under his eminent name, and finally those who reflected Zhuang Zhou's influence in their own writings. In the present book we may be said to have drawn the periphery of a periphery, the distanced appropriation of *Zhuangzi* tags and attitudes in the trading zone between

Chinese culture and alien cultures. It is perfectly legitimate for each of these disciplines—philosophy, philology, literary study, translatology—to map its universe around an origin-point. But such concern for unity is never the guiding principle for the translators into Chinese who use the *Zhuangzi* as bridge or transmitting membrane. Their pragmatism is extreme. And should we look into the available information about the real Zhuang Zhou, we find something more like a mirror blinking back at us.

References to Zhuangzi as thinker and hero of short anecdotes occur in a few early Chinese texts. The *Springs and Autumns of Lü Buwei* (*c*.239 BCE) tells a story about Zhuangzi and two geese, which presupposes knowledge of the argument about "the usefulness of uselessness"; Lü Buwei's older contemporary Xunzi (d. 235 BCE) catalogues among the victims of error "Master Zhuang, who is deluded by Nature and does not understand Man" 莊子蔽於天而不知人; the *Huainanzi*, compiled before 139 BCE, reproduces many stories and arguments also found in the *Zhuangzi*, reports on a few events of Master Zhuang's life, and even at one point raises the *Zhuangzi* to a position of authority elsewhere reserved for the *Daode jing*.[16] Master Zhuang thus enjoys a solid textual presence in Warring States and Han China. But the earliest extended discussion of Zhuang Zhou as author is found in chapter 63, "Laozi Han Fei liezhuan" 老子韓非列傳 ("The Lives of Laozi and Han Fei"), of Sima Qian's 司馬遷 *Shiji* 史記 (Records of the Grand Historian, *c*.90 BCE). It does not provide much support to the "Inner Chapters" as the core of Zhuang Zhou's authorship.[17] Then again, its sense of Zhuang Zhou as an author is both subordinated to another author and not entirely favorable where Zhuangzi's originality comes to the fore. Sima Qian's account of the life of Laozi, putative author of the *Daode jing*, concludes with a summary evaluation: "Those in the world who study Laozi reject the learning of the [Confucian] Scholars; the Scholars likewise reject Laozi. 'Those who follow different Ways cannot make plans for each other,' [as Confucius said], is it not so? Lao Er [taught] non-action and spontaneous change, with purity, stillness, and spontaneous correctness."[18] Then, without so much as a "For example," the historian continues:

As for Master Zhuang, he was a man from Meng, with the given name Zhou. For a time Zhou was clerk of the Lacquer Gardens in Meng. He lived during the reigns of kings Hui of Liang and Xuan of Qi [giving a range of 350–300 BCE]. His learning was all-encompassing, yet in essentials he looked back to the words of Laozi. His writings amount to over one hundred thousand words, mostly in the form of fictional dialogues. He wrote "The Fisherman," "Robber Zhi," and "Rifling Trunks" in order to castigate the followers of Confucius, in order to throw light on the techniques of Laozi. [His] "Weilei Xu," "Geng Sangzi," and the like are all empty words without substance in fact [i.e., fictions, not

historical documents].[19] Yet he was skilled at arranging words and mingling
terms, at adducing examples and analogizing situations, wherewith he excoriated the [Confucian] Scholars and the Mohists; even the most capable scholars
of the time were unable to extricate themselves [from his critiques]. His words
were like a powerful tide, indulging himself to suit his own [desires], and so
from the kings and grandees on down, none were able to make him their
instrument [i.e., employ him].

[As an illustration,] King Wei of Chu heard that Zhuang Zhou was a virtuous man and sent emissaries with precious offerings to greet him, begging
him to serve as prime minister. Zhuang Zhou laughed and told the Chu
emissaries: "A thousand-weight of gold is a rich offering; the prime ministership is a position of honor. But can it be that you alone have failed to
notice the ox-victims at the suburban sacrifices? They are fed with grain for
a number of years, then dressed in embroidered hangings to enter the great
temple. At that moment, even if they would rather have been [born as]
orphan piglets, it's no longer possible. Hurry away from here, do not pollute
me! I would rather sport and play in the mud for my own pleasure and not
wear the bridle of the masters of the state. To the end of my life I will refuse
office, and so satisfy my own will."

[The next thinker to be discussed,] Shen Buhai was a man from Jing...[20]

莊子者，蒙人也，名周。周嘗為蒙漆園吏，與梁惠王、齊宣王同時。
其學無所不闚，然其要本歸於老子之言。故其著書十餘萬言，大抵率
寓言也。作漁父、盜跖、胠篋，以詆訿孔子之徒，以明老子之術。
畏累虛、亢桑子之屬，皆空語無事實。然善屬書離辭，指事類情，
用剽剝儒、墨，雖當世宿學不能自解免也。其言洸洋自恣以適己，
故自王公大人不能器之。

楚威王聞莊周賢，使使厚幣迎之，許以為相。莊周笑謂楚使者曰：
「千金，重利；卿相，尊位也。子獨不見郊祭之犧牛乎？養食之數
歲，衣以文繡，以入大廟。當是之時，雖欲為孤豚，豈可得乎？子亟
去，無污我。我寧游戲污瀆之中自快，無為有國者所羈，終身不
仕，以快吾志焉」。

申不害者，京人也...

After narrating the lives of some more thinkers, Sima Qian summarizes
the Daoist school thus: "This is what Laozi honored: the Dao's emptiness
and not-having, relying on and responding to change in [the manner of]
non-action. So in his writings are phrasings and namings that are marvelous
and hard to understand. Zhuangzi scattered the Way and Virtue, discoursing
with abandon, [but] in the main he returned everything to Spontaneity
[or Nature]."[21]

The account of Zhuang Zhou has all the characteristics of an example: first demonstrating what it is like to be a follower of Laozi, then playing Zhuangzi against Laozi, whose pure emptiness contrasts with a discursive exuberance that "scatters the Way and Virtue." Like biographers in other ancient literary traditions, Sima Qian apparently had little to go on but the texts, and so his narrative of the life of Zhuang Zhou is essentially a response to and reflection of the work. The anecdote illustrating Zhuang Zhou's character is taken from the *Zhuangzi* itself ("Qiushui," chapter 15, one of the "Outer Chapters," and "Lie Yukou," one of the "Miscellaneous" ones), as are the references to Laozi's teaching. If the book *Zhuangzi* is imagined to have a core (authored by Zhuang Zhou himself) and a husk (writings of various provenance and authenticity), Sima Qian's narration credits Zhuang Zhou with several chapters that later editors placed among the husk—the "Outer" and "Miscellaneous" sections—and gives us little that is not already in the *Zhuangzi*. Shorn of the elements taken from the work, the residue of the life as given by Sima Qian consists of a few facts and a few literary judgments by the historian:

> [*Facts:*] Master Zhuang was a man from Meng, with the name Zhou. At one time Zhou was clerk of the Lacquer Gardens in Meng. He lived during the reigns of kings Hui of Liang and Xuan of Qi. [*Literary judgment:*] His learning was all-encompassing, yet in essentials he looked back to the words of Laozi.... He was skilled at arranging words and mingling terms, at adducing examples and analogizing situations, wherewith he excoriated the [Confucian] Scholars and the Mohists; even the most capable scholars of the time were unable to extricate themselves [from his critiques]. His words were like a powerful tide, indulging himself to suit his own [desires....] Zhuangzi scattered the Way and Virtue, discoursing with abandon, [but] in the main he returned everything to Spontaneity [or Nature].

When the "Life" is compared to the "Works," there is not much independent "Life" to go on. The essence of that "life" is a character judgment. Sima Qian's verdict on Zhuangzi mixes a stylistic assessment with ethical censure: Zhuangzi's words are "like a powerful tide, self-determined in order to suit his own [desires]" 其言洸洋自恣以適己; his rejection of employment says that he values one thing only, to be left alone "to satisfy my own will" 以快吾志焉. The central descriptive term, 自恣, appears many times in ancient historical and philosophical texts: typically applied to unruly princes or overbearing consorts, it means "extravagant, self-willed, self-indulgent, uncontrolled, arbitrary."[22] In those texts it is applied only to individuals, never to groups or abstractions. Zhuangzi's style is, as Oscar Wilde saw so well, "dangerous" in and of itself, because it obeys no law outside its self-enjoyment, and this, it seems, is clearly something Sima Qian wishes to condemn, by making Zhuangzi an ineffective, self-willed, and turbulent disciple of the quietist Laozi. Can one imagine Laozi "scattering the Way and Virtue"? If Laozi is the core of Daoist philosophy, Zhuangzi is already, for Sima Qian, a step away from that center, "scattered" by his inability to resist his own rhetorical brilliance.

In the eyes of Sima Qian, Zhuangzi's writing testifies to a moral failing.[23] A personal moral failing, moreover, a matter of character like that which befell so many undisciplined princes: only instead of wine, beautiful women, and revenge, his temptation is "a powerful tide" of fables, arguments, and likenesses. Zhuang Zhou's shortcoming, Sima Qian might say if he had our vocabulary to say it with, is too much individualism.[24] Gao You 高誘 (c.168–212), the Eastern Han commentator on the *Springs and Autumns of Lü Buwei*, seems to know of Zhuangzi only through Sima Qian's report: "Zhuangzi's personal name was Zhou: a man from Meng in the state of Song. He held the empire to be worthless; he belittled everything that exists 輕天下，細萬物. His technique valued emptiness and nonexistence. His writings amount to fifty-two items; he called them the [Book of] Master Zhuang."[25] This short sketch makes him out to be an eccentric, the person who rejects what everyone else admits as most valuable. The standard of relevance and irrelevance is set by Sima Qian's father Sima Tan, whose discussion of "The Essentials of the Six Schools" in chapter 130 of *Shiji* arranges the intellectual options of early-imperial China in a series of alternatives, capped and transcended by the flexible statecraft Sima Tan calls "the school of the Dao" (*daojia*):

The *Daojia* cause people to be concentrated in spirit, to move in accord with what is formless, and to be permeated by the fullness of the ten thousand things. Their techniques are based on the great sequence of Yin and Yang. Appropriating what is good among the Confucians and Mohists, condensing the principles of Nominalists and Legalists, changing with the times, responding to the alterations of things, establishing customs and executing policies, there is nothing to which [their art] is not suited. Their concepts are simple and easy to put into practice, their recommendations few and the results plenteous. With the Confucians it is the opposite: by taking the ruler as the gnomon of the entire world, [the Confucians] exalt the ruler and make the subject pliant, make the ruler lead and the subject follow. In this way, the ruler labors and the subject is at ease. As for the essentials of the Great Way, [the Daoists' recommendation is to] abjure force and display, to banish cleverness, abandoning all this and trusting in the techniques [of the Dao]....

The *Daojia* [exalt] non-action, yet they say that "no action is left unaccomplished," and their substance is easily carried out though their language is hard to understand. Their teaching takes non-existence as root and makes adaptability its method. As there is no complete rule, no constant form, they are thus able to get to the bottom of everything that exists. By not putting themselves before or after things, the *Daojia* can become masters of the ten thousand things. Their method is to have no method, to act as the times demand, to respond in particular ways and yet not to do so, to accord with circumstances. Thus it is said that "the Sage does not decay, but holds to the fact that times change." Emptiness is the constant feature of the Way, and adaptability the reference-point of the ruler.[26]

道家使人精神專一，動合無形，贍足萬物。其為術也，因陰陽之大順，采儒墨之善，撮名法之要，與時遷移，應物變化，立俗施事，無所不宜，指約而易操，事少而功多。儒者則不然。以為人主天下之儀表也，主倡而臣和，主先而臣隨。如此則主勞而臣逸。至於大道之要，去健羨，絀聰明，釋此而任術。...

道家無為，又曰無不為，其實易行，其辭難知。其術以虛無為本，以因循為用。無成埶，無常形，故能究萬物之情。不為物先，不為物後，故能為萬物主。有法無法，因時為業；有度無度，因物與合。故曰「聖人不朽，時變是守」。虛者道之常也，因者君之綱也。

This does not sound like most of the *Zhuangzi* at all. If that book has anything to say about governing, it is in an indirect, allegorical, or sarcastic way: the ruler who took Zhuangzi for a guide would quickly be deprived of all the traditional tools of coercion. What Sima Tan meant by "the school of Dao" is what today we call "Huang-Lao," a theory revolving around the creation of an invulnerable, elusive identity for the ruler, who becomes a "True Man" by being identified not against, but with or as change.[27] Such a program corresponds very imperfectly with the *Zhuangzi*, but quite well with the *Huainanzi*, that eclectic manual of Daoist arts of governance and natural observation compiled at the court of Liu An before 139 BCE, or around the time that Sima Tan was getting his education.[28] Zhuang Zhou's refusal to serve at King Huai's court and his literary self-indulgence, as outlined by Sima Qian, contrast even more pertinently with this ruler-centered "Daoism," an art of compelling obedience. Is Zhuangzi a "Daoist" at all, if these are the main features of that time's Daoism? Even with his gestures of discipleship toward Laozi, Zhuangzi is conspicuously isolated within the universe of Huang-Lao.

"Zhuang Zhou," then, can be only a marginal figure, if a self-important one, in an era of thought organized from end to end by the ambition of claiming, "I have the means to order the world" 我有以治天下.[29] Naming him and giving him such linguistic (but only linguistic) power may have been Sima Qian's way of limiting the Zhuang Zhou manner to its occurrence in one irreproducible individual.

But the *Zhuangzi* we have today shows the traces of many hands. Zhuang Zhou, if the originator was indeed Zhuang Zhou, had many imitators. And if Sima Qian's copy of *Zhuangzi* contained chapter 20, "The Mountain Tree," perhaps he should have revised the verdict of individualism that makes the *Zhuangzi* the expression of Zhuang Zhou's personality or pathology. The chapter opens with a play on one of the most famous arguments from the "Inner Chapters," "the usefulness of the useless":

Zhuangzi was traveling in the mountains, where he saw a huge tree. Its branches and leaves grew abundantly. The woodcutters stopped next to it and did not choose it. He asked them the reason, and they said, "It's not something we can use." Zhuangzi said: "Just because it's useless, this tree has been able to live out its natural span of years."[30]

莊子行於山中，見大木，枝葉盛茂，伐木者止其旁而不取也。問其故。曰：「無所可用」。莊子曰：「此木以不材得終其天年」。

So too the wise person should be slow to make himself "useful": the danger of being turned into "timber" is never far away. Chapter 1 of the *Zhuangzi* makes this point memorably. But the "Mountain Tree" chapter continues:

The Master left the mountains and took lodging in a friend's house. The friend, overjoyed, called his serving-boy to kill a goose and cook it. The boy asked: "There's one goose that cackles and one that can't, which one should I kill?" The householder said, "Just kill the one that can't cackle."

The next day, a disciple asked Zhuangzi: "That tree we saw yesterday in the mountain was able to live out its natural life because it was useless, and now the householder's goose was killed because it's useless; what is your position on this, sir?"

Zhuangzi said with a laugh, "My position—it's going to have to be somewhere between usefulness and uselessness. When something appears one way but isn't, you can't avoid entanglement..."

夫子出於山，舍於故人之家。故人喜，命豎子殺鴈而烹之。豎子請曰：「其一能鳴，其一不能鳴，請奚殺？」主人曰：「殺不能鳴者」。

明日，弟子問於莊子曰：「昨日山中之木，以不材得終其天年；今主人之鴈，以不材死。先生將何處？」莊子笑曰：「周將處夫材與不材之間。材與不材之間，似之而非也，故未免乎累。...」

Zhuangzi's answer (which I have cut short) seems evasive. And for good reason: his own student has found a way to make him contradict himself. If "the Master" in this story is the historical Zhuang Zhou, then Sima Qian can certainly not say that "not even the famous scholars of the time were able to extricate themselves" 雖當世宿學不能自解免也 from his skilled rhetorical attacks. The plot twist here—Zhuangzi being out-Zhuangzi'd by his student— reminds us that the *Zhuangzi* as a whole has the shape of an anthology amassed by repeated acts of self-parody or experiment. A limited number of "routines" expand through repetition, variation, and expansion into anecdotal examples: the arguments that start from a polarity and "make it equal," denying difference; the "usefulness of uselessness" and its inverse, the "futility of busyness"; the superman; the difference (and indifference) of large and small, right and wrong; the knack that eludes formulation in words (as we are told with words)—these germinal sketches prepare the reader to debate and defeat the non-Zhuangzian thinkers who still believe in the use of usefulness, the difference between differences, the adequacy of words, and so on. If "being Zhuangzi" does not mean to be the specific individual Zhuang Zhou, but to be the deployer of a certain rhetorical skill, then in the story from "The Mountain Tree" it is the student, not Zhuang Zhou, who "is Zhuangzi." Perhaps just number two in a series of Zhuangzis—but the principle is now established.

No current theory of the *Zhuangzi*'s authorship admits this episode as having been written by Zhuang Zhou. Its third-person narration and its position in one of the "Outer Chapters" distance it from the work's supposed core. Nonetheless, it is quoted in one of the earliest testimonia to Zhuangzi's existence, the *Lüshi chunqiu*. This might seem paradoxical, or else a proof that Zhuangzi had already achieved an unusual (though otherwise unrecorded) degree of fame, making him a household word by 250 BCE. Or it may be that our models of authorship are not well suited to imagining the composition-process of a book like the *Zhuangzi*. Let us follow the hint away from the usual precepts of textual criticism. Far from being a proof of inauthenticity, a reason for placing this segment far from the core, out on the derivative zone of the periphery, the overtly secondary character of this dialogue, its dependence on another argument presumed to have been made earlier, might show the way to unifying the *Zhuangzi* around something other than its "core beliefs" or originating author. The "Zhuangzi" whom we meet here for the first time in Chinese literature is from the beginning already identified with paradox: doubly so, as both maker and butt of paradoxes (a situation in itself paradoxical and parodic). We might conclude that what holds the *Zhuangzi* together is not an originating author (even if one trailed by epigones) but a set of procedures, a rhetoric. The pesky disciple teaches us how to read Zhuangzi inside out. If the property of "being Zhuangzi" can be transferred from the core to the periphery, from the original Zhuang Zhou to one of the rings of his reception, then the question "how much of *Zhuangzi* was written by Zhuangzi?" need not detain us long. What if we were to read Sima Qian's verdict differently, and treat 散道德放論 as meaning not a scattering, but an expansion, of the Way and Virtue in the release of discourse? A scattering, "as if to give back a hundredfold what the Great Clod had once joined together"? In bursts of strange translated music.

NOTES

Introduction

1. See for example Talal Asad, "The Concept of Cultural Translation in British Social Anthropology"; Homi K. Bhabha, *The Location of Culture*; Dipesh Chakrabarty, *Provincializing Europe*; Johannes Fabian, "The Other Revisited"; and for a retrospective assessment, Boris Buden et al., "Cultural Translation: An Introduction to the Problem." In history of science, see Xiang Chen, "Thomas Kuhn's Latest Notion of Incommensurability."

2. Susan Bassnett, *Comparative Literature: A Critical Introduction* (Oxford: Blackwell, 1993); Emily Apter, *The Translation Zone: A New Comparative Literature* (Princeton: Princeton University Press, 2006). For a perspective inspired by the "polysystems theory" of Itamar Even-Zohar, see Lieven d'Hulst, "Comparative Literature versus Translation Studies: Close Encounters of the Third Kind?" *European Review* 15 (2007): 95–104.

3. Walter Benjamin, "The Translator's Task," tr. Steven Rendall, in Venuti, ed., *The Translation Studies Reader*, 76, 79; original in Benjamin, "Die Aufgabe des Übersetzers," *Gesammelte Schriften*, 10, 16.

4. Prasenjit Gupta, "Introduction," *Indian Errant*, xxviii. I thank Adhira Mangalagiri for this reference.

5. Roman Jakobson, "On Linguistic Aspects of Translation" (428–35 in *Language in Literature*), 429 (emphasis in original).

6. One exception—spoken by a translator, of course: Dawne McCance, "Translation/Citation: An Interview with John P. Leavey, Jr."

7. Itamar Even-Zohar and Gideon Toury, *Theory of Translation and Intercultural Relations*; Even-Zohar, *Polysystem Studies*; Toury, *In Search of a Theory of Translation* and *Descriptive Translation Studies and Beyond.*

8. See John Goldsmith, "Unsupervised Learning of the Morphology of a Natural Language"; Nick Chater, Alexander Clark, John A. Goldsmith, and Amy Perfors, *Empiricism and Language Learnability.*

9. Ngũgĩ wa Thiong'o, *A Grain of Wheat*, 205. On the encoding of foreign languages as a feature of the tension between inset and frame, see Sternberg, "Polylingualism as Reality and Translation as Mimesis."

10. The distinction between transcription and translation in genetics was first formulated by John von Neumann, on purely logical grounds, before the discovery of DNA. See Moshe Sipper and James A. Reggia, "Go Forth and Replicate."

Chapter 1

1. Stefan George, "Das Wort," *Werke*, 1: 466–7, first published in 1919 and collected in *Das neue Reich* (1928); cited in Heidegger, "Das Wesen der Sprache," *Unterwegs zur Sprache*, 162–3. A second commentary on the poem occurs in "Das Wort," ibid., 220–8. On the contemporary resonances of George's imaginary "new Empire," see Klaus Schreiner, "Messianism in the Weimar Republic."
2. My translation. The sing-song meter and archaic vocabulary emulate the original; a certain debt to "Jabberwocky" must be recognized. Readers may wish to compare the translation (not reproduced here for copyright reasons) by Peter D. Hertz in Heidegger, *On the Way to Language* (hereafter *OWL*), 60.
3. *Encyclopedia Britannica*, eleventh edition, s.v.
4. Heidegger, *OWL*, 60. In the original: "Denn sie bringt das Wort der Sprache, diese selbst eigens zur Sprache und sagt etwas über das Verhältnis zwischen Wort und Ding." *Unterwegs zur Sprache*, 163.
5. Heidegger, *OWL*, 62 (emphasis in original).
6. *OWL*, 69; *Unterwegs zur Sprache*, 172.
7. Like George himself, or Rilke, or the early Gottfried Benn.
8. *OWL*, 62.
9. As in Heidegger, *An Introduction to Metaphysics*, 37.
10. See Max Vasmer, ed., *Russisches etymologisches Wörterbuch*, s.v. *put'*, 2: 469; Calvert Watkins, ed., *The American Heritage Dictionary of Indo-European Roots*, s.v. *pent-*., 67.
11. Friedrich Schleiermacher, "On the Different Methods of Translating," tr. Susan Bernofsky, in Venuti, ed., *The Translation Studies Reader*, 53–4.
12. Berman, *L'épreuve de l'étranger*, 297.
13. Schleiermacher, 54. On the "fine line," see Pym, *On Translator Ethics*, 17–35.
14. Walter Benjamin, "Die Aufgabe des Übersetzers," *Gesammelte Schriften*, 10: 9.
15. Venuti, *Scandals of Translation*, 1. For another view on the social and political effects of translation, including responses to Berman and Venuti, see Pym, *On Translator Ethics*.
16. Venuti, *Scandals of Translation*, 5.
17. Venuti, *The Translator's Invisibility*, 20. Similarly, Emily Apter ascribes to "the Untranslatable" qualities of "militant semiotic intransigence" (*Against World Literature*, 34) against more or less the same list of evils. In the perspective of "untranslatability," translation is always domesticating, indeed "neoliberal," for Apter. See Venuti, "Hijacking Translation," 203.
18. Venuti, *Scandals of Translation*, 165.
19. Ibid., 188.
20. Ibid., 71–5, 84–7.
21. Ibid., 174–6.
22. Berman, *La traduction et la lettre*, 29, 27.
23. Ibid., 74. For a parallel investigation, see Robert Eaglestone, "Levinas, Translation, and Ethics," 127–38 in Bermann and Wood, eds., *Nation, Language, and the Ethics of Translation*.
24. Jean-François Billeter, *Trois essais sur la traduction*, 108–9 (emphasis in original).
25. Ibid., 29–30 (emphases in original). "Hypertextual" as in Genette, *Palimpsestes*.
26. Cf. Berman, *La traduction et la lettre*, 75, on "the appropriating, annexing determination of the West" where "the logic of the Same" always triumphs. In order to dispel the illusion that translational violence is a unipolar thing with self-evident consequences, it is useful to consult Shadi Bartsch, "Roman Literature: Translation: Translation, Metaphor and Empire" and Sowon Park, "The Pan-Asian Empire and World Literatures." One might also think of the ways Herder's resistance to French universalism lent itself, in the course of time, to German and other chauvinisms.
27. Elizabeth Marie Young, *Translation as Muse*, 9, citing Siobhán McElduff, *Roman Theories of Translation*, 16 (emphasis in original). Young's first chapter (1–23) surveys the recent interest in the culturally specific aspects of Roman translating.
28. For Venuti's dismissal of descriptive translation studies, see *Scandals of Translation*, 26, 28–9.

29. On Lu Xun's "yingyi" 硬譯, see Leo Tak-hung Chan, "What's Modern in Chinese Translation Theory?"; for the debate, see Chan, ed., *Twentieth-Century Chinese Translation Theory,* 179–200. Lu Xun's own practice as a translator wavered among user-friendly and user-distant styles. On the Roman use of translation from Greek to supplement native "inopia," the adaptive devices applied to suit Greek literature to Roman mores, and anxieties about identity and control in the translators' culture, see Bartsch, "Roman Literature: Translation, Metaphor and Empire."
30. Jacques Derrida, "Qu'est-ce qu'une traduction 'relevante'?," echoed in Emily Apter, *The Translation Zone,* xi–xii.
31. James Joyce, *Ulysses,* 42.
32. Joyce, *Ulysse,* tr. Auguste Morel, with the assistance of Stuart Gilbert, Valéry Larbaud, and the author, 46–7. I have corrected a mistake ("flanc" for "flan," though I think the more exact term is "far breton").
33. "Gairmscoile," in MacDiarmid, *Collected Poems,* 57.
34. See Drew Milne, "Hugh MacDiarmid's Modernisms."
35. Jonson, *Timber, or Discoveries,* 89.
36. Derrida, *Le monolinguisme de l'autre,* 13, 42, 55–6.
37. *OED,* s.v. "askance."
38. "Loan word" is itself a calque, from German *Lehnwort:* see *OED,* s.v. "loanword." However, German *entlehnen* lacks the implication of a time-limit to the loan.
39. W. V. O. Quine, "Meaning and Translation."
40. Samuel Johnson, "Preface to the Dictionary" (1755), in McAdam and Milne, eds., *Johnson's Dictionary: A Modern Selection,* 27. Original spelling retained.
41. Apter, *The Translation Zone,* 245. As always, examples lead theory: consider the implications of substituting "Yiddish" for "Creole" in this statement, in the light of Benjamin Harshav, "Language: Multilingualism." (The coexistence of Yiddish and modern Hebrew in the Jewish state, greatly to the former's disadvantage, would however support Apter's implication about national languages.)
42. For the use of "creole" as a typological term see Robert A. Hall, Jr., *Pidgin and Creole Languages.* Hall's assumptions have been called into question. In the case of New World creoles, the creolization scenario often assumes an African grammatical substrate that empirical research has failed to uncover. For more recent discussions, see Salikoko S. Mufwene, "Creoles and Creolization" and "Jargons, Pidgins, Creoles, and Koines: What Are They?"
43. Mufwene, "Jargons, Pidgins, Creoles, and Koines," 57–60.
44. Apter, *The Translation Zone,* 227. The engineering point about the catalytic converter is elusive.
45. Manovich, *The Language of New Media,* xv, 47, 79.
46. See N. Katherine Hayles, *How We Became Posthuman;* Saussy, *The Ethnography of Rhythm.*

Chapter 2

1. Jacques Derrida, "La vérité blessante," 27.
2. Julia Kristeva, Σημειωτική, 85.
3. Kate Sturge reminds us that translators act "as lawyers or agents" on others' behalf (*Representing Others,* 177): misrepresentation, exploitation, or betrayal by these agents is one form of scandal. Another, foregrounded by Lawrence Venuti, points out how translation has long been "stigmatized as a form of writing, discouraged by copyright law, depreciated by the academy, exploited by publishers and corporations, governments and religious organizations" (*Scandals of Translation,* 1; and see *The Translator's Invisibility,* 20–1). Both Sturge and Venuti assert an "ethical" imperative for translators, Venuti adding that this ethics must be "theorized as contingent" (in other words, abstain from general rules) (*Scandals of Translation,* 6). Indeed the act of translating itself, as it appears in their own descriptions, seems unlikely to be contained by any a priori rule. But applying terms like "ethical" in a merely contingent way risks vacating the ethical force of the term "ethics."

4. "Une charogne," *Fleurs du mal* XXIX, in Charles Baudelaire, *Œuvres complètes*, 1: 31–2. English versions of the poem by William Aggeler, Roy Campbell, Richard Herne Shepherd, Jacques LeClercq, Jack Collings Squire, and Geoffrey Wagner may be consulted at http://fleursdumal. org/poem/126 (accessed January 20, 2017).

5. Xu Zhimo (1895–1931), one of the most influential poets of the early modernist movement in China, studied at Clark, Columbia, and Cambridge universities before returning in 1922 to teach at Peking University. In his time he was considered a Byronic figure for his scandalous divorce and remarriage. The preface and translation retranslated here appeared in *Yu si* 語絲 (Threads of Conversation), a little journal associated with Peking University. Many of the leading figures of modern Chinese literature—Lu Xun, Zhou Zuoren, Qian Xuantong, among others—published short essays there on controversial issues of literature and society. Flanking Xu Zhimo's article are, for example, a critical obituary of Lin Shu (the prolific translator of Dickens, Stowe, Dumas, and Defoe) and an exchange of letters between Zhou Zuoren and Jiang Shaoyuan discussing whether ritual characterizes primitive or highly evolved civilizations, and where China fits on that scale. Xu's preface and translation provoked a sarcastic response by Lu Xun in the next fortnight's number. On the history of the group, see Mark Miller, "The Yusi Society," 171–206 in Denton and Hockx, eds., *Literary Societies of Republican China*.

6. Guo Qingfan, ed., *Zhuangzi jishi*, 45. For an overview of the *Zhuangzi*, its textual history, reception, and wide influence in Chinese thought, see Victor Mair, "The *Zhuangzi* and Its Impact." On its twentieth-century echoes, see Liu Jianmei, *Zhuangzi and Modern Chinese Literature*.

7. *Yu si* 3 (1 December 1924), 5–7.

8. Aristotle, *De anima* 416 b 15; 424 a 18–24.

9. *De anima* 418 a 3–5; translation by J. A. Smith, from Jonathan Barnes, ed., *The Complete Works of Aristotle*, 1: 665. The bases for this theory of perception were laid down by Plato: see *Timaeus* 45 b. For a recent discussion, see Christopher Shields, "Controversies Surrounding Aristotle's Theory of Perception."

10. *Poetics* 1459 a 8.

11. *De anima* 416 b 27.

12. For thinking as the "form of forms," see *De anima* 432 a 1.

13. For one such account, see Manuel Castells, *The Rise of the Network Society*, 3–25.

14. Ray Kurzweil, *The Age of Spiritual Machines*, 133–56; also a frequent sci-fi plot device.

15. Hayles, *How We Became Posthuman*, 192–4.

16. Claude Shannon, "A Mathematical Theory of Communication," 379.

17. Shannon measures information as a function of the probability of a given message being selected. For the non-mathematician, the most easily deciphered pages of "The Mathematical Theory of Communication" are the most redundant ones: those in which the redundancy of written English (encompassing the range between Basic English and the language of *Finnegans Wake*) is evaluated.

18. See Richard Huelsenbeck, ed., *Dada Almanach*, 53.

19. This judgment is usually attributed to Robert Frost, but not quite accurately: see Cleanth Brooks and Robert Penn Warren, eds., *Conversations on the Craft of Poetry*, 7.

20. Dante, *The Divine Comedy*, vol. 2: *Purgatorio*, tr. and comm. Charles S. Singleton, 275. For a related passage continuing the metaphors of stamping ("suggellare") and receptive matter, see *Paradiso*, 13.64–81 (*The Divine Comedy*, 3: 144–7).

21. Xu's second-hand translation practice resembles that of Lin Shu 林紓 (1852–1924), who extensively rewrote paraphrases provided by assistants schooled in foreign languages. See Michael Gibbs Hill, *Lin Shu, Inc.: Translation and the Making of Modern Chinese Culture*, and Qian Zhongshu, "The Translations of Lin Shu," 104–19 in Leo Tak-hung Chan, ed., *Twentieth-Century Chinese Translation Theory*. On translation-style (absent originals) as a literary option, see Michel Hockx, *Questions of Style*, 176–86.

22. Curiously, this stanza has the most inelegant rhymes of the whole poem: *grâces/grasses, sacrements/ossements*. On the assumption that Baudelaire knew what he was doing, sarcasm may be intended.

23. Etymologically, "pure" and "putrid" derive from the same Indo-European root, as Mark Southern once kindly pointed out to me.

24. Cf. "Le Peintre de la vie moderne," on the sketching method of Constantin Guys: "at any moment of his progress [in making a drawing], every drawing appears thoroughly finished; you might call that a sketch if you want, but a perfected sketch." Baudelaire, *Œuvres complètes*, 2: 700.

25. I give Burton Watson's wording, adopted by many subsequent translators. But "piping" strikes my ear as too shrill, thin, and pastoral.

26. *Zhuangzi jishi*, 45–50; tr. Burton Watson in *The Complete Works of Chuang Tzu*, 36–7. This passage is quickly followed by another expressing skepticism about language, specifically the possibility of distinguishing a "this" from a "that"; assuming that the chapter forms a unit, a thematic link via the idea of indeterminacy may connect the two passages. I have rewritten Watson's last sentences to reflect the sense of some of the commentaries in Liu's edition. See also the translation by Victor H. Mair, *Wandering on the Way*, 10–12.

27. *Zhuangzi jishi*, 251; tr. Burton Watson, 85.

28. *Zhuangzi jishi*, 260, tr. Burton Watson, 80–1 (modified). If there is any personification in "The Maker of Things" or "Heaven," it is not strong; speculations about the intentions of these supernal authorities rarely go into detail. The word here translated as "hate" (Watson gives "resent") can also be rendered as "feel disgust"; by an ambiguity of the same word, Baudelaire's *Fleurs du mal* in Chinese can suggest "Flowers of disgust."

29. *Zhuangzi jishi*, 17.

30. By "Saussurian" I mean to refer to the views enshrined in the posthumous *Cours de linguistique générale* (1916). Saussure (unlike his students) was aware that the "systematic," self-bounded character of language was a collective convention, not a primary fact about languages. See Saussure, "Troisième conférence à l'Université de Genève (novembre 1891)," *Écrits de linguistique générale*, 163–73.

31. The image of intellectual and literary digestion is traditional since at least Seneca, *Epistulae morales* 84: "alimenta quae accepimus, quamdiu in sua qualitate perdurant et solida innatant stomacho, onera sunt; at cum ex eo quod erant mutata sunt, tunc demum in vires et in sanguinem transeunt.... Concoquamus illa..." (the food we take in, so long as it continues suspended in the stomach with its qualities intact, is a burden; but from the moment that it is changed from what it was, it goes over into energy and blood...We must digest [our mental food likewise]). Lucius Annius Seneca, *Lettere a Lucilio*, 530. For similar arguments in Erasmus and Montaigne, very much to my point, see Michel Jeanneret, "The Renaissance and its Ancients: Dismembering and Devouring." On modernity as re-chewing, see Rachel Galvin, "Poetry Is Theft."

32. On the relations of metaphor and metonymy and the curious reifications to which they give rise, see Jane Gallop, *Reading Lacan*, 114–32. For an account of metaphor as double synecdoche, see Groupe μ, *Rhétorique générale*, 108.

33. Dante, *Purgatorio* 25.37–45; *The Divine Comedy*, tr. Singleton, 271.

34. Bruno Nardi, *Dal "Convivio" alla "Commedia"* (1960), cited in Singleton's commentary, 595. See also John Freccero, *Dante: The Poetics of Conversion*, 199–204; Robert M. Durling, "Deceit and Digestion in the Belly of Hell," esp. 62, 68, 80–4. For the *Convivio* passages (amply documented in Singleton's commentary), see Dante Alighieri, *Convivio* IV.xxi, in *Opere minori*, 752–75.

35. *De generatione animalium* 729 a 20–32. On Aristotle's gynecology, see Sylviane Agacinski, "Le tout premier écart."

36. Aristotle, *De anima* 415 a 26–9.

37. See Aristotle, *De generatione animalium* 735 a 5–25, and St. Thomas Aquinas, *Summa theologica*, I, questions 75 and 90.

38. "Now, Hamlet, where's Polonius?"—"At supper...not where he eats, but where he is eaten." *Hamlet*, act 4, scene 3.

39. On Poe's "angelism" correlated with a poetic necrophilia, see Allen Tate, "Our Cousin, Mr. Poe," *Essays of Four Decades*, 385–400.

40. Baudelaire, "Le Confiteor de l'artiste," *Le Spleen de Paris*, III, in *Œuvres complètes*, 1: 279.

41. See Lu Xun's rejoinder, "'Yin yue'?": "If anyone should try to 'send him to the lunatic asylum,' I would leap to his defense and challenge the injustice   although from an utter mystic's point of view, to send music to music is no very great matter."

42. Walter Benjamin, "Die Aufgabe des Übersetzers," *Gesammelte Schriften*, 10: 9–21. Benjamin speaks of the original's *Fortleben* (ongoing life), *Überleben* (survival), and of the "völlig unmetaphorische Sachlichkeit" of its "Leben und Fortleben" (completely unmetaphorical reality of its life and continuing life), ibid., 10–11. Cf. the translation by Steven Rendall as "The Translator's Task," in Venuti, ed., *The Translation Studies Reader*, 75–83.

43. Precisely as Xu was later to put it in his manifesto for *Shi kan* 詩刊 (The Poetry Journal, 1926): "We recognize that within and without us there are numerous thoughts that seek embodiment. Our duty then is to build suitable bodies for them…. We believe that perfect form is the only manifestation of perfect essence" (cited in Kai-yu Hsu, ed., *Twentieth-Century Chinese Poetry*, 69).

44. Mandel'stam, *Complete Poetry*, tr. Burton Raffel and Alla Burago, 223 (translation modified); "Tatary, uzbeki i nentsy," poem 273 in Osip Mandel'stam, *Sobranie sochinenij*, 1: 427.

Chapter 3

1. Basic sources for Ricci's relation to Europe are Pietro Tacchi Venturi, ed., *Opere storiche del P. Matteo Ricci, S. J.*, and Pasquale M. d'Elia, SJ, ed., *Fonti Ricciane*. For an essay in retrieving Ricci's mental life, see Jonathan Spence, *The Memory Palace of Matteo Ricci*. Ricci's most widely circulated publication in Chinese has been translated by Timothy Billings as *On Friendship: One Hundred Maxims for a Chinese Prince*. More recently, Ronnie Po-chia Hsia, *A Jesuit in the Forbidden City: Matteo Ricci, 1552–1610* offers a theological and historical "thick description" of the man's bicultural enterprise.

2. On translation as the privileged model in Ricci studies, see Lionel Jensen, *Manufacturing Confucianism*, esp. 106–27, and Saussy, "In the Workshop of Equivalences."

3. These are the leading questions of Jacques Gernet's *Chine et christianisme: action et réaction*. On the consequences of Ricci's choice of cultural assimilation as the path for Chinese Catholicism to follow, see George Minamiki, *The Chinese Rites Controversy from its Beginning to Modern Times* and David E. Mungello, ed., *The Chinese Rites Controversy: Its History and Meaning*.

4. Wang Jiazhi 王家植, "Ti *Jiren shipian* xiao yin 題畸人十篇小引" (A short preface to *Ten Chapters from an Extraordinary Man*) in Li Zhizao, *Tianxue chuhan*, 1: 3a.

5. Li Zhi, "Yu youren shu 與友人書" (Letter to a friend), *Xu fen shu*, in *Fen shu, Xu fen shu*, 35; translation by Rivi Handler-Spitz in Li Zhi, *A Book to Burn and a Book to Keep (Hidden)*, 256–7.

6. Li Zhi, *Fen shu*, in *Fen shu, Xu fen shu*, 247; translation in Li Zhi, *A Book to Burn and a Book to Keep (Hidden)*, 223–4. On this poem, see Liu Yuelian 劉月蓮, "Li Zhuowu yu Li Xitai: Wanli zhong-xi chaoru zhi wu." Ricci's early appreciation for Li Zhi gave way to antagonism as Ricci found allies among the Chinese establishment. On this relationship see Saussy, *Great Walls of Discourse*, 21–32.

7. *Zhuangzi*, chapter 1 ("Xiaoyao you"). *Zhuangzi jishi*, 2.

8. Burton Watson, tr., *The Complete Works of Chuang Tzu*, 29.

9. See for example Emperor Jianwen of the Liang dynasty 梁簡文帝, "Congjun xing 從軍行," cited in Morohashi, *Dai Kan-Wa jiten*, s.v. 迤邐.

10. *Jiu Tang shu* 舊唐書, chapter 197, "Nan min zhuan 南閩傳," in *Ershiwu shi* 二十五史 (The Twenty-Five Dynastic Histories), 5: 634. On Chinese–Zhenla relations in the Ming, see Yan Congjian, *Shuyu zhouzi lu* (A Record of Thorough Investigations of Remote Areas, preface dated 1574), 270–8.

11. On Ricci's world map, see Pasquale d'Elia, SJ, *Il Mappamondo cinese del P. Matteo Ricci*, followed by d'Elia, "Recent Discoveries and New Studies (1938–1960) on the World Map in Chinese of Father Matteo Ricci S.J.," and Huang Shijian 黃時鑒, *Li Madou shijie ditu yanjiu* 利瑪竇世界地圖研究. Later missionaries made similar use of Western geographical information. See Bernard

Hung-kay Luk, "A Study of Giulio Aleni's 'Chih-fang wai-chi' " and Hartmut Walravens, "Father Verbiest's Chinese World Map (1674)."

12. Li Zhizao, "Ke *Zhifang waiji* xu" 科職方外紀序 (On Reprinting [Guido Aleni's] "Supplement to the Records of the Imperial Cartographer"), in *Tianxue chuhan*, 3: 1a–2b.

13. Wang Bi and Kong Yingda on the *Yijing* hexagram "Guan," *Zhou Yi zhengyi* 周易正義, in Ruan Yuan, ed., *Shisanjing zhushu*, 3/10a.

14. The point is made in memorials by Shen Que dated 1616. See Timothy Brook, "The Early Jesuits and the Late-Ming Border."

15. Banished immortals were much in favor at the close of the Ming: many young women of talent and eccentric personality were assumed, after their early deaths, to have been immortals banished to the human world for a space of years. See Ellen Widmer, "Xiaoqing's Literary Legacy and the Place of the Woman Writer" and Judith Zeitlin, "Spirit Writing and Performance in the Work of You Tong (1618-1704)."

16. *Zhuangzi jishi*, 40 (emphasis in translation added).

17. Ibid., 14.

18. Guo Xiang, cited, *Zhuangzi jishi*, 1 (emphasis in translation added). The basic meaning of *xiaoyao* in *Zhuangzi* is not in doubt, as the text practically glosses it by frequent use (for example, 逍遙乎 無為之業, ibid., 268) and putting it in parallel position with similar phrases (e.g. 彷徨 as in the "useless tree" passage of chapter 1, ibid., 40). For interpretations of *xiaoyao* contemporary with Li Zhi and Ricci, see for example Lu Xixing, *Nanhua zhenjing fumo*, 1/1a, where the moral of the "Nei pian" is paraphrased: "Only after a man has enlarged his mind can he enter on the Dao. So the 'Inner Chapters' begin with 'Xiaoyao you.'" For a collection of opinions current in the late Ming on the meanings of the phrase and chapter, see Jiao Hong, ed., *Zhuangzi yi* (1588), 1/12a–14a. Bi Sheng 筆乘 there interprets *xiao* as 消, "dissolving," and *yao* as 搖, "shaking," which would seem to impart a new and violent tone to the word, but his point is that the person who "embodies the Dao" can go through shaking and dissolving without being shaken or dissolved (1/2a). For another selection of traditional commentaries on the passage, see Ziporyn, *Zhuangzi: The Essential Writings*, 3–5, 129–32.

19. Li Zhi, *Xu fen shu*, 35.

20. A point of clarification here. My lack of specialized knowledge of Daoism obliges me to a certain nominalism. Here "Daoism" is a rhetoric of concepts, justifications, and critical attitudes about other rhetorics in the intellectual situation; it builds on interpretations of a set of favored texts; it has institutional consequences (temples, monasteries, isolated virtuosi, liturgies, consultants, etc.), a group of more or less dedicated exponents, and a degree of influence on other groups. Readers should not assume that "Daoism" is an airtight ideology or a "church" in the sense of that word familiar to Christianity since Luther. One recognizes "Daoism" as one recognizes a genre or style in a literary text; like styles and genres, it is open to counterfeiting, parody, and mixture.

21. Jacques Gernet, *Chine et christianisme*, 27.

22. *Jiren shipian*, in Li Zhizao, comp., *Tianxue chuhan*, 1: 93–282. On its publication and success, see d'Elia, *Fonti Ricciane*, 2: 301–6. Li Zhizao's edition takes one of the many later reprints as its basis. For a modern typeset edition with punctuation, see Zhu Weizheng, ed., *Li Madou zhongwen zhuyiji*, 503–98.

23. D'Elia, *Fonti Ricciane*, 2: 302. The term *jiren* has lost much of its power over the years. In chapter 63 of *Dream of the Red Chamber*, the Daoist nun Miaoyu calls herself *jiren*, glossing the term as "one beyond the threshold" (Cao Xueqin and Gao E, *Honglou meng*, 2: 898). Lu Xun used it to translate "hermits" in his first, classical-language version (1918) of the prologue to Nietzsche's *Also sprach Zarathustra*—the hermits being precisely not the coming Superman (Lu Xun, tr., "Chaluodusideluo xuyan" 察羅堵斯德羅緒言, *Lu Xun zhu yi biannian quanji*, 3: 109–13). Sherwood Anderson's *Winesburg, Ohio* is known in Chinese as *Xiaocheng jiren* 小城畸人 (The Loners [or: Eccentrics] of a Small Town).

24. D'Elia, *Fonti Ricciane*, 2: 301–2.

25. Victor Mair, tr., *Wandering on the Way*, 61.

26. *Zhuangzi*, "Da zong shi," in Guo Qingfan, *Zhuangzi jishi*, 264–8. In my translation I have taken some expressions from Burton Watson's version Chuang Tzu, 86–7.

27. See for example chapters 2 ("Qi wu lun"), 3 ("Yangsheng zhu"), 6 ("Da zongshi"), and 18 ("Zhi le," where the hero is Zhuang Zhou himself).

28. On the allegorical strategy of reading both the Old Testament and the Chinese classics as veiled prophecies of things to come, see Zhang Longxi, "Jewish and Chinese Literalism," *Mighty Opposites*, 84–116. It is possibly the New Testament's revisionary reading of the Old that suggested to Ricci a way of accommodating, while not totally accepting, some Chinese philosophical ideas. On this figurative logic, see Erich Auerbach's essay "Figura," 11–76 in *Scenes from the Drama of European Literature*.

29. On the connotations of *shanren*, see Hsia, *A Jesuit in the Forbidden City*, 156; Chow, *Publishing, Culture, and Power in Early Modern China*, 107–9; and Greenbaum, *Chen Jiru (1558–1639): The Development and Subsequent Uses of Literary Personae*, 172–6. For a contemporary's dim view of self-styled "mountain recluses," see Shen Defu (1578–1642), "Shanren minghao" 山人名號 (The Name and Style of "Mountain Recluse"), *Wanli yehuo bian* 萬曆野獲編 (A Round-up of Occasional Notes from the Wanli Era), 23/6b–7a.

30. Zhou Bingmou, "Chongkan *Jiren shipian* yin 重刊畸人十篇引," *Tianxue chuhan* 1: 107–10; here, 107. See also Zhu Weizheng, ed., *Li Madou zhongwen zhuyiji*, 589–90. On the prefaces to *Jiren shipian*, see d'Elia, "Sunto poetico-ritmico di *I dieci paradossi* di Matteo Ricci S. I."

31. Echoing *Daode jing*, chapter 79 (天道無親, 常與善人): *Laozi daode jing*, in *Xinbian zhuzi jicheng*, 3: 49.

32. Zhou Bingmou, preface, 108. Zhou alludes to two passages from the "Qian" hexagram of the *Yijing*: 時乘六龍以御天 ("ascending to heaven on six dragons") and 首出庶物 ("emerging to observe the world"): see *Zhou Yi zhengyi* in Ruan Yuan, *Shisanjing*, 1/18b, 7b. I have emended one character in the text; compare Zhu Weizheng, ed., *Li Madou zhongwen zhuyiji*, 590.

33. Zhou Bingmou, preface, 109. For the further *Yijing* allusion, 百姓日用之而不知, 故君子之道鮮矣 ("the common people use it every day without understanding, thus the Way of the noble person is exceptional"), see *Zhou Yi zhengyi* in Ruan Yuan, *Shisanjing*, 7/12a.

34. Zhou Bingmou, preface, 107; *Zhuangzi jishi*, 17; Burton Watson, *The Complete Works of Chuang Tzu*, 32.

35. On this group, see Heinrich Busch, "The Tung-lin Academy"; Benjamin Elman, *A Cultural History of Examinations in Late Imperial China*, 208–11; Cynthia Brokaw, *The Ledgers of Merit and Demerit*, 22–8.

36. See d'Elia, "Sunto poetico-ritmico," 115, notes 1, 3, 4; 116, par. 4 and notes 7 and 8; 118, par. 1.

37. Gernet, *Chine et christianisme*, 153–70; see also Brook, "The Early Jesuits and the Late-Ming Border." For Ricci's understanding of the "White Lotus" sect, see *Fonti Ricciane* 2: 458.

38. Directly citing Han Yu 韓愈, "Lun fogu biao" 論佛骨表 (Memorial on a Bone of the Buddha), *Han Changli wenji*, 354–6.

39. *Ming shi* 明史, chapter 326 ("Wai guo zhuan: Yidaliya" 外國傳, 意大利亞), in *Ershiwu shi*, 10: 929–30. For Ricci's account of the presentation, see *Fonti Ricciane*, 2: 107–51, esp. 147 n.3, with d'Elia's translation of a related memorial. On the motif of "novelty-seeking" as a feature of the late Ming, see Tina Lu, *A Coin, A Severed Head*.

40. Matthew 5:5; 5:44; 20:16; I Corinthians 1:27–8; *Daode jing*, sections 31, 36, 7, 40. Perhaps this flickering similarity accounts for the popularity of the *Daode jing* in erstwhile Christian countries: it is the most often translated of all Chinese books, and not only because it is one of the shortest.

41. For a sense of the materials among which the present New Testament books circulated early in their history, collections such as Montague Rhodes James, ed., *The Apocryphal New Testament*, are useful in showing the close cousinage of the Gospels with the exotic popular fiction of the late Empire. On the social and intellectual history of the period, see Peter Brown, *The Making of Late Antiquity*.

42. On the Pauline rhetoric of position and mobilization, see Olga Solovieva, *Christ's Subversive Body*. If the Tianzhu religion had not remained tethered to its origins in Rome, might it not

have adopted a different syncretic path? Taiping millennialism, it may be said, confirms the predictions of the *Ming History*, though it took shape in a different dynastic and international context. See Jonathan Spence, *God's Chinese Son*.

43. See d'Elia, ed., *Fonti Ricciane*, 1: 115, 127–31, for Ricci's summary of "the sect of Laozi."

44. For the monikers, see *Jiaoyou lun*, 1a, in Li Zhizao, ed., *Tianxue chuhan*, 1: 299; *Tianzhu shiyi* 1a, ibid., 1: 377. For the seals, see e.g. "*Tianzhu shiyi* yin" 天主實義引 (Preface to *The Substantive Doctrine of the Lord of Heaven*), 4a, ibid., 1: 371.

45. *Daode jing*, sections 1, 2, 45, 55, etc.

46. For the early history of Daoist religion (*Daojiao*), see Robinet, *Daoism: History of a Religion*, and Bokenkamp, *Early Daoist Scriptures*.

47. On "egocentricity" as a flaw of translation, see Berman, *L'épreuve de l'étranger*, 17–24.

Chapter 4

1. Liang Qichao, "Fanyi wenxue yu fodian" (1920), collected in *Yinbingshi wenji* 61/1a–24b; here, 24b. The essay is reprinted in full in Zhang Mantao, ed., *Fojiao yu Zhongguo wenxue*, 345–82, and in part in Luo Xinzhang, ed., *Fanyi lunji*, 95–110.

2. On this vast subject, see Lydia Liu, *Translingual Practice*; Andrew F. Jones, "Chinese Literature in the 'World' Literary Economy"; Gang Zhou, *Placing the Modern Chinese Vernacular in Transnational Literature*; Mark Gamsa, *The Reading of Russian Literature in China*; James St. André and Peng Hsiao-yen, eds., *China and Its Others*; Michael Gibbs Hill, *Lin Shu, Inc.*

3. Liang Qichao, "Fanyi wenxue," 3a.

4. Hu Shi, *The Chinese Renaissance*, 85. On Hu Shi's persistent drive to reverse this obedience, see his "The Indianization of China: A Case Study in Cultural Borrowing," and John A. McRae, "Religion as Revolution in Chinese Historiography: Hu Shih (1891–1962) on Shen-hui (684–758)."

5. Liang Qichao, "Fanyi wenxue," 21a, 24a.

6. Hu Shi, *Baihua wenxue shi*, 1: 133–80.

7. For Liang's enormously influential essay of 1902, "Lun xiaoshuo yu qunzhi zhi guanxi" 論小說 與群治之關係 (On the Novel and Government), see *Yinbingshi heji*, 10/6–10. For a translation, see Kirk Denton, ed., *Modern Chinese Literary Thought*, 74–82.

8. Liang Qichao, "Fanyi wenxue," 12b, apparently quoting Dao'an's preface to An Shigao, tr., *Renben yusheng jing* 人本欲生經 (T 0014) as cited in Sengyou 僧祐, *Chusanjing jijixu* 出三經記序, chapter 6 (T 2145), 55: 45a; moreover closely paralleled in Sengyou's biography of An Shigao, (T 2145), 55: 95. On the genre of the "translator's biography," see Tanya Storch, *The History of Chinese Buddhist Bibliography*, 141–72.

9. Hundun, in the *Zhuangzi*, was a primordial being, wholly round, whose friends misguidedly decided to give him eyes and ears and a mouth. Once they had pierced his spherical form, he died (chapter 7). The meaning here is that meddling with a perfect original only causes it to degenerate.

10. Liang Qichao, "Fanyi wenxue," 13b. Liang lifts many expressions from Dao'an's brief history of Buddhist translation in *Zongli zhongjing mulu* 總理眾經目錄 (Inventory of the Many Sutras, Ordered and Classified), now incorporated in Sengyou 僧祐, ed., *Chu sanzang jiji* 出三藏記集 (Collected Notes on the Tripitaka Vulgate), (T 2145), 55: 1–114.

11. *Si shi er zhang jing* (T 784: 17.722a–24a). "Jiaochenru" is a Chinese transliteration of Kaundinya, the Buddha's first convert, who is said to have become an arhat (*aluohan*). Other technical terms I have left in Chinese form. I have consulted the translation by Robert Sharf, but rebarbarized it and reinserted some sentences on the basis of other editions. On the textual history of this work, whose attributed date clearly made it a tempting target for forgery and interpolations in later periods, see Tang Yongtong, "The Editions of the *Ssu-shih-erh-chang ching*." Liang Qichao's remarks apply especially to some of these interpolated versions, but in

some degree to the less questionable ones as well. For example, a partisan of Chan inserted the following at some point:

> [18] The Buddha said: My dharma consists in meditating a meditation without meditation, practicing a practice without practice, speaking a speech without speech, disciplining a discipline without discipline. Understand this, and you are close; misunderstand it, and you are far off. The way of words and speech breaks off, and material things no longer impede one. Miss it by a fraction of a hair, and you have lost it in a moment.
>
> 佛言：吾法念無念念，行無行行，言無言言，修無修修，會者近爾，迷者遠乎，言語道斷，非物所拘，差之毫釐，失之須臾。

On the sutra's reception-history in Europe, see Urs App, "Arthur Schopenhauer and China."

12. *Si shi er zhang jing*, T 784: 17.722c.
13. Zürcher, *The Buddhist Conquest of China*, 30, 329. With time, familiarity with the Sanskrit lexicon and Buddhistic literary genres increased to the point that convincing apocryphal translations could be written in Chinese and even "restored" to Sanskrit form: see Robert E. Buswell, Jr., *The Formation of Ch'an Ideology*, and Jan Nattier, "The *Heart Sūtra*: A Chinese Apocryphal Text?" Such Tlönian practices should also be included in the wider scope of "translation" in China.
14. *Xiao jing*, section 12, trans. James Legge, *The Sacred Books of China, Part I*, 481–2 (with modifications).
15. *Mao Shi zhengyi*, "Shi da xu," in Ruan Yuan, ed., *Shisanjing zhushu*, 1: 1/8b; *Zhou Yi zhengyi*, "Xi ci," ibid., 7/18a; *Xiaojing*, "Guang yao dao," ibid., 6/4b; *Chunqiu Zuo zhuan zhengyi*, Zhao gong, year 13, ibid., 46/11b; *Xunzi*, "Jie bi" (On Removing Ignorance), in *Xunzi jijie*, 267.
16. *Si shi er zhang jing*, T 784: 17.722c; cf. "The Scripture in Forty-Two Sections," tr. Robert Sharf, section 9: "Feeding ten billion solitary buddhas is not as good as liberating one's parents in this life by means of the teaching of the three honored ones.... But the merit of feeding a good man is [still] very great. It is better for a common man to be filial to his parents than for him to serve the spirits of Heaven and Earth, for one's parents are the supreme spirits" (*Coming to Terms with Chinese Buddhism*, 366).
17. Liang, "Fanyi wenxue," 14a.
18. For the canonical pairing of *zhi* (substance) and *wen* (pattern), see *Lunyu* 6:18.
19. Zürcher, *The Buddhist Conquest of China*, 2.
20. Sengyou, *Chusanzang jiji*, chapter 13 (T 2145), 55: 95a. In the *Gaoseng zhuan* version, An's ability to speak animal languages makes possible his miraculous conversion of a python who had been his enemy in a past life (5–6). On An's biography, see Antonino Forte, *The Hostage An Shigao and His Offspring*.
21. Thus giving rise to "a third type of literature which falls between a Chinese translation and a Chinese composition or compilation.... It was difficult for those in attendance at a lecture to tell whether the lecture by the Indian authority was composed of only views he learned from his own teacher, or mixed with additions originating from his own interpretation, let alone when the Indian master read the lecture from memory, and when he had to communicate through the medium of an interpreter." Funayama Tōru, "Masquerading as Translation: Examples of Chinese Lectures by Indian Scholar-Monks in the Six Dynasties Period," 39, 55.
22. On An Shigao's two main areas of teaching, see Zürcher, *The Buddhist Conquest of China*, 33. Stefano Zacchetti has explored the translation-corpus of An Shigao ("Teaching Buddhism in Han China" and "Inventing a New Idiom"). The use of lists, a feature common to Indian and Chinese Buddhisms, is emphasized by Zacchetti as a mental "flowchart" around which the speaker can freely "improvise" ("Teaching Buddhism," 220).
23. Zürcher, *The Buddhist Conquest of China*, 202.
24. Ibid., 321.
25. Jan Nattier, *A Guide to the Earliest Chinese Buddhist Translations*, 22 (emphasis in original). On authorship and the tenuous quality of Sino-Indian "dialogue," see Robert Sharf, *Coming to Terms with Chinese Buddhism*, 18, 24.
26. Zürcher, *The Buddhist Conquest of China*, 202–3. On the lasting effects of Dao'an's synoptic ambitions for Buddhist literature, see Zacchetti, "Notions and Visions of the Canon in Early Chinese Buddhism."

27. See nonetheless Dao'an's advice for translators as rendered in Leon N. Hurvitz and Arthur E. Link, "Three Prajñāparamitā Prefaces of Tao-an," 426–32; Martha Cheung, ed., *An Anthology of Chinese Discourse on Translation*, 1: 69–87; Michael Lackner, "Circumnavigating the Unfamiliar," 358–65; and Christoph Harbsmeier, "Early Chinese Buddhist Translators on Translation."
28. Zürcher, *Buddhism in China*, 551; on the organization of the workshops see also 540, 589–90.
29. Ibid., 320; see also Jiang Wu, "The Chinese Buddhist Canon Through the Ages," in Jiang Wu and Lucille Chia, eds., *Spreading Buddha's Word in East Asia*, 15–45.
30. Zürcher, *Buddhism in China*, 118.
31. On "rhetorical communities," see Nattier, *A Guide*, 166–8.
32. Zürcher, *Buddhism in China*, 344; see also 93–5.
33. Ibid., 436.
34. Ibid., 427–8.
35. Huijiao, *Gaoseng zhuan*, ed. Tang Yongtong, chapter 4 ("The Explicators" 義解), 152–3. Kang Falang, mentioned as Faya's associate in *geyi*, later conceived the desire to go to Western countries and acquire scriptures at first hand. The other members of his party stopped their journey at an abandoned monastery in the sands, restoring it and dwelling there; he continued and was never heard from again (153–4). Kang Falang's biography suggests a cautionary tale.
36. Chen Yinke, "Zhi Mindu xueshuo kao" 支愍度學說考 (An Examination of Zhi Mindu's Theories), first published as 1–18 in the 1933 Festschrift for Cai Yuanpei (Zhongyanyuan [collective author], *Qingzhu Cai Yuanpei xiansheng liushiwusui lunwenji*), and "Qingtan wuguo (fu 'geyi')" 清談誤國, 附 '格義' (Pure Conversation and the Loss of the Realm, with a Discussion of "geyi"), lecture notes from 1942 taken down by Zhang Weigang 張為綱 and first published in *Xingdao ribao*, January 26, 1949 (see Jiang Tianshu, *Chen Yinke xiansheng biannian shiji*, 182, 191–3). The name "Yinke" is sometimes transcribed "Yinque." On *geyi* generally, see T'ang Yungtung, "On 'Ko-yi' "; Tsukamoto Zenryū, *A History of Early Chinese Buddhism*, 1: 297–310, 712, 796; Chen Tixian, "Wei-Jin-Nanbeichao fojiao de chuanbo yu quxiang," 124–7; Cai Zhengfeng, "Dao'an jingxu sixiang de zhuanzhe ji zai geyi wentishang de yiyi"; Li Xingling, "Geyi xintan"; Lin Chuanfang, "Geyi fojiao sixiang zhi shi de kaizhan"; Liu Jingguo, "*Ge-yi* in Buddhist Scripture Translations"; Sharf, *Coming to Terms with Chinese Buddhism*, 4–10; Cheung, *An Anthology of Chinese Discourse on Translation*, 1: 66–7, 95–9, 123–4, 130–5, 159–61; Miao Ri, "Dao'an geyi fojiao sixiang shuping"; and Chi Yi Chu, "Chinese Translation of Buddhist Terminology: Language and Culture." Victor Mair has recently raised doubts about the pertinence of the term: see "What Is *Geyi*, After All?" In the following I shall use "geyi" to designate the term, and *geyi* to designate the practices supposed to be its referent, but will not alter Roman-letter quoted texts to reflect this distinction.
37. T'ang Yung-t'ung [= Tang Yongtong], "On 'Ko-yi,' " 276.
38. Mair, "What Is Geyi," 231.
39. Chen Yinke, "Zhi Mindu xueshuo kao," *Chen Yinke xiansheng lunji*, 431.
40. Chen, "Zhi Mindu xueshuo kao," 433.
41. Tang Yongtong, "On 'Ko-yi,' " 276–9. I have changed the romanization.
42. Ge Zhaoguang, *An Intellectual History of China*, 1: 327–8.
43. Mair, "What is Geyi," 260.
44. Ibid., 227.
45. Ibid., 227, 233. Earlier scholars have also held that the term "geyi" refers to the coordination of numbered lists: see substantive discussions in Zürcher, *The Buddhist Conquest of China*, 184, and Robinson, *Early Mādhyamika in India and China*, 254.
46. Mair, "What is Geyi," 241–3.
47. Ibid., 243–7.
48. Cf. Zürcher, *The Buddhist Conquest of China*, 184: "the practice which is commonly supposed to be *geyi*, viz., the presentation of Buddhist ideas in terms of *Laozi, Zhuangzi*, and the *Yijing*, is abundantly attested not only in Dao'an's later works, but also in those of Huirui and other members of Kumārajīva's school. We can hardly assume that these authors did not know what they were talking about…"
49. Mair, "What is Geyi," 243.

50. On the early masters of the Daoist religion and their emulation of Buddhist precedents, see Zürcher, "Buddhist Influence on Early Daoism: A Survey of Scriptural Evidence," *Buddhism in China*, 105–64.

51. Mair, "What is Geyi," 250–1.

52. Thus Hu Shi responded positively to Chen's analysis of *geyi* on receiving a draft of the 1933 publication: see Hu, letter of August 20, 1931, cited in Bian Senghui, ed., *Chen Yinke xiansheng nianpu changbian*, 138. On Chen Yinke's response to May Fourth cultural polemics, see Q. Edward Wang, *Inventing China Through History*, 190–4.

53. On these conditions, see Étienne Balazs, "Entre révolte nihiliste et évasion mystique"; Mou Zongsan, *Wei-Jin xuanxue*; Liu Guijie, *Zhi Daolin sixiang zhi yanjiu*; Zhou Shaoxian, *Wei-Jin qingtan shulun*; Mark Edward Lewis, *China Between Empires*.

54. Fan Xuan, a specialist in the Confucian *Records of Ritual*, had retired from the world to study in peace. See Zürcher, *The Buddhist Conquest of China*, 403.

55. I have altered these two sentences from Zürcher's rendering. Zürcher has it that Huiyuan "once attended a sermon" by Dao'an where a guest raised objections, but this deprives the mention of Huiyuan's age (and the particle 便) of any pertinence. *Shixiang* 實相, glossed by Zürcher as "transcendent truth" and by Mair (235) as "ultimate reality," has not been traced back to a Sanskrit corresponding term. It occurs frequently in Dao'an's and Kumārajīva's writings. Nor is it known to which *Zhuangzi* passage Huiyuan correlated it. Two likely passages are in chapters 1 ("A name is the guest of a reality" 名者，實之賓也, *Zhuangzi jishi*, 24) and 18 ("The former sages...limited names by the corresponding realities, established meanings by their suitability" 先聖...名止於實，義設於適, ibid., 621–2).

56. Huijiao, *Gaoseng zhuan*, 211–12; translation from Zürcher, *The Buddhist Conquest of China*, 240–1, with slight changes (mostly for the sake of greater literalness).

57. Zürcher, *The Buddhist Conquest of China*, 114.

58. On this commentary-literature, see Chen Yinke, "Xiaoyao you Guo Xiang yi ji Zhi Dun yi tanyuan" 逍遙遊郭象義及支遁義探源 (An Enquiry into the Origins of the Meanings Guo Xiang and Zhi Dun Ascribed to "Xiaoyao you"), *Chen Yinke xiansheng wenshi lunji*, 195–200; Livia Knaul, "Kuo Hsiang and the *Chuang Tzu*"; Rudolf Wagner, *The Craft of a Chinese Commentator* and *A Chinese Reading of the Daodejing*; Brook Ziporyn, *Zhuangzi: The Essential Writings*, ix–xi, and *The Penumbra Unbound*; and Richard John Lynn, "The Influence of Guo Xiang's Commentary to the *Zhuangzi*."

59. *Gaoseng zhuan* 6, cited in Chen Yinque, "Zhi Mindu xueshuo kao," 432–3. The passage is also cited by Mair, who adds that the use of the passage to support the assertion "that *geyi* was a technique used by Buddhists for borrowing from Daoism is completely fallacious" (235–6).

60. Huijiao, *Gaoseng zhuan*, 194–5. Some editions give the older monk's name as Sengguang 僧光; I follow Tang's edition. "The Shi clan's disorder" here refers to the twenty-odd years of civil war beginning in the 320s, not the later episode that blocked Huiyuan from going to the South.

61. See chapter 3 for this gloss. It seems likely that the anecdote originally showed the inconsequentiality of "small" things by contrasting them to "great" ones (thus Zhuangzi's picayune opponents are likened to chittering sparrows). In a second move, commentators in the era of Wang Bi and Guo Xiang relativized this relativism, denying that the difference between small and great was consequential and thereby "out-Zhuangzi-ing" Zhuangzi. See also the parable of the frog in the well and the turtle of the Eastern Sea in *Zhuangzi*, chapter 17 (Guo Qingfan, *Zhuangzi jishi*, 597–603). On the competitive relativism of the *Zhuangzi* commentators, see further in chapter 5.

62. Zhi Mindu, Dao'an's contemporary, called this practice *heben* 合本, "collating the editions." The primary purpose was establishing a reliable text by determining the filiation of "mother" texts and "child" texts. See Zürcher, *The Buddhist Conquest of China*, 99–100. The pairing of *geyi* and *heben*, like the foregrounding of "geyi," derives from Chen Yinke's inaugural essay, part 5 of which gives a description of the two practices. Chen finds the technical term "child" first occurring in a prefatory remark to the *Weimichijing* 微密持經 translated by Zhi Qian (T 1011; remark in T 2145). Zhi Mindu's great literary achievement was the compilation of the bibliography *Jinglun dulu*, as Dao'an's was the compilation of the *Zongli zhongjing mulu*. But the two

contemporaries seem never to have met. Chen adds that for his discovery of the *heben* method, Zhi Mindu deserves to be recognized as the forerunner of modern comparative linguistics. On *heben* vs. *geyi*, see Miao Ri, "Dao'an geyi fojiao sixiang shuping"; Liu Jingguo, "*Ge-yi* in Buddhist Scripture Translations"; and for a different perspective on the meaning of the term "heben," see Gao Mingdao, "Cong 'huiyi' tanqi 'heben.'"

63. On transculturation, see Fernando Ortiz, *Cuban Counterpoint: Tobacco and Sugar.*

64. Priority in discovering the truth common to Buddhism and other teachings was a matter of controversy. A theory flattering to Chinese national pride posited Confucius, Laozi, and Zhuangzi as originators of Buddhism; but Buddhists could also claim those Chinese worthies as "disciples or manifestations of the Buddha, sent to or evoked in the East in order to convert the Chinese" (Zürcher, *The Buddhist Conquest of China*, 280). On the ensuing debates, see Livia Kohn, *Laughing at the Dao*, 77–80, 101–5, 163, 166.

65. Susan Leigh Star and James R. Griesemer, "Institutional Ecology, 'Translations,' and Boundary Objects," 393.

66. Liu Yiqing (403–44), comp., *Shishuo xinyu*, 179. See the translation by Richard B. Mather, *A New Account of Tales of the World*, 402.

67. *Zhuangzi jishi*, 1063.

68. Confucius, as reported in the *Book of Rites*: "Tan gong," part 1, *Li ji zhengyi*, chapter 3, in Ruan Yuan, ed., *Shisanjing zhushu*, 8/5b–6a.

69. Sigmund Freud, *Jokes and Their Relation to the Unconscious* (1905), 120. Roman Jakobson's view that puns or sound–sense linkages, as a defining property of poetry, prove that poetry cannot be translated but only creatively transposed ("On Linguistic Aspects of Translation," *Language in Literature*, 434), assumes the narrow definition of "translation proper" as occurring between two languages. If languages are porous, however, the difference between translation and transposition fades, as I think it should. On puns as the nucleus of a literary genre often assimilated to extended metaphor, see Maureen Quilligan, *The Language of Allegory: Defining the Genre.*

70. On this recurrent point of friction, see Zürcher, *The Buddhist Conquest of China*, 106–8, 231–2.

71. *The Book of Poetry*, ode 205, "Bei shan": *Mao Shi zhengyi* in Ruan Yuan, ed., *Shisanjing shuzhu*, 13: 1/19b; abundantly cited in *Xunzi*, *Mengzi*, *Lüshi chunqiu*, and other early doctrinal texts.

72. Zürcher, *The Buddhist Conquest of China*, 231–6. Huiyuan's response is translated and discussed in Hurvitz, "'Render Unto Caesar'"; Zürcher, *The Buddhist Conquest of China*, 238–9, 251–2, 258–64, 310; Robinson, *Early Mādhyamika*, 102–3, 196–9.

73. Huiyuan, "Shamen bujing wangzhe lun," 30b, in Sengyou, ed., *Hongming ji* 宏明集 (T 2102), chapter 5: *Taishō shinshū daizōkyō*, 52: 29–32. On "effacing one's traces," see *Zhuangzi*, chapter 4; on those "who wander outside the bounds," see chapter 6 (*Zhuangzi jishi*, 150, 267) and page 53.

74. This transliteration is common to several Eastern and Western Jin sutra-translations, e.g. T5, T6, T144.

75. Huiyuan, "Shamen bujing wangzhe lun," 31a.

76. Ibid., 31b, 30c.

77. Huiyuan, "Shamen bujing wangzhe lun," 31a; cf. Hurvitz, "'Render unto Caesar,'" 105–6.

78. Huiyuan, "Shamen bujing wangzhe lun," 31b; cf. Hurvitz, "'Render unto Caesar,'" 106–7.

79. Huiyuan, "Shamen bujing wangzhe lun," 31b; cf. Hurvitz's translation, 107. The *Zhuangzi* quotation, truncated and garbled, is from chapter 22, "Zhi bei you" (*Zhuangzi jishi*, 733). I translate the garbled wording rather than correct it. If corrected, the passage would read: "Life is the follower of death; death is the beginning of life, and who knows their connecting thread? Human life is a gathering of vital breaths: when they gather, there is life; when they disperse there is death. If life and death are followers [of each other], why should I be anxious about them?" The Guo Xiang commentary adds: "Anxiety is born from [the mistaken perception of] difference."

80. I.e. karmic attributes, the residues of actions performed over one's lifetime; but Huiyuan uses a term that is not exclusive to Buddhist teaching.

81. Huiyuan, "Shamen bujing wangzhe lun," 31c; cf. Hurvitz, "'Render unto Caesar,'" 109–11.

82. Huiyuan, "Shamen bujing wangzhe lun," 32a; cf. Hurvitz, "'Render unto Caesar,'" 112. For "carriages and clothing," symbols of imperial reward, see Ban Gu, *Hou Han shu*, chapters 39–40.

"Peoples of ninefold translation" were foreigners so distant from China that a relay of nine translators (each one shunting a message between two languages) was needed to communicate with them.

83. For *shengdian*, in the dominant sense of "Confucian classics," see *Qian fu lun*, 1: 7, *Lunheng*, 85: 5, *Hou Han shu*, chapter 30 (biography of the scholar Chen Yuan 陳元). On Buddhist instances of the "wood and fire" simile, see Robinson, *Early Mādhyamika*, 278.

84. *Zhuangzi jishi*, 242, repeated on 262. I italicize the phrases emphasized in Huiyuan's essay.

85. *Zhuangzi jishi*, 243–4. The phrase 萬化而未始有極 also appears in chapter 21, "Tian Zifang," *Zhuangzi jishi*, 714, in a passage denigrating honors.

86. Chapter 6, "Da zong shi," *Zhuangzi jishi*, 258.

87. Ibid., 266. It is possible that the copy Huiyuan read from had 鞊 in place of 猗: this would account for his attributing to Zhuangzi the otherwise broadly plausible view that "human life is a bridle."

88. Chapter 23, "Gengsang Chu," *Zhuangzi jishi*, 802.

89. Chapter 2, "Qi wu lun," *Zhuangzi jishi*, 66.

90. Chapter 33, "Tianxia," *Zhuangzi jishi*, 1102.

91. *Zhuangzi jishi*, 1112, emphasizing here Huiyuan's key phrases.

92. Ibid., 129.

93. Ibid., 130. See also Brook Ziporyn, *Zhuangzi: The Essential Writings*, 169–71, for the continuation of Guo Xiang's reasoning and several other explanations. The Guo Xiang interpretation is indebted to Wang Bi's exegesis of the phrase from the *Book of Changes* to the effect that "that which gives life to life we call change" 生生之謂易 (*Zhou Yi zhengyi*, "Xi ci," in Ruan Yuan, ed., *Shisanjing zhushu*, 7/13b). Some modern interpreters replace "fingers" (*zhi* 指) with "fat" or "resin" (*zhi* 脂).

94. Bloom, *Anxiety of Influence*, 66.

95. Burton Watson, tr., *The Complete Works of Chuang Tzu*, 85, 84; *Zhuangzi jishi*, 261, 260. I have conflated two passages and reversed their order.

96. I.e. the "gross and elementary heresy" of *ātmavāda*: see Robinson, *Early Mādhyamika*, 101–8.

Chapter 5

1. For general or partial histories of translation in China, see Luo Xinzhang, *Fanyi lunji*; Martha Cheung, *An Anthology of Chinese Discourse on Translation*; Chan Sin-wai and David Pollard, eds., *An Encyclopedia of Translation*; Harbsmeier, "Early Chinese Buddhist Translators On Translation"; Denis Twitchett and Herbert Franke, "Introduction," *The Cambridge History of China*, 6: 30–6; Lackner, Amelung, and Kurtz, eds., *New Terms for New Ideas*; Leo Tak-hung Chan, *Twentieth-Century Chinese Translation Theory*.

2. Lewis and Short, *A New Latin Dictionary*, s.v. "sponsor": "one who becomes answerable for another." The archaic Roman rite of promising required one party to ask the other, "spondes?" and the other to reply, "spondeo" (meaning roughly: "I answer for it"). On the linguistic background, see Benveniste, *Le Vocabulaire des institutions indo-européennes*, 2: 214–15.

3. Thomas Cranmer et al., *The Book of Common Prayer*, 327.

4. On the formula "dari spondes? Spondeo," see Gaius, *Institutiones*, III, par. 92, in Mears, ed., *The Institutes of Gaius and Justinian*, 157.

5. *Zhuangzi*, chapter 1, "Xiaoyao you"; *Zhuangzi jishi*, 31.

6. According to *Analects* 11.26: *Lunyu zhushu*, in Ruan Yuan, ed., *Shisanjing zhushu*, 11/10b.

7. *Zhuangzi jishi*, 28–31. Zhuangzi's designation of "True Man" (with its fellows, "Ultimate Man" and "spirit-man") was one of the first terms to be appropriated for Buddhist teaching, there applied to the Buddha and to followers of the Buddhist Way: see e.g. Zhi Qian 支謙, tr., *Fo shuo zhai jing* 佛說齋經 (The Sutra on Fasting, Pronounced by the Buddha), T 87 (1: 910c–912a); Zhi Loujiaqian 支婁迦讖, tr., *Za piyu jing* 雜譬喻經 (The Sutra of Diverse Similes), T 204 (4: 499b–502a).

8. For "transvaluation" ("Entwertung aller Werte"), see Friedrich Nietzsche, *Ecce Homo*, "Warum ich ein Schicksal bin," part 1 (*Kritische Studienausgabe*, 6: 365). On the meeting of Nietzsche and

Zhuangzi in the work of the translator Richard Wilhelm, see Helen Huiwen Zhang, "Die Begegnung des chinesischen *Sonderlings* mit dem deutschen Übermenschen" and "Übertragung als Prophezeiung und Inszenierung."

9. *Zhuangzi jishi*, 271; translation from Mair, tr., *Wandering on the Way*, 61. On these fables, see Romain Graziani, *Fictions philosophiques du Tchouang-tseu*.

10. Liu Yiqing, *Shishuo xinyu*. For an analysis and an appreciation of "the Wei-Jin spirit" as per-petuated in succeeding ages, see Nanxiu Qian, *Spirit and Self in Medieval China*. On *qingtan*, see Zhou Shaoxian, *Wei-Jin qingtan shulun*. On *xuanxue*, see Mou Zongsan, *Wei-Jin xuanxue*.

11. Li Ziming, cited in Yu Jiaxi, ed., *Shishuo xinyu* 1: 125–6, as quoted and translated in Qian Nanxiu, *Spirit and Self*, 58.

12. Oscar Wilde, "A Chinese Sage" (1890), 537, 529.

13. A. C. Graham, "How Much of *Chuang-tzu* Did Chuang-tzu Write?"; reprinted as 283–321 of Graham, *Studies in Chinese Philosophy and Philosophical Literature*.

14. Harold D. Roth, "*Chuang tzu*," 56. This essay provides a survey of available editions and of the-ories on the work's composition. In "Who Compiled the *Chuang-tzu*?," 114–23, Roth further conjectures that the earliest version of the *Zhuangzi* must have taken shape at the court of Liu An *c*.130 BCE.

15. See among other valuable works Victor Mair, ed., *Experimental Essays on Chuang-tzu*; Robert E. Allinson, *Chuang-tzu for Spiritual Transformation*; Paul Kjellberg and Philip J. Ivanhoe, *Essays on Skepticism, Relativism, and Ethics in the Zhuangzi*.

16. See Xu Weiyu, ed., *Lüshi chunqiu jishi*, 14/34b–35b; *Xunzi jijie*, 262; Liu Wendian, ed., *Huainan honglie jijie*, 391, 404, 654. In the chapter "Daoying xun" (Artful Responses) a remark from Zhuangzi is cited as the final verdict on an anecdote, a role elsewhere performed only by quota-tions from the *Laozi* (*Huainan honglie jijie*, 410; see also John S. Major et al., trans., *The Huainanzi*, 472). On the transformation of *Zhuangzi* passages in the course of their integration into the *Huainanzi*, see Michael Puett, "Violent Misreadings."

17. Sima Qian's references are to chapters later classed as "Outer" and "Miscellaneous." See Brooks, "Jwangdz Editions" and "The Disunity of the Jwangdz 'Inner' Chapters"; Lynn, "Reexamination of the Biography of Master Zhuang in the *Shiji* (Records of the Historian)."

18. Sima Qian, *Shiji*, 2143. Lao Er is Laozi.

19. It is uncertain whether the quoted phrases refer to imaginary persons or chapters of a non-historical import.

20. Sima Qian, *Shiji*, 2143–6.

21. Ibid., 2156.

22. See for example Dong Zhongshu, *Chunqiu fanlu* 27: 1; *Han Feizi* 8.5; *Huainan zi* 9.20, 23; and especially the closing anecdote of chapter 49 ("The Hereditary Houses of the Imperial Consorts") in Sima Qian, *Shiji*, 1986.

23. See the similar analysis in terms of Marxist historical materialism in Ren Jiyu, *Zhongguo zhexue shi*, 1: 153–67: "Zhuangzi's Idealism and Relativism." Zhuangzi is there described as a decadent *déclassé* aristocrat who can find consolation for his loss of status only in aesthetic detachment from the world of real action. I somewhat suspect that the individual biography in both Sima Qian and such narratives as Ren Jiyu's has been constructed in order to mask the existence of a whole tribe of Zhuangzis, exerting their skeptical reasoning and disorienting examples to throw the ordered world into confusion.

24. Zhuangzi as "individualist" is a chestnut of histories of Chinese philosophy.

25. Gao You, cited in Xu Weiyu, ed., *Lüshi chunqiu jishi*, 14/34b–35a.

26. Sima Qian, *Shiji*, 3285, 3292.

27. For materials and discussion relevant to these theories, see Randall P. Peerenboom, *Law and Morality in Ancient China*.

28. On the composition of *Huainanzi*, see Charles Le Blanc, "Huai Nan Tzu," 189–95 in Loewe, ed., *Early Chinese Texts*; Harold Roth, *The Textual History of the Huai-nan Tzu*.

29. Sima Qian, *Shiji*, 3292.

30. *Zhuangzi jishi*, 667; see for example chapter 1, ibid., 39.

BIBLIOGRAPHY

Agacinski, Sylviane. "Le tout premier écart." 117–32 in Philippe Lacoue-Labarthe and Jean-Luc Nancy, eds., *Les fins de l'homme: à partir du travail de Jacques Derrida*. Paris: Galilée, 1981.

Allinson, Robert E. *Chuang-tzu for Spiritual Transformation: An Analysis of the Inner Chapters*. Albany: State University of New York Press, 1989.

App, Urs. "Arthur Schopenhauer and China: A Sino-Platonic Love Affair." *Sino-Platonic Papers* 200 (2010).

Apter, Emily. *The Translation Zone: A New Comparative Literature*. Princeton: Princeton University Press, 2006.

Apter, Emily. *Against World Literature: On the Politics of Untranslatability*. London: Verso, 2013.

Asad, Talal. "The Concept of Cultural Translation in British Social Anthropology." 141–64 in James Clifford and George F. Marcus, eds., *Writing Culture: The Poetics and Politics of Ethnography*. Berkeley: University of California Press, 1986.

Auerbach, Erich. *Scenes from the Drama of European Literature*. Gloucester, MA: Peter Smith, 1973.

Balazs, Étienne. "Entre révolte nihiliste et évasion mystique: les courants intellectuels en Chine au IIIe siècle de notre ère." *Asiatische Studien* 2 (1948): 27–55.

Barnes, Jonathan, ed. *The Complete Works of Aristotle*. 2 vols. Princeton: Princeton University Press, 1985.

Bartsch, Shadi. "Roman Literature: Translation, Metaphor and Empire." *Daedalus* 145 (2016): 30–9.

Bassnett, Susan. *Comparative Literature: A Critical Introduction*. Oxford: Blackwell, 1993.

Baudelaire, Charles. *Œuvres complètes*. 2 vols. Ed. Claude Pichois. Paris: Gallimard, 1975.

Beecroft, Alexander. "When Cosmopolitanisms Intersect: An Early Chinese Buddhist Apologetic and World Literature." *Comparative Literature Studies* 47 (2010): 266–89.

Benjamin, Walter. *Gesammelte Schriften.* Ed. Rolf Tiedemann and Hermann Schweppenhäuser. 12 vols. Frankfurt am Main: Suhrkamp, 1980.

Benveniste, Émile. *Le Vocabulaire des institutions indo-européennes.* 2 vols. Paris: Minuit, 1969.

Berman, Antoine. *L'épreuve de l'étranger.* Paris: Gallimard, 1984.

Berman, Antoine. *Pour une critique des traductions: John Donne.* Paris: Gallimard, 1995.

Berman, Antoine. *La traduction et la lettre ou l'auberge du lointain.* Paris: Seuil, 1999.

Bermann, Sandra, and Michael Wood, eds. *Nation, Language, and the Ethics of Translation.* Princeton: Princeton University Press, 2005.

Bhabha, Homi K. *The Location of Culture.* London: Routledge, 1994.

Bian Senghui 卞僧慧. *Chen Yinke xiansheng nianpu changbian* 陳寅恪先生年譜長編 (A Chronological Biography of Chen Yinke). Beijing: Zhonghua shuju, 2010.

Billeter, Jean François. *Trois essais sur la traduction.* Paris: Allia, 2014.

Birnbaum, Jean. "Étienne Balibar: 'L'universel ne rassemble pas, il divise.'" *Le Monde,* Idées, February 9, 2017.

Bloom, Harold. *The Anxiety of Influence: A Theory of Poetry.* New York: Oxford University Press, 1973.

Bokenkamp, Stephen. *Early Daoist Scriptures.* Berkeley: University of California Press, 1999.

Boucher, Daniel. "Dharmaraksa and the Transmission of Buddhism to China." *Asia Major,* third series, 19 (2006): 13–37.

Brokaw, Cynthia. *The Ledgers of Merit and Demerit: Social Change and Moral Order in Late Imperial China.* Princeton: Princeton University Press, 1991.

Brook, Timothy. "The Early Jesuits and the Late-Ming Border." 19–38 in Xiaoxin Wu, ed., *Encounters and Dialogues: Changing Perspectives on Chinese-Western Exchanges from the Sixteenth to the Eighteenth Centuries.* Sankt Augustin: Monumenta Serica, 2005.

Brooks, Cleanth, and Robert Penn Warren, eds. *Conversations on the Craft of Poetry.* New York: Holt, Rinehart, Winston, 1959.

Brooks, E. Bruce. "The Disunity of the Jwangdz 'Inner' Chapters." *Warring States Papers* 3. E-publication, 2012.

Brooks, E. Bruce. "Jwangdz Editions." *Warring States Papers* 3. E-publication, 2012.

Brower, Reuben A., ed. *On Translation.* Cambridge, MA: Harvard University Press, 1959.

Brown, Peter. *The Making of Late Antiquity.* Cambridge, MA: Harvard University Press, 1968.

Buden, Boris, Stefan Nowotny, Sherry Simon, Ashok Bery, and Michael Cronin. "Cultural Translation: An Introduction to the Problem," with "Responses." *Translation Studies* 2 (2009): 196–219.

Burke, Kenneth. *Perspectives by Incongruity.* Ed. Stanley Edgar Hyman. Bloomington: Indiana University Press, 1964.

Busch, Heinrich. "The Tung-lin Academy and Its Political and Philosophical Significance." *Monumenta Serica* 14 (1955): 1–163.

Buswell, Robert E., Jr. *The Formation of Ch'an Ideology in China and Korea: The Vajrasamâdhi-Sûtra, A Buddhist Apocryphon*. Princeton: Princeton University Press, 1989.

Buswell, Robert E., Jr., and Donald S. Lopez, Jr., eds. *The Princeton Dictionary of Buddhism*. Princeton: Princeton University Press, 2014.

Cai Zhengfeng 蔡振豐. "Dao'an jingxu sixiang de zhuanzhe ji zai geyi wentishang de yiyi" 道安經序思想的轉折及在格義問題上的意義. *Taiwan daxue wenshizhe xuebao* 48 (1998): 251–92.

Cao Xueqin 曹雪芹 and Gao E 高鶚. *Honglou meng* 紅樓夢 (Dream of the Red Chamber). 3 vols. Beijing: Renmin wenxue, 1985.

Cassin, Barbara, ed. *Vocabulaire européen des philosophies: Dictionnaire des intraduisibles*. Paris: Seuil, 2004.

Cassin, Barbara, ed. *Dictionary of Untranslatables: A Philosophical Lexicon*. Tr. Steven Rendall, Christian Hubert, Jeffrey Mehlman, Nathaneal Stein, and Michael Syrotinski; translation edited by Emily Apter, Jacques Lezra, and Michael Wood. Princeton: Princeton University Press, 2014.

Castells, Manuel. *The Rise of the Network Society*. Oxford: Oxford University Press, 1996.

Chakrabarty, Dipesh. *Provincializing Europe: Postcolonial Thought and Historical Difference*. Princeton: Princeton University Press, 2000.

Chan, Leo Tak-hung. "What's Modern in Chinese Translation Theory? Lu Xun and the Debates on Literalism and Foreignization in the May Fourth Period." *TTR: traduction, terminologie, rédaction* 14 (2001): 195–223.

Chan, Leo Tak-hung, ed. *Twentieth-Century Chinese Translation Theory: Modes, Issues and Debates*. (Benjamins Translation Library, 51.) Amsterdam: Benjamins, 2004.

Chan Sin-wai and David Pollard, eds. *An Encyclopedia of Translation: Chinese-English, English-Chinese*. Hong Kong: Hong Kong University Press, 1995.

Chao Yuen Ren. "Interlingual and Interdialectal Borrowings in Chinese." 39–51 in Roman Jakobson and Shigeo Kawamoto, eds., *Studies in General and Oriental Linguistics Presented to Shirô Hattori on the Occasion of his Sixtieth Birthday*. Tokyo: TEC Company, 1970.

Chater, Nick, Alexander Clark, John A. Goldsmith, and Amy Perfors. *Empiricism and Language Learnability*. Oxford: Oxford University Press, 2015.

Chen Tixian 陳悌賢. "Wei-Jin-Nanbeichao fojiao de chuanbo yu quxiang" 魏晉南北朝的佛教傳播與趨向 (The Transmission and Tendencies of Buddhism in the Wei, Jin, and Nanbeichao Periods). 115–36 in Zhang Mantao, ed., *Zhongguo fojiaoshi zhuanji, 1: Han Wei liang Jin Nanbeichao pian*. Taipei: Dacheng wenhua chubanshe, 1978.

Chen, Xiang. "Thomas Kuhn's Latest Notion of Incommensurability." *Journal for General Philosophy of Science* 28 (1997): 257–73.

Chen Yinke (or Yinque). "Zhi Mindu xueshuo kao" 支愍度學說考 (An Examination of Zhi Mindu's Theories). *Qingzhu Cai Yuanpei xiansheng liushiwusui lunwenji*, 1–18; subsequently republished as 1: 273–300 in *Chen Yinke xiansheng wenshi lunji* (Hong Kong: Wenwen chubanshe, 1972–73); 426–43 in *Chen Yinke xiansheng lunji* (Taipei:

Zhongyang yanjiu yuan lishi yuyan yanjiu suo, 1977); 2: 1229–54 in *Chen Yinke xiansheng quanji* (Taipei. Jiusi chubanshe, 1977); 1: 141–67 in *Chen Yinke xiansheng wenji* (Taipei: Liren chubanshe, 1981).

Chen Yinke (or Yinque) 陳寅恪. *Chen Yinke xiansheng wenshi lunji* 陳寅恪先生文史論集 (Essays on Literature and History by Chen Yinke). 2 vols. Hong Kong: Wenwen chubanshe, 1972–73.

Chen Yinke (or Yinque). *Chen Yinke xiansheng lunji* 陳寅恪先生論集 (A Collection of Chen Yinke's Essays). (Zhongyang yanjiu yuan lishi yuyan yanjiu suo te kan, 3.) Taipei: Zhongyang yanjiu yuan lishi yuyan yanjiu suo, 1977.

Chen Yinke (or Yinque). *Chen Yinke xiansheng quanji* 陳寅恪先生全集 (The Complete Writings of Chen Yinke). Ed. Yu Dawei 俞大維. 2 vols. Taipei: Jiusi chubanshe, 1977.

Chen Yinke (or Yinque). *Chen Yinke xiansheng wenji* 陳寅恪先生文集 (The Writings of Chen Yinke). Ed. Yu Dawei 俞大維. 2 vols. Taipei: Liren chubanshe, 1981.

Chen Yinke (or Yinque). *Wei Jin Nanbeichao shi jiangyanlu* 魏晉南北朝史講演錄 (Lectures on the History of the Wei, Jin, and Nanbeichao Periods). Ed. Wan Shengnan 萬繩楠. Hefei: Huangshan shushe, 1987.

Chen Yinke (or Yinque). "Qingtan wuguo (fu 'geyi')" 清談誤國 (附'格義'). 49–72 in Wan Shengnan 萬繩楠, ed., *Chen Yinke Wei Jin Nanbeichao shi jiangyan lu* 陳寅恪魏晉南北朝史講演錄 (Lectures on the History of the Wei, Jin, and Nanbeichao Periods). Taipei: Zhishufang chubanshe, 1995.

Chen Yinke (or Yinque). *Jiangyi ji zagao* 講義及雜稿 (Lectures and Manuscripts). (*Chen Yinke ji* 陳寅恪集, vol. 14.) Beijing: Sanlian, 2001.

Cheung, Martha P. Y., ed. *An Anthology of Chinese Discourse on Translation, Volume One: From Earliest Times to the Buddhist Project.* Manchester, UK: St. Jerome Publishing, 2006.

Cheung, Martha P. Y., comp.; Robert Neather, ed. *An Anthology of Chinese Discourse on Translation, Volume Two: From the Late Twelfth Century to 1800.* London: Routledge, 2014.

Chinese Buddhist Electronic Text Association. *CBETA dianzi fodian jicheng kuapingtai banben* CBETA 電子佛典集成跨平台版本. Taipei: CBETA, 2011. Electronic resource.

Chow, Kai-wing. *Publishing, Culture, and Power in Early Modern China.* Stanford: Stanford University Press, 2004.

Chu, Chi Yi. "Chinese Translation of Buddhist Terminology: Language and Culture." 39–51 in Luo Xuanmin and He Yuanjian, eds. *Translating China.* Bristol: Multilingual Matters, 2009.

[Cranmer, Thomas, et al.] *The Book of Common Prayer.* Oxford: Oxford University Press, 1969.

d'Elia, Pasquale M., SJ. *Il Mappamondo cinese del P. Matteo Ricci.* Rome: Biblioteca apostolica vaticana, 1938.

d'Elia, Pasquale M., SJ, ed. *Fonti Ricciane.* 3 vols. Rome: Libreria dello Stato, 1942–9.

d'Elia, Pasquale M., SJ. "Sunto poetico-ritmico di *I dieci paradossi* di Matteo Ricci S. I." *Rivista degli studi orientali* 27 (1952): 111–38.

d'Elia, Pasquale M., SJ. "Recent Discoveries and New Studies (1938-1960) on the World Map in Chinese of Father Matteo Ricci S.J." *Monumenta Serica* 20 (1961): 82–164.

d'Hulst, Lieven. "Comparative Literature versus Translation Studies: Close Encounters of the Third Kind?" *European Review* 15 (2007): 95–104.

Dante Alighieri. *Opere minori*. Eds. Cesare Vascoli and Domenico de Robertis. 2 vols. Milan: Riccordi, 1979.

Dante Alighieri. *The Divine Comedy*. Tr. and comm. Charles S. Singleton. 3 vols. Princeton: Princeton University Press, 1982.

Denton, Kirk A., ed. *Modern Chinese Literary Thought: Writings on Literature, 1893–1945*. Stanford: Stanford University Press, 1996.

Denton, Kirk A., and Michel Hockx, eds. *Literary Societies of Republican China*. Lanham: Rowan and Littlefield, 2008.

Derrida, Jacques. *Le monolinguisme de l'autre*. Paris: Galilée, 1996.

Derrida, Jacques. "Qu'est-ce qu'une traduction 'relevante'?" 21–48 in *Quinzièmes Assises de la traduction littéraire*. Arles: Actes Sud, 1999.

Derrida, Jacques. "La vérité blessante" (interview with Evelyne Grossman). *Europe* 901 (2004): 8–28.

Durling, Robert M. "Deceit and Digestion in the Belly of Hell." 61–93 in Stephen Greenblatt, ed., *Allegory and Representation*. Baltimore: Johns Hopkins University Press, 1986.

Elman, Benjamin A. *A Cultural History of Examinations in Late Imperial China*. Berkeley: University of California Press, 2000.

Encyclopedia Britannica. Eleventh edition. Cambridge, UK: Cambridge University Press, 1911.

Ershiwu shi 二十五史 (The Twenty-Five Dynastic Histories). 12 vols. Shanghai: Guji, 1991.

Even-Zohar, Itamar. "The Position of Translated Literature Within the Literary Polysystem." 45–51 in Itamar Even-Zohar, *Polysystem Studies*. Tel Aviv: Porter Institute for Poetics and Semiotics, 1990.

Even-Zohar, Itamar, and Gideon Toury, eds. *Theory of Translation and Intercultural Relations*. Tel Aviv: Porter Institute for Poetics and Semiotics, 1981.

Fabian, Johannes. "The Other Revisited: Critical Afterthoughts." *Anthropological Theory* 6 (2006): 139–52.

Fichte, Gottlob. *Der geschlossene Handelsstaat* (1800). Tr. Anthony Curtis Adler as *The Closed Commercial State*. Albany: State University of New York, 2012.

Forte, Antonino. *The Hostage An Shigao and His Offspring: An Iranian Family in China*. Kyoto: Istituto italiano di cultura, 1995.

Freccero, John. *Dante: The Poetics of Conversion*. Cambridge, MA: Harvard University Press, 1986.

Freud, Sigmund. *Jokes and their Relation to the Unconscious.* James Strachey, chief ed., *The Standard Edition of the Complete Psychological Works of Sigmund Freud, vol. 8.* London: The Hogarth Press, 1962.

Fukunaga Mitsuji 福永光司. "No-Mind in *Chuang-tzu* and *Chan* Buddhism." Tr. Leon Hurvitz. *Zinbun* 12 (1969): 9–45.

Funayama Tōru. "Masquerading as Translation: Examples of Chinese Lectures by Indian Scholar-Monks in the Six Dynasties Period." *Asia Major,* third series, 19 (2006): 39–55.

Gallop, Jane. *Reading Lacan.* Ithaca: Cornell University Press, 1987.

Galvin, Rachel. "Poetry Is Theft." *Comparative Literature Studies* 51 (2014): 18–54.

Gamsa, Mark. *The Reading of Russian Literature in China.* New York: Palgrave, 2010.

Gao Mingdao 高明道 [Friedrich Grohmann]. "Cong 'huiyi' tanqi 'heben'" 從「會譯」談起「合本」 (Using "Huiyi" as a Starting Point to Discuss "Heben"). *Foguang* 320 (2016): 2–4.

Ge Zhaoguang 葛兆光. *An Intellectual History of China. Volume 1: Knowledge, Thought and Belief before the Seventh Century CE.* Tr. Michael S. Duke and Josephine Chiu-Duke. Leiden: Brill, 2014.

Genette, Gérard. *Palimpsestes.* Paris: Gallimard, 1982.

George, Stefan. *Werke.* 2 vols. Munich/Düsseldorf: Helmut Kupper, 1958.

Gernet, Jacques. *Chine et christianisme: action et réaction.* Paris: Gallimard, 1982. Tr. Janet Lloyd as *China and the Christian Impact.* Chicago: University of Chicago Press, 1985.

Goldsmith, John. "Unsupervised Learning of the Morphology of a Natural Language." *Computational Linguistics* 27 (2001): 153–98.

Graham, A. C. "How Much of *Chuang-tzu* Did Chuang-tzu Write?" *Journal of the American Academy of Religion* 47 (1980): 459–501.

Graham, A. C., tr. *Chuang-tzu: The Seven Inner Chapters and Other Writings from the Book Chuang-tzu.* London: Allen & Unwin, 1981.

Graham, A. C. *Studies in Chinese Philosophy and Philosophical Literature.* Albany: State University of New York Press, 1986.

Graziani, Romain. *Fictions philosophiques du Tchouang-tseu.* Paris: Gallimard, 2006.

Greenbaum, Jamie. *Chen Jiru (1558–1639): The Development and Subsequent Uses of Literary Personae.* Leiden: Brill, 2007.

Groupe μ. *Rhétorique générale.* Paris: Larousse, 1970.

Guo Qingfan 郭慶藩, ed. *Zhuangzi jishi* 莊子集釋 (*Zhuangzi* with Collected Commentaries). Reprint, Taipei: Lianjing, 1981.

Gupta, Prasenjit, tr. *Indian Errant: Selected Stories of Nirmal Verma.* New Delhi: Indialog Publications, 2002.

Hall, Robert A., Jr. *Pidgin and Creole Languages.* Ithaca: Cornell University Press, 1966.

Han Yu 韓愈. *Han Changli wenji jiaozhu* 韓昌黎文集校注 (The Writings of Han Yu, Collated and Annotated). Ed. Ma Tongbo 馬通伯. Hong Kong: Zhonghua shuju, 1972.

Harbsmeier, Christoph. "Early Chinese Buddhist Translators on Translation: A Brief Introduction with Textual Data." 259–73 in Émilie Aussant, ed., *La Traduction dans l'histoire des idées linguistiques: représentations et pratiques.* Paris: Geuthner, 2015.

Harshav, Benjamin. 2011. "Language: Multilingualism." *YIVO Encyclopedia of Jews in Eastern Europe*, available at http://www.yivoencyclopedia.org/article.aspx/Language/Multilingualism (accessed July 12, 2016).

Hayles, N. Katherine. *How We Became Posthuman: Virtual Bodies in Cybernetics, Literature, and Informatics*. Chicago: University of Chicago Press, 1999.

Heidegger, Martin. *An Introduction to Metaphysics*. Tr. Ralph Manheim. New Haven: Yale University Press, 1959.

Heidegger, Martin. *Unterwegs zur Sprache*. Pfullingen: Neske, 1959.

Heidegger, Martin. *On the Way to Language*. Tr. Peter D. Hertz. New York: Harper & Row, 1971.

Hill, Michael Gibbs. *Lin Shu, Inc.: Translation and the Making of Modern Chinese Culture*. New York: Oxford University Press, 2012.

Hockx, Michel. *Questions of Style: Literary Societies and Literary Journals in Modern China, 1911–1937*. Leiden: Brill, 2003.

Hsia, Ronnie Po-chia. *A Jesuit in the Forbidden City: Matteo Ricci, 1552–1610*. New York: Oxford University Press, 2010.

Hsu, Kai-yu, ed. *Twentieth-Century Chinese Poetry: An Anthology*. Garden City, NY: Doubleday, 1963.

Hu Shi 胡適 (Hu Shih). *The Chinese Renaissance: The Haskell Lectures, 1933*. Chicago: University of Chicago Press, 1934.

Hu Shi 胡適 (Hu Shih). "The Indianization of China: A Case Study in Cultural Borrowing." 219–47 in Harvard Tercentenary Conference of Arts and Sciences, ed., *Independence, Convergence and Borrowing in Institutions, Thought and Art*. Cambridge, MA: Harvard University Press, 1937.

Hu Shi 胡適 (Hu Shih). *Baihua wenxue shi* 白話文學史 (A History of Chinese Vernacular Literature). 2 vols. Taipei: Meiya, 1969.

Huainanzi: see Liu Wendian.

Huang Shijian 黃時鑒. *Li Madou shijie ditu yanjiu* 利瑪竇世界地圖研究 (A Study of Matteo Ricci's World Map). Shanghai: Shanghai guji, 2004.

Huelsenbeck, Richard, ed. *Dada Almanach*. Berlin: Reiss, 1920.

Huijiao 慧皎. *Gaoseng zhuan* 高僧傳 (Biographies of Eminent Monks). Ed. Tang Yongtong 湯用彤. Beijing: Zhonghua shuju, 1992.

Hurvitz, Leon. "'Render Unto Caesar' in Early Chinese Buddhism." 80–114 in Kshitis Roy, ed., *Liebenthal Festschrift*. Sino-Indian Studies, vol. 5. Santiniketan: Visvabharati, 1957.

Hurvitz, Leon. "Chih Tun's Notions of Prajñā." *Journal of the American Oriental Society* 88 (1968): 243–61.

Hurvitz, Leon N., and Arthur E. Link. "Three Prajñaparamita Prefaces of Tao-An." 405–49 in *Mélanges de Sinologie offerts à Monsieur Paul Demiéville*, vol. 2. Paris: Institut des Hautes Études Chinoises, 1974.

Inge, W. R., L. P. Jacks, M. Hiriyanna, E. A. Burtt, and P. T. Raju, eds. *Radhakrishnan: Comparative Studies in Philosophy Presented in Honor of His Sixtieth Birthday*. London: Allen & Unwin, 1968.

Jakobson, Roman. *Language in Literature*. Eds. Krystyna Pomorska and Stephen Rudy. Cambridge, MA: Harvard University Press, 1987.

James, Montague Rhodes, ed. *The Apocryphal New Testament*. Oxford: Oxford University Press, 1924.

Jeanneret, Michel. "The Renaissance and Its Ancients: Dismembering and Devouring." *MLN* 110 (1995): 1043–53.

Jensen, Lionel. *Manufacturing Confucianism*. Durham, NC: Duke University Press, 1997.

Jiang Tianshu 蔣天樞. *Chen Yinke xiansheng biannian shiji* 陳寅恪先生編年事輯 (A Year-by-Year Biography of Chen Yinke). Shanghai: Guji, 1981.

Jiao Hong 焦竑, ed. *Zhuangzi yi* 莊子翼. Preface dated 1588. Reprinted, Zhongguo zixue mingzhu jicheng series, 56. Taipei: Zhongguo zixue mingzhu jicheng bianyin jijinhui, 1977.

Johnson, Samuel. *Johnson's Dictionary: A Modern Selection*. Eds. E. L. McAdam, Jr. and George Milne. New York: Pantheon, 1963.

Jones, Andrew F. "Chinese Literature in the 'World' Literary Economy." *Modern Chinese Literature* 8 (1994): 171–90.

Jonson, Ben. *Timber, or Discoveries*. London: Dent, 1902.

Joyce, James. *Ulysse*. Tr. Auguste Morel, with the assistance of Stuart Gilbert, Valéry Larbaud, and the author. Paris: Gallimard, 1930.

Joyce, James. *Ulysses*. New York: Random House, 1961.

Karashima, Seishi. *A Critical Edition of Lokakṣema's Translation of the Aṣṭasāhasrikā Prajñāpāramitā*. Bibliotheca Philologica et Philosophica Buddhica, 12. Tokyo: International Research Institute for Advanced Buddhology—Soka University, 2011.

Kieschnick, John, and Meir Shahar. *India in the Chinese Imagination: Myth, Religion, and Thought*. Philadelphia: University of Pennsylvania Press, 2013.

Kjellberg, Paul, and Philip J. Ivanhoe, eds. *Essays on Skepticism, Relativism, and Ethics in the Zhuangzi*. Albany: State University of New York Press, 1996.

Knaul, Livia. (= Livia Kohn.) "Lost *Chuang-tzu* Passages." *Journal of Chinese Religions* 10 (1982): 53–79.

Knaul, Livia. "The Habit of Perfection—A Summary of Fukunaga Mitsuji's Studies on the *Chuang-tzu* Tradition." *Cahiers d'Extrême-Asie* 1 (1985): 71–85.

Knaul, Livia. "Kuo Hsiang and the *Chuang Tzu*." *Journal of Chinese Philosophy* 12 (1985): 429–47.

Knaul, Livia. "Chuang-tzu and the Chinese Ancestry of Ch'an Buddhism." *Journal of Chinese Philosophy* 13 (1986): 411–28.

Kohn, Livia. *Laughing at the Dao: Debates among Buddhists and Daoists in Medieval China*. Princeton: Princeton University Press, 1995.

Kristeva, Julia. Σημειωτικὴ: *recherches pour une sémanalyse*. Paris: Seuil, 1969.

Kurzweil, Ray. *The Age of Spiritual Machines*. New York: Penguin, 2000.

Lackner, Michael. "Circumnavigating the Unfamiliar: Dao'an (314–85) and Yan Fu (1852–1921) on Western Grammar." 357–70 in Michael Lackner, Iwo Amelung, and

Joachim Kurtz, eds., *New Terms for New Ideas: Western Knowledge and Lexical Change in Late Imperial China*. Leiden: Brill, 2001.

Lefkowitz, Mary R. *The Lives of the Greek Poets*. Second edition. Baltimore: Johns Hopkins University Press, 2012.

Legge, James, tr. *The Sacred Books of China. The Texts of Confucianism, Part I: The Shû King, The Religious Portions of the Shih King, The Hsiâo King*. Oxford: Clarendon Press, 1879.

Lewis, Charlton T., and Charles Short. *A New Latin Dictionary*. Oxford: Clarendon Press, 1882.

Lewis, Mark Edward. *China Between Empires: The Northern and Southern Dynasties*. Cambridge, MA: Harvard University Press, 2009.

Li Xiaoben 李孝本. "Fulu: Nanbei chao zhi fojiao (ziliao pian)" 附錄：南北朝之佛教 (資料篇) (Appendix: Buddhism in the Northern and Southern Dynasties [Materials]). 155–211 in Zhang Mantao, ed., *Zhongguo fojiaoshi zhuanji, 1: Han Wei liang Jin Nanbeichao pian*. Taipei: Dacheng wenhua chubanshe, 1978.

Li Xingling 李幸玲. "Geyi xintan" 格義新探. *Zhongguo xueshu niankan* 18 (1997): 127–57.

Li Zhi 李贄. *Fen shu, Xu fen shu* 焚書，續焚書 (A Book to Burn and Another Book to Burn). Beijing: Zhonghua shudian, 1975.

Li Zhi 李贄. *A Book to Burn and a Book to Keep (Hidden): Selected Writings of Li Zhi (1527–1602)*. Tr. and eds. Rivi Handler-Spitz, Pauline Chen Lee, and Haun Saussy. New York: Columbia University Press, 2016.

Li Zhizao 李之藻, comp. *Tianxue chuhan* 天學初函 (A First Collection of Celestial Studies). 1628. 4 vols. Reprinted, Zhongguo shixue congshu series. Taipei: Xuesheng, 1964.

Liang Qichao 梁啟超. "Fanyi wenxue yu fodian" 翻譯文學與佛典 (The Literature of Translation and the Buddhist Canon, 1920). 61/1a–24b in *Yinbingshi wenji* 飲冰室文集. Shanghai: Zhonghua shuju, 1926.

Liang Qichao 梁啟超. *Yinbingshi heji* 飲冰室合集 (Collected Writings from the Ice-Drinker's Studio). 12 vols. 1936. Reprinted, Beijing: Zhonghua shuju, 1989.

Liebenthal, Walter. "Chinese Buddhism During the 4th and 5th Centuries." *Monumenta Nipponica* 11 (1955): 44–83.

Lin Chuanfang 林傳芳. "Geyi fojiao sixiang zhi shi de kaizhan" 格義佛教思想之史的開展. *Huagang foxue xuebao* 2 (1972): 45–96.

Liu Guijie 劉貴傑. *Zhi Daolin sixiang zhi yanjiu: Wei Jin shidai xuanxue yu fojiao zhi jiaorong* 支道林思想之研究：魏晉時代玄學與佛教之交融 (A Study of Zhi Daolin's Thought: The Confluence of "Dark Learning" and Buddhism in the Wei-Jin Period). Taipei: Taiwan shangwu chubanshe, 1980.

Liu Jianmei. *Zhuangzi and Modern Chinese Literature*. New York: Oxford University Press, 2016.

Liu Jingguo. "*Ge-yi* in Buddhist Scripture Translations." *Perspectives: Studies in Translatology* 14 (2006): 206–13.

Liu, Lydia H. *Translingual Practice: Literature, National Culture, and Translated Modernity, China, 1900–1937*. Stanford. Stanford University Press 1994.

Liu Wendian 劉文典, ed. *Zhuangzi buzheng* 莊子補正 (*Zhuangzi*, with Supplements and Corrections). Shanghai: Shangwu, 1947. Reprinted, Kunming: Yunnan renmin chubanshe, 1980.

Liu Wendian 劉文典, ed. *Huainan honglie jijie* 淮南鴻烈集解 (The Resplendent Work of the Master of Huainan, with Collected Commentaries). 2 vols. Beijing: Zhonghua shuju, 1989.

Liu Yiqing 劉義慶. *Shishuo xinyu* 世說新語. Comm. Liu Xiaobiao 劉孝標. Beijing: Zhonghua shuju, 1982. Tr. Richard B. Mather as *A New Account of Tales of the World*. Second edition. Ann Arbor: Center for Chinese Studies, University of Michigan, 2002.

Liu Yuelian 劉月蓮. "Li Zhuowu yu Li Xitai: Wanli zhong-xi chaoru zhi wu" 李卓吾與利西泰：萬曆中西超儒之晤 (Li Zhuowu [Li Zhi] and Li Xitai [Matteo Ricci]: The Meeting of Two Great Scholars of East and West in the Wanli Period). *Wenhua zazhi* 43 (2002), available at http://www.icm.gov.mo/deippub/rcMagC.asp.

Loewe, Michael, ed. *Early Chinese Texts: A Bibliographical Guide*. Berkeley, CA: The Society for the Study of Early China and the Institute of East Asian Studies, 1993.

Lopez, Donald S., Jr., ed. *Religions of China in Practice*. Princeton: Princeton University Press, 1996.

Lu, Tina. *A Coin, A Severed Head: Experiencing the Material in Early Modern China*. Cambridge, MA: Harvard University Asia Center, 2017.

Lu Xixing 陸西星. *Nanhua zhenjing fumo* 南華真經副墨 (Supplementary Jottings on the Immortal Classic of the Southern Flowery Realm). Zhongguo zixue mingzhu jicheng series, 58. Taipei: Zhongguo zixue mingzhu jicheng bianyin jijinhui, 1977.

Lu Xun 魯迅. "'Yin yue'?" 《音樂》？("Music"?), *Yu si* 5 (December 15, 1924), 4–5.

Lu Xun 魯迅. *Lu Xun quanji* 魯迅全集 (Collected Works of Lu Xun). 16 vols. Beijing: Renmin wenxue chubanshe, 1981.

Lu Xun 魯迅. *Lu Xun zhu yi biannian quanji* 魯迅著譯編年全集 (Lu Xun's Writings and Translations, Arranged by Year of Composition). 20 vols. Eds. Wang Shijia 王世家 and Zhi An 止庵. Beijing: Renmin chubanshe, 2009.

Luk, Bernard Hung-kay. "A Study of Giulio Aleni's 'Chih-fang wai-chi.'" *Bulletin of the School of Oriental and African Studies* 40 (1977): 58–74.

Lung, Rachel. *Interpreters in Early Imperial China*. Benjamins Translation Library, 96. Amsterdam: Benjamins, 2011.

Luo Xinzhang 羅新璋, ed. *Fanyi lunji* 翻譯論集 (Essays on Translation). Beijing: Shangwu, 1984.

Luo Xuanmin and He Yuanjian, eds. *Translating China*. Bristol: Multilingual Matters, 2009.

Lüshi chunqiu: see Xu Weiyu.

Lynn, Richard John. "The Influence of Guo Xiang's Commentary to the *Zhuangzi* on Chinese Literary Thought of the Six Dynasties Era." *Journal of Chinese Studies* 1 (2001): 13–38.

Lynn, Richard John. "Reexamination of the Biography of Master Zhuang in the *Shiji* (Records of the Historian)." Presentation at the meeting of the Western Branch of the American Oriental Society, October 2013.

McCance, Dawne. "Translation/Citation: An Interview with John P. Leavey, Jr." *Mosaic* 35 (2002): 1–20.

MacDiarmid, Hugh. *Collected Poems*. Michael Grieve and W. R. Aitken, eds. 2 vols. Manchester: Carcanet, 2017.

McRae, John A. "Religion as Revolution in Chinese Historiography: Hu Shih (1891-1962) on Shen-hui (684-758)." *Cahiers d'Extrême-Asie* 12 (2001): 59–102.

Mair, Victor H., ed. *Experimental Essays on Chuang-tzu*. Honolulu: University of Hawai'i Press, 1983.

Mair, Victor H., tr. *Wandering on the Way: Early Daoist Tales and Parables of Chuang Tzu*. Honolulu: University of Hawai'i Press, 1998.

Mair, Victor H. "The *Zhuangzi* and Its Impact." 30–52 in Livia Kohn, ed., *Daoism Handbook*. Leiden: Brill, 2000.

Mair, Victor H. "What is *Geyi*, After All?" 227–64 in Alan Chan and Yuet-keung Lo, eds., *Philosophy and Religion in Early Medieval China*. Albany: SUNY Press, 2010. Reprinted as 449–97 of Mair, *China and Beyond: A Collection of Essays*. Amherst, NY: Cambria Press, 2013.

Mair, Victor H. *China and Beyond: A Collection of Essays*. Eds. Rebecca Shuang Fu, Matthew Anderson, Xiang Wan, and Sophie Ling-Chia Wei. Amherst, NY: Cambria Press, 2013.

Major, John S., Sarah A. Queen, Andrew Seth Meyer, and Harold D. Roth, eds. and tr. *The Huainanzi: A Guide to the Theory and Practice of Government in Early Han China*. New York: Columbia University Press, 2010.

Mandel'stam, Osip. *Sobranie sochinenij*. 3 vols. Washington, DC: Mezhdunarodnoe literaturnoe sodruzhestvo, 1967.

Mandel'stam, Osip. *The Complete Poetry of Osip Emilevich Mandelstam*. Tr. Burton Raffel and Alla Burago. Albany: State University of New York Press, 1973.

Manovich, Lev. *The Language of New Media*. Cambridge, MA: MIT Press, 2002.

Mears, T. Lambert, ed. *The Institutes of Gaius and Justinian*. London: Stevens and Sons, 1882.

Miao Ri 妙日. "Dao'an geyi fojiao sixiang shuping" 道安格義佛教思想述評. *Pumen xuebao* 5 (2001): 1–22.

Milne, Drew. "Hugh MacDiarmid's Modernisms: Synthetic Scots and the Spectre of Robert Burns." 142–59 in Neal Alexander and James Moran, eds., *Regional Modernisms*. Edinburgh: Edinburgh University Press, 2013.

Minamiki, George, SJ. *The Chinese Rites Controversy from its Beginning to Modern Times*. Chicago: Loyola University Press, 1985.

Morohashi, Tetsuji 諸橋轍次, ed. *Dai Kan-Wa jiten* 大漢和辞典 (Kanji Dictionary). Tokyo: Taishûkan, 1984-6.

Mou Zongsan 牟宗三. *Wei-Jin xuanxue* 魏晉玄學 (The "Dark Learning" of the Wei-Jin Period). Taizhong: Donghai daxue chubanshe, 1961.

Mufwene, Salikoko S. "Creoles and Creolization." In Jan-Ola Östman and Jef Verscheuren, eds., *Handbook of Pragmatics Manual. Amsterdam:* John Benjamins 1997; available at http://benjamins.com/online/hop/.

Mufwene, Salikoko S. "Jargons, Pidgins, Creoles, and Koines: What Are They?" 35–69 in Arthur K. Spears and Donald Winford, eds., *The Structure and Status of Pidgins and Creoles*. Amsterdam: John Benjamins, 1997.

Mungello, David E., ed. *The Chinese Rites Controversy: Its History and Meaning*. Nettetal: Steyler, 1995.

Nattier, Jan. "The *Heart Sūtra*: A Chinese Apocryphal Text?" *Journal of the International Association of Buddhist Studies* 15 (1992): 153–223.

Nattier, Jan. *A Guide to the Earliest Chinese Buddhist Translations: Texts from the Eastern Han and Three Kingdoms Periods*. Bibliotheca Philologica et Philosophica Buddhica, 10. Tokyo: International Institute for Advanced Buddhist Research, 2008.

Ngũgĩ wa Thiong'o. *A Grain of Wheat*. Revised edition. Oxford: Heinemann, 1987.

Nietzsche, Friedrich. *Sämtliche Werke: Kritische Studienausgabe*. Eds. Giorgio Colli and Mazzino Montinari. 15 vols. Berlin: de Gruyter, 1988.

Ortiz, Fernando. *Cuban Counterpoint: Tobacco and Sugar*. Tr. Harriet de Onís. 1947. Reprint, Durham, NC: Duke University Press, 1995.

Park, Sowon S. "The Pan-Asian Empire and World Literatures." *CLCWeb: Comparative Literature and Culture* 15 (2013), available at http://docs.lib.purdue.edu/clcweb/vol15/iss5/15/ (accessed June 19, 2016).

Peerenboom, Randall P. *Law and Morality in Ancient China: The Silk Manuscripts of Huang-Lao*. Albany: State University of New York Press, 1993.

Puett, Michael. "Violent Misreadings: The Hermeneutics of Cosmology in the *Huainanzi*." *Bulletin of the Museum of Far Eastern Antiquities* 72 (2000): 29–46.

Pym, Anthony. *On Translator Ethics*. Tr. Heike Walker. Amsterdam: Benjamins, 2012.

Qian, Nanxiu. *Spirit and Self in Medieval China: The* Shih-shuo hsin-yü *and Its Legacy*. Honolulu: University of Hawai'i Press, 2001.

Quilligan, Maureen. *The Language of Allegory: Defining the Genre*. Ithaca: Cornell University Press, 1979.

Quine, Willard Van Orman. "Meaning and Translation." 148–72 in Reuben A. Brower, ed., *On Translation*. Cambridge, MA: Harvard University Press, 1959.

Ren Jiyu 任繼愈, ed. *Zhongguo zhexue shi* 中國哲學史 (A History of Chinese Philosophy). 4 vols. Beijing: Renmin chubanshe, 1979.

Ricci, Matteo. *On Friendship: One Hundred Maxims for a Chinese Prince*. Tr. Timothy Billings. New York: Columbia University Press, 2009.

Robinet, Isabelle. *Daoism: Growth of a Religion*. Stanford: Stanford University Press, 1997.

Robinson, Richard H. *Early Mādhyamika in India and China*. Madison: University of Wisconsin Press, 1967.

Roth, Harold D. "The Taoist Influence on Buddhism in the Fourth Century: Case Study, Chih Tun's Understanding of the *Prajñāpāramitā*." MA Thesis, McMaster University, 1973.

Roth, Harold D. *The Textual History of the Huai-nan Tzu*. Ann Arbor: Association for Asian Studies, 1992.

Roth, Harold D. "Who Compiled the *Chuang-tzu*?" 79–128 in Henry Rosemont, Jr., ed., *Chinese Texts and Philosophical Contexts: Essays Dedicated to Angus C. Graham*. La Salle, IL: Open Court, 1999.

Roth, Harold D. "*Chuang tzu*." 56–66 in Michael Loewe, ed., *Early Chinese Texts: A Bibliographical Guide*. Berkeley, CA: The Society for the Study of Early China and the Institute of East Asian Studies, 1993.

Ruan Yuan 阮元, ed. *Shisanjing zhushu* 十三經注疏 (The Thirteen Classics, with Notes and Commentaries). 1815. Reprinted in 8 vols., Taipei: Dahua, 1987.

Saussure, Ferdinand de. *Cours de linguistique générale* [1916]. Paris: Payot, 1972.

Saussure, Ferdinand de. *Écrits de linguistique générale*. Paris: Gallimard, 2002.

Saussy, Haun. *Great Walls of Discourse and Other Adventures in Cultural China*. Harvard East Asian Monographs, 212. Cambridge, MA: published by the Harvard University Asia Center and distributed by Harvard University Press, 2001.

Saussy, Haun. "In the Workshop of Equivalences: Translation, Institutions and Media in the Jesuit Re-Formation of China." 163–81 in Samuel Weber and Hent de Vries, eds., *Religion and Media*. Stanford: Stanford University Press, 2001.

Saussy, Haun. *The Ethnography of Rhythm: Orality and its Technologies*. New York: Fordham University Press, 2016.

Schreiner, Klaus."Messianism in the Weimar Republic." 311–62 in Peter Schäfer and Mark Cohen, eds., *Toward the Millennium: Messianic Expectations from the Bible to Waco*. Leiden: Brill, 1998.

Sen, Tansen. "The Spread of Buddhism." 447–79 in Benjamin Z. Kedar and Merry Wiesner-Hanks, eds., *The Cambridge World History*, vol. 5: *Expanding Webs of Exchange and Conflict, 500 CE–1500 CE*. Cambridge, UK: Cambridge University Press, 2015.

Seneca, Lucius Annius. *Lettere a Lucilio*. Ed. Umberto Boella. Turin: Unione tipografico-editrice torinese, 1969.

Shannon, Claude. "A Mathematical Theory of Communication." *The Bell System Technical Journal* 27 (1948): 379–423, 623–56.

Sharf, Robert H. *Coming to Terms with Chinese Buddhism: A Reading of the 'Treasure Store Treatise'*. Honolulu: University of Hawai'i Press, 2002.

Shen Defu 沈德符. *Wanli yehuo bian* 萬曆野獲編 (A Round-Up of Occasional Notes from the Wanli Era). N.p.: Fuli shanfang, 1869.

Shields, Christopher. "Controversies Surrounding Aristotle's Theory of Perception." *Stanford Encyclopedia of Philosophy*, available at http://plato.stanford.edu/entries/aristotle-psychology/suppl3.html (Accessed October 2, 2006).

Sima Qian 司馬遷. *Shiji* 史記 (Records of the Grand Historian). 10 vols. Beijing: Zhonghua shuju, 2014.

Sipper, Moshe, and James A. Reggia. "Go Forth and Replicate." *Scientific American* 285 (2001): 35–43.

Sishi'er zhang jing 四十二章經 (The Sutra in Forty-Two Sections). Shanghai: Shanghai dazhong shuju, n.d.

Solovieva, Olga V. *Christ's Subversive Body.* Evanston, IL: Northwestern University Press, 2017.

Spence, Jonathan. *The Memory Palace of Matteo Ricci.* Harmondsworth: Penguin, 1983.

Spence, Jonathan. *God's Chinese Son: The Taiping Heavenly Kingdom of Hong Xiuquan.* New York: Norton, 1996.

St. André, James, and Peng Hsiao-yen, eds. *China and Its Others: Knowledge Transfer Through Translation, 1829–2010.* New York: Rodopi, 2012.

Star, Susan Leigh, and James R. Griesemer. "Institutional Ecology, 'Translations,' and Boundary Objects: Amateurs and Professionals in Berkeley's Museum of Vertebrate Zoology, 1907-39." *Social Studies of Science* 19 (1989): 387–420.

Sternberg, Meir. "Polylingualism as Reality and Translation as Mimesis." *Poetics Today* 2 (1981): 221–39.

Storch, Tanya. *The History of Chinese Buddhist Bibliography: Censorship and Transformation of the Tripitaka.* Amherst, NY: Cambria Press, 2014.

Sturge, Kate. *Representing Others: Translation, Ethnography, and the Museum.* Manchester, UK: St. Jerome Publishing, 2007.

T'ang Yung-tung [= Tang Yongtong]. "The Editions of the *Ssu-shih-er-chang jing.*" *Harvard Journal of Asiatic Studies* 1 (1936): 147–55.

T'ang Yung-tung [= Tang Yongtong]. "On 'Ko-yi,' The Earliest Method by Which Indian Buddhism and Chinese Thought Were Synthesized." 276–86 in W. R. Inge, L. P. Jacks, M. Hiriyanna, E. A. Burtt, and P. T. Raju, eds., *Radhakrishnan: Comparative Studies in Philosophy Presented in Honor of His Sixtieth Birthday.* London: Allen & Unwin, 1968.

Tacchi Venturi, Pietro, ed. *Opere storiche del P. Matteo Ricci, S. J.* 2 vols. Macerata: Giorgetti, 1911-13.

Takakusu Junjirō 高楠順次郎, et al., eds. *Taishō shinshū Daizōkyō* 大正新脩大藏經 (The Newly Edited Tripitaka of the Taishō Era). 100 vols. Tokyo: Taishō Issaikyō kankōkai, 1924-34.

Tang Yongtong 湯用彤. *Tang Yongtong quanji* 湯用彤全集 (Complete Works of Tang Yongtong). 7 vols. Shijiazhuang: Hebei renmin chubanshe, 2000.

Tate, Allen. *Essays of Four Decades.* Chicago: Swallow, 1968.

Toury, Gideon. *In Search of a Theory of Translation.* Tel Aviv: Porter Institute for Poetics and Semiotics, 1980.

Toury, Gideon. *Descriptive Translation Studies and Beyond.* Philadelphia: Benjamins, 1995.

Tripitaka: see Takakusu Junjirō et al., eds.

Tsukamoto Zenryū. *A History of Early Chinese Buddhism from its Introduction to the Death of Hui-yüan.* Tr. Leon Hurvitz. 2 vols. Tokyo: Kodansha, 1985.

Twitchett, Denis, and Herbert Franke, eds. *The Cambridge History of China,* vol. 6: *Alien Regimes and Border States, 907–1368.* Cambridge, UK: Cambridge University Press, 1994.

Vasmer, Max, ed. *Russisches etymologisches Wörterbuch.* 3 vols. Heidelberg: Winter, 1953-8.

Venuti, Lawrence. *The Translator's Invisibility: A History of Translation.* New York: Routledge, 1995, second edition 2008.

Venuti, Lawrence. *Scandals of Translation: Towards an Ethics of Difference.* London: Routledge, 1998.

Venuti, Lawrence, ed. *The Translation Studies Reader.* New York: Routledge, 2005.

Venuti, Lawrence. "Hijacking Translation: How Comp Lit Continues to Suppress Translated Texts." *boundary 2* 43 (2016): 179–204.

Wagner, Rudolf G. *The Craft of a Chinese Commentator: Wang Bi on the* Laozi. Albany: State University of New York Press, 2000.

Wagner, Rudolf G. *A Chinese Reading of the* Daodejing: *Wang Bi's Commentary on the* Laozi *with Critical Text and Translation.* Albany: State University of New York Press, 2003.

Walravens, Hartmut. "Father Verbiest's Chinese World Map (1674)." *Imago Mundi* 43 (1991): 31–47.

Wang, Q. Edward. *Inventing China Through History: The May Fourth Approach to Historiography.* Albany: State University of New York Press, 2001.

Watkins, Calvert, ed. *The American Heritage Dictionary of Indo-European Roots.* Boston: Houghton Mifflin Harcourt, 2011.

Watson, Burton, tr. *The Complete Works of Chuang Tzu.* New York: Columbia University Press, 1968.

Widmer, Ellen. "Xiaoqing's Literary Legacy and the Place of the Woman Writer." *Late Imperial China* 13 (1992): 111–55.

Wilde, Oscar. "A Chinese Sage" (1890). 528–38 in *Reviews.* London: Methuen, 1908.

Wu, Jiang, and Lucille Chia, eds. *Spreading Buddha's Word in East Asia: The Formation and Transformation of the Chinese Buddhist Canon.* New York: Columbia University Press, 2016.

Xinbian zhuzi jicheng (Newly Edited Canon of Philosophical Masters). Taipei: Shijie shuju, n.d.

Xu Kangsheng 許抗生. *Wei-Jin sixiang shi* 魏晉思想史 (An Intellectual History of the Wei-Jin Period). Taipei: Guiguan, 1996.

Xu Weiyu 許維遹, ed. *Lüshi chunqiu jishi* 呂氏春秋集釋 (The Springs and Autumns of Mr. Lu, With Collected Commentaries). 2 vols. Beijing: Zhongguo shudian, 1985.

Xunzi (Xun Qing 荀卿). *Xunzi jijie* 荀子集解 (*Xunzi*, With Collected Explanations). Ed. Wang Xianqian 王先謙. Taipei: Huazheng, 1988.

Yan Congjian 嚴從簡. *Shuyu zhouzi lu* 殊域周咨錄 (A Record of Thorough Investigations of Remote Areas). Beijing: Zhonghua, 1993.

Young, Elizabeth Marie. *Translation as Muse: Poetic Translation in Catullus's Rome.* Chicago: University of Chicago Press, 2015.

Yu Shiyi. "Reading the *Chuang-tzu* in the T'ang Dynasty: The Commentary of Ch'eng Hsüan-ying (fl. 631–52)." PhD dissertation, University of Colorado, 1998.

Zacchetti, Stefano. "Teaching Buddhism in Han China: A Study of the *Ahan koujie shi'er yinyuan jing* (T 1508) Attributed to An Shigao." *Annual Report of the International Research Institute for Advanced Buddhology* 7 (2004): 197–224.

Zacchetti, Stefano. "Inventing a New Idiom: Some Aspects of the Language of the *Yin chi ru jing* 陰持入經 (T 603) Translated by An Chigao." *Annual Report of the International Research Institute for Advanced Buddhology* 10 (2007): 395–416.

Zacchetti, Stefano. "Notions and Visions of the Canon in Early Chinese Buddhism." 81–108 in Jiang Wu and Lucille Chia, eds. *Spreading Buddha's Word in East Asia: The Formation and Transformation of the Chinese Buddhist Canon*. New York: Columbia University Press, 2016.

Zeitlin, Judith F. "Spirit Writing and Performance in the Work of You Tong (1618–1704)." *T'oung Pao* 84 (1998): 127–79.

Zhang Huiwen. "Die Begegnung des chinesischen *Sonderlings* mit dem deutschen Übermenschen. Ein Phänomen der interkulturellen Übertragung" (The Encounter of the Chinese Eccentric and the German Superman: A Phenomenon of Intercultural Translation). *Orientierungen* 1 (2008): 9–36; 2 (2008): 5–44.

Zhang Huiwen. "Übertragung als Prophezeiung und Inszenierung: Richard Wilhelms Einführung des *Übermensch*-Konzepts in die daoistische Gedankenwelt" (Translation as Prophecy and mise-en-scène: Richard Wilhelm's Introduction of the *Übermensch* Concept into the Daoistic Thought World). 495–518 in Walter Sparn, ed., *Kulturhermeneutik: Interdisziplinäre Beiträge zum Umgang mit kultureller Differenz*. Munich: Fink, 2008.

Zhang Longxi. *Mighty Opposites: From Dichotomies to Differences in the Comparative Study of China*. Stanford: Stanford University Press, 1998.

Zhang Mantao 張曼濤, ed. *Fojiao yu Zhongguo wenxue* 佛教與中國文學 (Buddhism and Chinese Literature). Taipei: Dacheng wenhua chubanshe, 1977.

Zhang Mantao 張曼濤, ed. *Zhongguo fojiaoshi zhuanji, 1: Han Wei liang Jin Nanbeichao pian* 中國佛教史專集，1:漢魏兩晉南北朝篇 (Studies in the History of Chinese Buddhism, 1: Han, Wei, the Former and Latter Jin, and the Nanbeichao Period). Taipei: Dacheng wenhua chubanshe, 1978.

Zhongyanyuan 中研院 (i.e. Academia Sinica, collective author). *Qingzhu Cai Yuanpei xiansheng liushiwusui lunwenji* 慶祝蔡元培先生六十五歲論文集 (A Festschrift for Cai Yuanpei's Sixty-Fifth Birthday). 2 vols. Beijing: Zhongyang yanjiu yuan, 1933.

Zhou, Gang. *Placing the Modern Chinese Vernacular in Transnational Literature*. Stanford: Stanford University Press, 2005.

Zhou Shaoxian 周紹賢. *Wei-Jin qingtan shulun* 魏晉清談述論 (An Account of Wei-Jin "Pure Conversations"). Taipei: Shangwu, 1965.

Zhu Weizheng 朱維錚, ed. *Li Madou zhongwen zhuyiji* 利瑪竇中文著譯集 (Matteo Ricci's Collected Chinese Writings and Translations). Hong Kong: City University of Hong Kong Press, 2001.

[Zhuang Zhou 莊周, attr.] *Zhuangzi* 莊子. For editions, see Jiao Hong, Liu Wenjian, and Guo Qingfan; for translations, see Burton Watson, A. C. Graham, Victor Mair, and Brook Ziporyn.

Ziporyn, Brook. *The Penumbra Unbound: The Neo-Taoist Philosophy of Guo Xiang*. Albany: State University of New York Press, 2003.

Ziporyn, Brook, tr. and ed. *Zhuangzi: The Essential Writings with Selections from Traditional Commentaries.* Indianapolis: Hackett, 2009.

Zürcher, Erik. *The Buddhist Conquest of China: The Spread and Adaptation of Buddhism in Early Medieval China.* Third edition. Leiden: Brill, 2007.

Zürcher, Erik. *Buddhism in China: Collected Papers of Erik Zürcher.* Ed. Jonathan A. Silk. Leiden: Brill, 2013.

INDEX